Quantitative Methods of Educational Planning

Quantitative Methods
of Educational
Planning

HÉCTOR CORREA

This edition has been authorized by IIEP *and* UNESCO.

INTERNATIONAL TEXTBOOK COMPANY
Scranton, Pennsylvania

Standard Book Number 7002 2249 9

© **UNESCO 1969**

Library of Congress Catalog Card Number: 70-86869

Preface

This book by Dr. Héctor Correa[1] is intended primarily as a learning aid for present and future practitioners of educational planning, though hopefully others may also find it useful.

It focuses on the *quantitative* aspects and methodologies, but recognizes that in coming years educational planners must be equally concerned with the *qualitative* aspects. The two, in fact, are frequently inseparable and undistinguishable, and to treat them as separate categories is false.

Dr. Correa is concerned here not simply with diagnosing and planning the *internal* affairs of an educational system, but with showing how the vital input and output linkages and interactions between an educational system and its social and economic environment must be taken into account in integrating educational development with overall national economic and social development.

This volume is not intended to be a "cookbook" from which any planner can select a recipe to fit his particular country. Every nation must obviously create its own recipe to fit his particular country. Every nation must obviously create its own recipe appropriate to its own special circumstances.

Yet there are certain basic concepts, principles, and methodologies that can be useful and valid in a wide range of countries, provided they are appropriately interpreted and applied. It is these which Dr. Correa attempts to make clear and to demonstrate here, through the device of a hypothetical country which he uses as a working model.

Naturally, he had less trouble getting the facts he needed for this hypothetical country than planners in real countries have in getting the facts they need. The practicing planner frequently has to splice together the best available facts, then fill the gaps as ingeniously as he can. The assumption behind this book is that he will do these things better if he understands clearly the basic logic that underlies educational planning and its various essential methodologies. The book is aimed at revealing this

[1] Formerly a staff member of the International Institute for Educational Planning (IIEP) and subsequently Professor of Economics at Tulane University in New Orleans, La.

v

logic. (Another book on educational planning methodologies, prepared by Mr. John Chesswas of the IIEP,[2] is oriented toward the practical problems of diagnosing an educational system and projecting its future dimensions, in situations where the available facts may be scarce, incomplete, and untidy).

An earlier version of Dr. Correa's manuscript was submitted to a wide range of critics, who made many useful suggestions for its improvement. It was also subjected to the practical test of usage in several training programs at the IIEP, the four UNESCO regional training centers for educational planning, and in a number of universities. To all those who helped in this critical review and testing exercise, the Institute expresses its thanks. We are especially grateful to Dr. Correa who, even after leaving the Institute's staff to serve in a university, continued to devote his personal time to bringing this manuscript to its present form.

A final word of caution and encouragement should perhaps be said to those potential readers who, like so many of us are inclined to drop a psychological curtain the moment they are confronted with an algebraic formula. An earlier draft attempted to avoid all use of such frightening symbols and equations, using fully worked-out arithmetic examples instead, in the tradition of primary school teaching. It was a noble effort, but the results, quite frankly, seemed demeaning to the adult reader, covered too many pages with simple calculations, and threatened to drive more readers away from it out of boredom than out of fear of algebra.

This revised version, therefore, retreats to a modest use of simple equations which anyone who has conquered first-year algebra should be able to follow. Getting through this book may indeed be a good test for those who think they want to be educational planners. Planning does not require one to be a higher mathematician; but there is no escape from getting one's hands dirty with a good deal of quantitative data, if one is going to be a good educational planner. If this allergy to statistics and simple mathematics is too strong, the aspiring planner may be well advised to consider another career.

PHILIP H. COOMBS
Former Director, IIEP

October, 1969

[2] J. D. Chesswas, *Methodologies of Educational Planning for Developing Countries,* Paris, UNESCO/IIEP, 1969.

Contents

List of Tables

*Quantitative Methods
of Educational
Planning*

chapter 1

Introduction

1-1   Purpose of This Chapter

As the title of this book suggests, not all the aspects of educational planning are considered here. An attempt is made to locate the content of this book within the general context of educational planning. First, the aspects of society and of education that are considered are described. In this description the quantitative aspects are differentiated from the qualitative ones. Next, the aspects of the planning process covered by the present methodology as well as those omitted are mentioned.

1-2   Point of View Adopted on Social Development

An appropriate analysis of educational planning and, actually, of any kind of planning should begin with a conceptual description of society as a whole and the place of education in it. Such a conceptual framework will permit us to see in the proper perspective items such as population, education, polity, or economics, and the interrelations among them. Only with reference to such a general framework is it meaningful to ask questions about social development, and educational planning for social development.

However, to present such a general frame of reference and to locate education in it falls outside the scope of this book. In fact, limitations of scientific knowledge make it impossible at the present time to construct such a general frame of reference. Yet policy decisions are made and must continue to be made taking into consideration society as a whole. Rigorous scientific methods can be applied to certain aspects of the social processes; and in these aspects, a planner can help the policy-makers. There is very little a planner can do with respect to the other aspects. Foresight and intuition are still the best guides for the policy-makers.

In this book we will consider some of the interrelations among three aspects of social life: education, population, economy. A description of these aspects will be given later. The main reason for the limited point of view adopted here is that I am not qualified to cover a wider field. However, I strongly believe that an educational plan should not be prepared considering only the thrée aspects of education, population, and economy.

1-3   The View of Education Adopted in This Book

In every human society, large or small, the new members undergo a process of socialization—learning to be a participating member of the society. This is particularly true in the case of national societies, with which most of our analysis will be concerned.

This socialization process takes different forms: preschool education of children; education in formal educational institutions and at home for children, teenagers and adults; and in institutions not directly related to education, such as the army or in business firms. Literacy campaigns and mass media used for educational purposes should also be noted. In this book *we will focus mainly on the formal educational institution, in brief, the school system, both general and vocational.* The methods presented below can be successfully applied to other forms of education, for instance, on-the-job training; however, this possibility is not explored in detail. On the other hand, the method below could not be applied to the socialization process in the family or through mass media.

The analysis further is restricted to the quantitative aspects of educational planning and of its integration with economic planning. It is customary to contrast quantitative and qualitative. However, I do not think that this dichotomy with respect to aspects of education can be accepted without qualification. The problem of education from the point of view of society as a whole and from that of a classroom are discussed below.

From the first point of view, I show that the aspects of quantity and content must be considered together to judge the quality of an educational system. Later I show that a similar approach cannot be used when the question is studied from the point of view of the classroom.

In studying the educational system from the point of view of the society as a whole one should be aware that the educational system is subject to pressures originating in two types of social needs. The first social need is the desire by many individuals to be instructed in certain subjects. The second social need is seen in the demand from firms, governments, and families for a number of persons who have met certain educational qualifications. The first type can be called demand for education; the second, demand for educated persons. Social rewards such as prestige or income bring about adjustments between the two types of demands.

From the previous observations it follows that to judge the quality of an educational system both quantitative and content aspects must be considered.

Unfortunately, when a more refined analysis is attempted, the dichotomy, defined as relationship of quantitative and content aspects contributing to the qualitative aspect, does not hold. To see this one need only examine quantity, content, and quality on a classroom level.

In order to satisfy the social demands on the educational system, a certain number of teachers with certain qualifications is required. Similar statements can be made with respect to buildings, laboratories, and equipment. This means that when an analysis is made from the viewpoint of a classroom, it is reasonable to distinguish between quantitative and qualitative aspects.

In this book special attention is given to numerical measures of aspects of the educational process and of its integration with population and the economy. Thus questions such as number of students, number of graduates, or number of classrooms receive most of the attention. However, only marginal attention is given to the question of the correspondence between the content of the education received by students and the social needs and qualifications of teachers.

1-4 Planning

Two main questions will be considered below with respect to planning: the functions that have to be performed in the planning process and the level of aggregation in which the planning functions are performed.

In planning, three main functions must be performed: (a) decision making, (b) technical preparation of the plan, and (c) implementation and control.

By decision making, we mean here the determination of the main goals of the educational system. For instance, the decision to provide elementary education for all children of school age is part of the decision making in educational planning. Usually this function is performed by the highest governmental authorities.

To achieve the goal decided on, the educational system needs certain inputs—teachers, buildings, equipment. In the technical preparation of the plan, the quality and quantity of inputs required are estimated, and an estimate is made as to whether or not these inputs will be available. If the inputs are not available at all, the goals will have to be revised downward; but if they are available, the planners can proceed to more detailed planning. Such planning will include not only estimates of quantities of inputs needed to reach the goals but also a timetable showing when the inputs need to be available. In this sense, a plan can be summarized in terms of a sequence of steps that have to be taken in order to achieve the goals. The technical preparation of a plan is usually the duty of a group of experts whom we shall call "planners."

In the implementation and control of a plan, the steps needed to attain the goals are taken and control is exerted in order to insure that the steps are taken. This operation is carried out by the administration of a country.

Of the three functions described above, the second—the technical planning process—is the main topic of this book. Two different approaches can be used in dealing with the technical aspects of planning. In the first approach, it is assumed that there is only one way to obtain the desired ends. In reality, of course, this simply is not true. For instance, to obtain a larger number of graduates it is possible to increase the number of new entrants or to reduce dropouts and repeaters. In order to increase production, it might be possible to substitute one engineer for several technicians, or vice versa. Bad teachers might be able to obtain the same number of graduates from a larger group of students as good teachers from a smaller group. As a final example, the preparation of curriculum involves the choice of a set of subjects and a time distribution and the implicit rejection of all other sets of subjects and time distributions.

In the second approach, the different alternative methods available to obtain the targets of the plans are explicitly taken into consideration. Such analysis permits us to choose rationally the best possible alternative. In particular, this procedure might reduce substantially the expenditures required to achieve the targets.

The present work is devoted mainly to the first approach because the mathematical tools required are less sophisticated and there are fewer unknown areas in the adaptation of these techniques to the study of education. In the final chapter, examples of the mathematical analysis required to solve a problem involving choice among alternative possibilities is presented.

Another aspect of planning that should be considered is the level of aggregation. The approach described below permits the preparation of a *general overall long-term educational plan integrated with an economic plan.* Many details which have not been considered here would have to be taken into account in the preparation and utilization of a complete educational plan for a country's educational system.

A more detailed study of such questions as the distribution of resources between the different levels, between general and vocational, and between public and private education, is required. Disaggregation in space provide more detailed attention to the distribution of educational needs and resources by regions and by urban and rural areas. Finally, an extremely important step in the preparation of any plan is its disaggregation in time, i.e., the plan should be broken down into a clear sequence of steps that should be taken in order to attain the goals.

In the process of disaggregation of an overall plan, it is important to take into consideration the subdivisions of the institutions charged with the administration of education. The disaggregation should continue to the point that the different governmental departments know which part of the plan they must carry out. Little can be said in general of the way that this procedure should be carried out. Implementation depends to a large extent on the particular organization of the government of the country for which the plan is prepared. However, this step is perhaps the most important one when the enactment of the plan is considered.

In the preparation of detailed plans, a global plan should prove highly useful, especially because the results of the global plan can be taken as data for those aspects not being studied in a detailed plan.

Suppose, for instance, that a detailed regional plan for elementary education is to be prepared. In this case the results of the overall plan for high school and college-level education can be accepted along with the estimates of total funds available for the elementary school level. The detailed study can be compared to looking at a picture with a magnifying glass: we obtain more information about one part of the picture while accepting as it is a large part of the picture that does not especially interest us.

As a result of detailed studies, some modification of the overall plan might be found necessary. Unless these modifications are important ones, it is convenient to introduce them in the overall plan only after the results of all the detailed studies are known. When this second formulation of the general plan, introducing all the results of the detailed studies, has been accomplished, it is possible to say that the plan is ready.

The two steps are necessary. The initial preparation of the overall plan gives terms of reference for the detailed studies, which otherwise would be inconsistent and uncoordinated. The detailed studies, on the other hand, give confirmation to the overall plan, for without them the overall plan would be too general and schematic and it would not be possible to implement it.

In order to prepare the plans by sectors, the methods described for the overall plan can be used. When more detailed information is required, however, it is possible and convenient to use more judgment and less pure mathematics than in the case of the global plan. For instance, in the detailed plans, it is possible and convenient to use judgment to modify the parameters of certain equations when the statistical information available does not seem to take full account of important factors. In all of this it should be remembered that mathematics, statistics, and models are an aid for thinking but are not a substitute for thought.

Finally, a comment on organization for planning: the overall plan such as the one described in this book can and should be prepared by a central planning organization. However, the detailed plans should normally be prepared by the agencies charged with implementing them. There are two important reasons for this. First, only in this way is it possible to obtain the emotional identification with the plan required to obtain its implementation. Second, only the persons directly in charge of a section have the experience and familiarity necessary to make detailed judgments required in sectoral planning.

1-5   Outline of This Study's Approach to Educational Planning

We begin with the presentation of the basic ideas of demographic and economic analysis. The object of this presentation is to familiarize the reader with the methods used in demography and economics, but not to provide a working knowledge in these two fields.

Next, the influence of population growth and economic development on flows of students in the educational system is considered. We then proceed to consider the influence of these student flows on the output of the educational system and the manner in which this output modifies the educational structure of the population.

The next step involves consideration of the adaptation of the educational system to the economic development plans. After this analysis of the educational requirements of the economic development plan, a set of provisional targets for education output is determined. They take into account both the automatic growth of the student flows and the needs of the economic plan.

The teachers and buildings needed to attain the provisional targets are our next concern. Finally, the sources and uses of funds for the educational plan are considered.

As we make our step-by-step study of the process of educational planning, we shall prepare a complete, aggregated plan for an imaginary country which we call Planiland. In this way, all the interrelations among the different elements in the formulation of a plan can be exhibited.

As mentioned above, in actual planning, in addition to the aggregated plan presented here, a more detailed analysis of the educational process and of its interaction with population and the economic process is required. Fortunately, in this disaggregated analysis, the methodology presented here does not need any basic modification. Examples of this fact are presented below. This stability of the methodology when the level of aggregation is changed is one of the main advantages of the use of mathematics.

1-6   Knowledge of Elementary Mathematics and Statistics Required for the Understanding of This Book

The object of this book is to present the basic framework that should be used in educational planning. This can be done on two levels; first, describing what steps must be taken to prepare a plan; second, explaining how these steps should be taken.

The first level is introduced at the beginning of each chapter. These introductions describe in detail the objective of each chapter, but do not indicate how to reach it. In the remaining portion of each chapter the process required to obtain the objective is presented. This process is essentially mathematical and statistical. However, an effort has been made to simplify the mathematics and statistics as much as possible.

In this book mathematics is used essentially as a form of shorthand. Formulas permit us to express concisely ideas that would otherwise require pages to present. It is usually easier to understand an idea concisely expressed in a formula than it is to grasp the same idea expressed in several pages of prose. To understand the simple mathematics used in this book, only an understanding of elementary arithmetic is required.

Confining mathematical exposition to its simplest levels has not handicapped the book in any important way. Possibly the only important consequence is that the book is somewhat longer than it would be otherwise. Although some things can only be said with higher mathematics, I believe that all the important points in educational planning are included here without resort to mathematics beyond the elementary level.

The situation is somewhat different where statistical theory is concerned. Statistical theory does not aid in the presentation of the basic framework of educational planning. It is needed to apply such a framework to a particular country; but we are not here concerned with this problem. As a consequence, no formal statistical theory is used in this book, and readers do not need any preparation in the field. Statistical theory could be used in the application of the general framework of educational planning to the imaginary country Planiland. In particular, there are many cases where the use of regression, correlation, and econometric methods could yield more reliable results than the methods actually employed. However, these methods are not employed for the sake of simplicity.

Where the framework introduced here is used for actual planning, the educational planners acquainted with this book could ask the help of a statistician or use some of the books mentioned in the reference at the end of this chapter.

References

The most advisable reference in statistics:

Werdelin, I., *Educational Statistics Methods and Problems.* Parts A, B, C, and D. Regional Centre for the Advanced Training of Educational Personnel in the Arab States. (Processed) December 1964.

Another elementary textbook is:

Yamane, T., *Statistics: An Introductory Analysis.* 2d ed. New York: Harper, 1967.

A higher level of mathematics is required for:

Hoel, P. G., *Introduction to Mathematical Statistics.* 2d ed. New York: Wiley, 1954.

Mood, A. M., and F. A. Graybill, *Introduction to the Theory of Statistics.* 2d ed. New York: McGraw-Hill, 1963.

Johnston, J., *Econometric Methods.* New York: McGraw-Hill, 1963.

An attempt to study social planning in the way described in Sec. 1-2 appears in

Correa, H., "Social Development and Social Planning," in E. Reimer, (ed.), *Social Planning*, University of Puerto Rico Press, 1968.

chapter 2

Population and Labor Force

2-1   Content of This Chapter

The interrelations between population and the educational system are one of the main elements that must be considered in an educational plan. In order to be able to consider these interrelations, the educational planners should be able to describe the information that they need to the demographers; hence, the planners need some idea of the methods that demographers use to obtain that information.

The first type of population information of interest to the educational planners is the number of persons of school age. This number is used to determine whether or not all the children are receiving an education. In addition, a projection of this number is used to determine the educational facilities that will be required in the future.

The population of school age and that part of it actually enrolled in the educational system do not give a complete picture of the educational conditions in a country. The educational characteristics of the adult population, in general, and of the labor force, in particular, are the missing elements. These additional elements are especially necessary if one of the targets of an educational plan is to provide the educated workers required for economic development.

In this chapter the methods used by demographers to study populations, their characteristics, and their development over time are briefly described. First, the approach used to determine the size and characteristics of a population at a designated time is presented. Next, the techniques used to forecast future population at given times are considered.

The description below deals mainly with the rationale of the techniques used by demographers. In the short space available, it is not possible to do justice to the detailed aspects of the methodology. Educational planners who have an elementary acquaintance with demography as presented here will need the assistance of professional demographers in the preparation of specific educational plans.

2-2   A Photographic View of the Population

2-2.1   Why a Photographic View of the Population?

At first glance, populations would seem to be solid and tangible. It might be thought that the only difficulty lies in establishing their size. In practice, however, the demographer's task is extremely complex and the real population of a country cannot even be studied at all.

Why should this be so? An example of part of the answer could be seen at the 1964–65 World's Fair in New York, where a huge clock indicated the size of the United States' population. Every minute, the figures changed as deaths, births, and migrations altered the population. Moreover, it is not only the total size which changes: other characteristics of the population such as the proportion of men and women may likewise vary. In other words, far from being solid and unchanging, populations are very fleeting subjects of study.

It is possible, nonetheless, to obtain a "picture" or "image" of the population at any given moment, a picture that takes the form of statistical tables and graphs and from which useful information may be extracted.

2-2.2   Statistical Methods of Obtaining Population Data

The "cameras" used to obtain pictures of the population are *census and sample survey*.

A great deal of information is required in order to prepare a census. Area maps of the country are needed and should be sufficiently detailed to show even individual houses. Some idea of the number of persons living in each area is also necessary since each interviewer can be expected to deal only with a reasonable number of people in a specific area. In rural sectors, delimitation of such areas is a complex task. All hills, houses, and trees look very much alike; yet delimitations must be made in such a way that interviewers can recognize such landscape features from written instructions.

The moment of the census is usually defined as the first minute after midnight on a given day. Early in the morning of the day selected, therefore, the interviewers will set out from thousands of headquarters throughout the country and complications will immediately arise: in one house, the head of the family has just died (he should be included in the census); in another, a baby has just been born (he should not be included); and so on, all over the country.

When the actual compilation of information is completed, it must then be processed, tabulated, and published. The "picture" of the population about which we have been speaking is printed in the census volumes.

Yet, how accurate is this picture? Certain maps may have been in-adequate, with the result that some areas were covered twice and others not at all; elsewhere, there may have been a shortage of interviewers; some people may have refused to be interviewed while others may have given deliberately false answers. The fact is that *any census will contain errors*.

A sample survey differs from a census in that only a small fraction of the population is interviewed, samples of 10 or 20 percent usually being considered large enough.

This does not mean, unfortunately, that the work involved is only 10 or 20 percent of that required for a census. Better maps are needed, for instance, since any small error will be magnified when a sample is taken; more precise advance information about the population is required; al-though fewer interviewers will be engaged, they must be more highly skilled.

Two types of errors may occur in a sample survey. On the one hand, there are the errors arising from inaccurate maps, faulty interviewing, misleading answers, and the like. Such errors are common to both cen-suses and sample surveys and can be reduced through careful preparation, while the fact that the sample covers only part of the population makes it easier to keep down the significance of such errors.

On the other hand, the necessity to generalize from the sample ex-amined to the entire population opens the door to a second type of error. The methods used in preparing sample surveys may reduce but cannot eliminate these so-called sampling errors.

2-2.3 Final Results

In preparing an educational plan, it is useful to use the results of sev-eral population surveys. In Planiland three surveys are available, corre-sponding to the first minutes of years -10, -5 and 0. The results of each of these surveys are given below.

Population by sex and age in Planiland

These data are shown in Table 2-1. The age intervals involved, i.e., the age groups into which the population has been divided, appear in the first column. The body of the table is divided into three main parts, rep-resenting the three surveys. Under each survey heading the total of both sexes, the number of men and the number of women, within each age in-terval is given. For instance, opposite the age interval 20–24 in columns 2, 3, and 4 are the numbers 282, 137, and 145, meaning that within that age interval, Planiland in year -10 had a total of 282,000 people, consist-ing of 137,000 men and 145,000 women. Figures for the total population and male and female populations in each year studied are shown at the bottom of the table.

The distribution of the population in age and sex intervals is called *structure of the population.* For instance, women 35–39 is an age and sex interval; 50–54 is an age interval; and finally, men and women are the sex intervals. In the case of Planiland, the total population of 4,160,000 inhabitants in year 0 is divided into 2,079,000 men and 2,081,000 women. This subdivision is the sex structure of the population. The age structure can be established in the same way.

Table 2-1.   Planiland: Population by Sex and Age (thousands)

Age Intervals (1)	Year $t = -10$			Year $t = -5$			Year $t = 0$		
	Total (2)	Men (3)	Women (4)	Total (5)	Men (6)	Women (7)	Total (8)	Men (9)	Women (10)
0–4	526	267	259	647	327	320	736	373	363
5–9	498	228	220	491	249	242	611	309	302
10–14	369	190	179	440	224	216	483	245	238
15–19	316	158	158	360	185	175	430	219	211
20–24	282	137	145	305	152	153	350	180	170
25–29	238	116	122	272	132	140	295	147	148
30–34	197	97	100	229	111	118	262	127	135
35–39	173	85	88	189	93	96	220	107	113
40–44	143	69	74	165	81	84	181	89	92
45–49	117	57	60	135	65	70	158	77	81
50–54	100	51	49	109	53	56	126	60	66
55–59	77	39	38	90	45	45	99	47	52
60–64	59	28	31	67	33	34	79	39	40
65–69	43	20	23	49	23	26	55	27	28
70–74	29	13	16	31	14	17	37	17	20
75–79	16	7	9	18	8	10	20	9	11
80–84	15	6	9	7	3	4	9	4	5
85+	12	5	7	10	4	6	6	2	4
Total P_t	3,156	1,571	1,585	3,614	1,803	1,811	4,160	2,079	2,081

Population data covering those between ages 5 and 14 in intervals of one year are used in the preparation of projections of school enrollment. These figures are given for Planiland in Table 2-2. It is to be noted that children between ages 9 and 10 are included in the 5–9 interval and that the children 14 years old, but not yet 15, are included in the 10–14 interval. If the information in Table 2-2 is not available, it can be easily obtained by a demographer by using as a starting point the figures in Table 2-1. It should be observed that the data in Table 2-2 refer to years −12 to 0 though the census information available, presented in Table 2-1, refers

Table 2-2.   *Planiland: Population Between 5 and 14 Years of Age (thousands)*

Age Intervals	Year												
	0	-1	-2	-3	-4	-5	-6	-7	-8	-9	-10	-11	-12
5-6	132.44	127.64	122.82	117.98	113.12	102.28	101.01	99.72	98.40	97.06	95.92	93.47	90.98
6-7	127.32	122.51	117.68	112.83	102.02	100.24	98.96	97.65	96.32	95.19	92.76	90.29	87.77
7-8	122.20	117.38	112.54	101.76	99.91	98.20	96.90	95.58	94.46	92.26	89.60	87.10	84.56
8-9	117.08	112.25	101.50	99.58	97.87	96.16	94.85	83.74	91.76	89.33	86.44	83.92	81.35
9-10	111.96	101.24	99.25	97.55	95.74	94.12	93.02	91.27	89.06	86.40	83.28	80.73	78.14
10-11	101.00	98.92	97.23	93.32	93.83	92.36	90.78	88.79	86.36	83.19	80.12	77.55	74.93
11-12	98.60	96.91	94.90	93.54	92.07	90.32	88.52	86.32	83.10	80.03	76.96	74.37	71.72
12-13	96.60	84.49	93.25	91.78	80.04	88.28	86.28	83.01	79.94	76.87	73.80	71.18	68.51
13-14	94.10	92.96	91.50	89.76	88.01	86.23	82.92	79.85	76.78	73.72	70.64	68.00	65.45
14-15	92.70	91.22	89.48	87.74	85.96	82.81	79.76	76.69	73.64	70.56	67.48	64.96	62.52

to years − 10 up to 0. As a consequence, in any case, the help of a demographer is needed to obtain estimates for years − 11 and − 12. The use of these figures is explained in Chapter 5.

It will be noted that Planiland carried out a population survey in year 0, simultaneously with the commencement of planning. In practice, of course, it rarely happens that countries have actually conducted a survey and published the results in the same year as that in which preparation of a plan was begun. But the absence of an exactly contemporaneous survey does not mean that it is impossible to apply quantitative methods to educational planning. What is usually done is to estimate population for the year in which planning is due to begin and this can be done by competent demographers who will use the methods outlined below for estimating the growth of the population.

In order to simplify the presentation below, some mathematical notations will be used:

P_t = total population in year t

P_{ht} = population in the age interval h in year t

For instance, in Table 2-1,

$$P_0 = 4,160,000$$
$$P_{30-34; -5} = 229,000$$

Educational structure of the population

Data on the educational structure of the population, that is, on the population broken down by level of education, is shown in Table 2-3. In this table, all those with between one day up to six years—the whole cycle of elementary education, are included in the elementary stratum. Similarly, the high school and college data include all those who have received the relevant education whether for one day or for the duration of the cycle.

Any other subdivision of the population by educational level would be equally valid and could be handled without difficulty. An alternative method of dealing with the educational structure of the population, for instance, could include all those who had been graduated from a particular level in the stratum corresponding to that level; e.g., the elementary stratum would include all graduates from that level plus all those who had had some high school education but had not been graduated from high school.

Despite the flexibility in the definition of the educational strata, it is crucial to maintain the same definition in all the studies pertaining to the same educational plan. Any adequate definition is sufficient as long as it is not changed.

Table 2-3.   Planiland: Educational Structure of the Population of Six and
More Years of Age (thousands)

Educational Strata	Year				
	0	−5	−6	−10	−12
Without education	744.5	966.2	1,012.1	1,109.4	1,152.8
Elementary (0 to 6 years of schooling)	2,250.8	1,662.6	1,557.4	1,227.8	1,077.6
High school (over 6 to 12 years of schooling)	260.9	209.5	199.8	176.5	165.2
College (over 12 years of schooling)	35.8	26.4	24.7	20.4	18.4
Total population over six years of age	3,292.0	2,864.7	2,794.0	2,534.1	2,414.0

It should be observed that the data in Table 2-3 refer to the total
population, including the population outside the educational system. In
some cases below we consider the educational structure of the population
outside the educational system.

In Table 2-3 we see under the column corresponding to year −10, for
example, that 1,109.4 thousand persons* over six years of age had received
no formal education; 1,227.8 thousand had received or are receiving formal education at the elementary level; 176.5 thousand had received or are
receiving at least some secondary schooling, but nothing beyond the secondary level; and 20.4 thousand had received or are receiving some education beyond the secondary level.

Besides the data on the educational structure of the population in
years −10, −5 and 0, Table 2-3 presents the structure for years −12 and
−6. A demographer can obtain these values by extrapolating or interpolating from the census values.

The sceptical reader will naturally feel that planning presents no dif-
ficulties when all the necessary data can be assumed to exist; but he will
perhaps argue that nothing comparable to Table 2-3 could be prepared
for his own country. In this he is most likely mistaken. What is needed
is *at least one* population survey with information about the educational
structure of the population together with data on enrollment in different
years in the various educational levels. In due course (Chapter 6), we will
see how these two elements may be combined to provide data on the educational structure of the population for several years.

*Here and throughout for simplicity we use the British or Continental form of
"thousand thousand" instead of "million." In the United States, "1,109.4 thousand" would
be taken to mean 1.1094 million.

Educational structure of the labor force

One of the basic sets of statistical information needed for the preparation of an educational plan is the educational structure of the labor force.
In collecting the data for the educational structure of the labor force, it
is important to take care that the definitions of the educational strata used
coincide with those used in the data about the educational structure of the
population.

It is often true that such information is difficult to obtain since it has
not been collected in most countries. An approximately correct picture
can, however, be drawn if the educational structure of the total population
is known. The data for Planiland are presented in Table 2-4.

In Table 2-4 the following notation is used:

L_t = total number of persons in the labour force in year t

L_t^i = total number of workers with educational level i in year t

i = 0 without education

i = 1 with elementary education

i = 2 with high school education

i = 3 with college education

Table 2-4.   Planiland: Educational Structure of the Labor Force (thousands)

i	Educational Strata	Year -10 (2) L_{-10}^i	Year -5 (3) L_{-5}^i	Year 0 (4) L_0^i
0	Without education	523	537	580
1	Elementary	580	686	781
2	High school	75	103	149
3	College	11	15	22
	Total L_t	1,189	1,341	1,532

2-3   Changes of the Population over Time

Demographers are all too well aware that not very much can be
learned from one picture of the population or even from several pictures.
As mentioned at the outset, account must be taken of the changes which
occur in populations over time. For the present we must first decide in
*which changes of the population we are interested, what factors determine
these changes and what methods can be used to measure both the changes
and the governing factors.* We are mainly concerned in this context with
*population growth and its influence on the age and sex structure of the
population.*

*The factors determining population growth are birth, immigration,
death, and emigration.* The ways in which these factors affect the total
population are obvious as are the methods of measuring them. Data on

births and deaths are usually assembled by government offices of vital statistics while information about the movement of people into and out of the national territory may be obtained in immigration offices.

Let us concentrate first on *the total population.* As regards Planiland in year −12, this amounted to 3,026,000. If we add births and immigrations and subtract deaths and emigrations during −12, we obtain the total population at the beginning of −11. We can repeat this operation to establish the total population at the beginning of −10, −9, and so on.

Table 2-5. *Planiland: Total Population and Rates of Growth Between Years −12 and 0 (thousands)*

Years (1)	Total Population (thousands) (2)	Rate of Growth (3)
−12	3,026	
−11	3,081	0.0182
−10	3,156	0.0243
−9	3,241	0.0269
−8	3,329	0.0272
−7	3,421	0.0276
−6	3,515	0.0275
−5	3,614	0.0282
−4	3,715	0.0279
−3	3,823	0.0290
−2	3,933	0.0288
−1	4,045	0.0285
0	4,160	0.0284
Average rate of growth = 0.0270		

Table 2-5 shows the total population of Planiland for each year between −12 and 0. With these data, and the formula

$$\frac{P_t - P_{t-1}}{P_{t-1}}$$

the rate of growth from one year to the next can be computed. For instance, the rate of growth between year −10 and year −9 is

$$\frac{3,241 - 3,156}{3,156} = 0.0269$$

So far we have considered only changes in total population over time, but *changes in the different age and sex groups are also important.* The basis for calculating such changes consists of information about the population similar to that contained in Table 2-1. Our aim is to establish the relationship between one group in an interval of age and sex in, for example, year − 10 and the group in the next interval of age and the same interval of sex in year − 5.

Let us begin by considering the age interval 0–4 in year − 5. Between the years − 10 and − 5 there are five years, and none of those in the 0–4 age interval has attained five years of age. In other words, all of them were born after the beginning of year − 10 and are not included in the figures for year − 10 given in Table 2-1.

When any age interval other than 0–4 is considered, the figures for year − 10 give a slightly distorted picture of the next age interval for year − 5. Let us take the case, for instance, of the 20–24 age interval, composed of 282 thousand persons in year − 10, as shown in Table 2-1. The same table indicates that in year − 5 the group has decreased to 272 thousand in the 25–29 age interval. The difference between the two,

$$282 - 272 = 10 \text{ thousand}$$

is due mainly to mortality (immigration and emigration may also have affected somewhat the size of the difference).

2-4   Population Projections

2-4.1   Method to Be Used

A projection of the population is an estimate of its future growth. The method to prepare such an estimate is similar to the method used for any projection in any science. First, we must find out through observation the factors controlling the growth of the population and the relationship between such factors and the population. Second, an estimate of the development of these determining factors must be obtained. Finally, the knowledge of the development of the determining factors and of the relationship between them and the population permits us to obtain an estimate of the future growth of the population.

The factors determining the growth of the population are well known: births, deaths, immigrations and emigrations. Their relationship to population is simple: Births and immigrations add to the existing population; deaths and emigrations reduce it.

It has been observed that the future development of these four factors is closely related to the present population. So the following causal sequence can be used to project population: present population is directly related to births, deaths and migrations; hence, in turn, these factors are directly related to future populations. Thus, we must begin with the projection of births, deaths, and migrations, using present population as a starting point.

An attempt is made below to present the major elements of the methods used to estimate the future of births, deaths and migrations. The procedures described below should not be used to carry out projections except when the lack of demographers forces the educational planner to obtain rough first approximations. The methods used by demographers expand upon these basic elements in order to eliminate sources of error that are not considered below.

2-4.2   Projections of Births

The number of births bears a more or less constant relationship to the total population. In other words, if the total population increases by one-third, the number of births per year will also increase by approximately one-third. There is an even closer statistical relationship between the number of births and the number of women of childbearing age (between 15 and 44 years).

The relationship between births, on the one hand, and total population of women between 15 and 44, on the other, is numerically measured in terms of *birth rates*. By way of example we will concentrate on the relationship between the number of births and the number of women between ages 15 and 44. The birth rate in this case consists of the number of births per woman between 15 and 44 per unit of time. To obtain the figure, the number of births in, for example, year −10 is divided by the number of women in the 15–44 age interval at the beginning of that year.

In order *to project the number of births*, we use the birth rate observed in the past and the number of women between 15 and 44 existing at the present. Establishing the number of births per year is merely a question of multiplication; if each woman has, say, 0.22 births per year, what is the annual number of births for 687 thousand women? The answer is obtained by multiplying 0.22 by 687 thousand.

More refined projections can be obtained by making valid assumptions about the way in which birth rates will change over a period of time; for example, there is a tendency for an overall decrease in birth rates to occur with the passage of time.

Other factors besides the number and age of women might also be considered in projecting births; e.g., education tends to reduce natality. The inclusion of such factors would give rise to new methods of projection and lead to different results.

2-4.3   Projections of Deaths

The situation is more or less similar with regard to deaths. The only prerequisite for dying in the future is to be living now. People in each age and sex interval tend to die in roughly constant proportions. Among those in the age and sex interval, for instance, of women between ages 20–24 in year −10, a certain proportion will die; this proportion is approximately the same as that observed for the same age and sex interval in, say, year −8. On the other hand, the proportions change from one interval to another. *The death rate is the number of deaths of persons within an age and sex interval per person in the age and sex interval per unit of time.* This rate can be calculated by dividing the number of deaths among those between, say, 20 and 25 during year −5 by the total number of persons in that age interval at the beginning of that year.

Once the death rate is known, the number of deaths can be projected. Let us take the age and sex interval of men as 30–35 in year 0. If we multiply the death rate of that age interval by the number of persons in it, we obtain the number of deaths.

In preparing projections of deaths, it may be useful to assume different death rates so as to provide for various unforeseen contingencies. This technique is frequently employed in order to allow for changes in the factors determining the death rates even though such factors could be explicitly considered. For more refined projections, it is essential to give explicit consideration to these factors; mortality, for example tends to decrease with increase of income.

In some cases it is easier to use survival rates instead of death rates. This rate is the number of survivors within an age and sex interval per person in the age and sex interval per unit of time. The survival rate in Table 2-6 will be used later.

Table 2-6.   Survival Rates of the Population of Six and More
Years of Age from − 12 to −6 and from −6 to 0

Period	Six-Years Rates	Yearly Rates
−12 to −6	0.9289	0.996
−6 to 0	0.934	0.996

2-4.4   Projections of Migrations

Migration rates can likewise be computed for the different age and sex intervals. When these rates are multiplied by population in the corresponding age and sex intervals, one obtains a projection of migrations. Migration rates, too, are subject to other influences such as income and are considerably less stable over time than birth and death rates.

2-4.5   Population Projections

Given projections of births, deaths and migrations, do we have enough to make population projections? Not altogether. An important factor is still missing: the order in which the components must be combined. In order to project the population, we must proceed by stages. And, for each stage we must project the whole population. Beginning in the year 0, we can obtain births, deaths and migrations up to, say, year 5 so that we can construct the population in that year and obtain the second column of Table 2-7. Once all the figures for year 5 are available, it becomes possible to go to year 10 and so on.

Demographers normally make several projections—in most cases, a maximum, medium, and minimum. In the first of these, higher birth and immigration rates and/or lower death and emigration rates are assumed. As regards the medium projection, the most likely developments are assumed. For the minimum projections, the assumptions made for the maximum are reversed. The alternatives for the population projections in Planiland are given in Table 2-7 where only birth rate assumptions are varied.

In setting out the population data required for educational planning, we noted that detailed census information for the 5–14 age interval was needed. This information must be supplemented by detailed projections for that age interval; as regards Planiland, these projections are shown in Table 2-8.

2-4.6   Projections of the Educational Structure of the Population

For the preparation of the population projections, we have used the factors determining population growth—births, deaths and migrations. In the case of the projections of the educational structure of the population, we must also consider its determinants, the output of the educational system. For this reason, before preparing projections of the educational structure of the population, we must study the future growth of the educational system. This is done in Chapter 5. The projections of the educational structure of the population must wait until Chapter 6.

2-5   Labor Force Projections

Educational planners are not expected to prepare labor force projections; it is therefore unnecessary to give a detailed description of the methods used to make such projections. It should be noted simply that while population projections require the rates of birth, death, and migration, labor force projections call for the rates of labor force participation. What is this rate? It is established by taking the population and labor force figures for a given age and sex interval. Labor force divided by population gives the rate of participation; in other words, the rate of participation is the number of persons in the labor force per person in the population within a given age and sex interval. For projection purposes, rates of participation are assumed to be more or less constant.

Table 2-7.   Planiland: Population Projections by Sex and Age (thousands)

Age Intervals (1)	Year 5			Year 10			Year 15			Year 20		
	Total (2)	Men (3)	Women (4)	Total (5)	Men (6)	Women (7)	Total (8)	Men (9)	Women (10)	Total (11)	Men (12)	Women (13)
						The Medium Assumptions						
0- 4	808	409	399	893	453	440	1,005	510	495	1,146	582	564
5- 9	702	355	347	777	393	384	865	438	427	980	497	483
10-14	602	305	297	694	351	343	769	389	380	859	434	423
15-19	475	241	234	593	300	293	685	346	339	760	384	376
20-24	420	214	206	464	235	229	582	294	288	673	340	333
25-29	341	175	166	409	208	201	454	230	224	569	287	282
30-34	287	143	144	331	170	161	500	203	197	444	225	219
35-39	254	123	131	279	139	140	322	165	157	390	198	192
40-44	212	103	109	246	119	127	270	134	136	313	160	153
45-49	172	84	88	203	98	105	237	114	123	260	129	131
50-54	148	72	76	163	79	84	193	92	101	224	107	117
55-59	115	54	61	136	65	71	151	72	79	180	85	95
60-64	88	41	47	103	48	55	123	58	65	136	64	72
65-69	66	32	34	74	34	40	88	40	48	105	48	57
70-74	42	20	22	51	24	27	58	26	32	68	30	38
75-79	23	10	13	28	13	15	33	15	18	39	17	22

80–84	10	4	6	12	5	7	14	6	8	18	8	10
85+	5	2	3	6	2	4	8	3	5	9	4	5
	4,771	2,837	2,384	5,462	2,735	2,726	6,255	3,135	3,120	7,174	3,599	3,575
The Maximum Assumptions												
0– 4	850	431	419	990	502	488	1,173	595	578	1,409	716	693
5– 9				818	414	404	959	486	473	1,142	579	563
10–14							809	409	400	950	481	469
15–19										801	405	396
	4,814	2,409	2,405	5,600	2,805	2,795	6,557	3,288	3,269	7,733	3,883	3,850
The Minimum Assumptions												
0– 4	790	400	390	871	441	430	961	487	474	1,060	537	523
5– 9				763	386	377	841	426	415	928	470	458
10–14							737	373	364	816	411	405
15–19										712	360	352
	4,753	2,378	2,375	5,425	2,715	2,709	6,155	3,084	3,071	6,947	3,480	3,467

Table 2-8.   Planiland: Projections of Population Between Ages 5 and 14 (thousands)

Age Intervals	Year										
	0	1	2	3	4	5	6	7	8	9	10
5–6	132.44	135.26	138.60	141.90	145.17	148.40	151.20	153.94	156.67	159.37	162.04
6–7	127.32	131.74	134.54	137.86	141.15	144.40	147.80	150.59	153.32	156.03	158.72
7–8	122.20	126.85	131.04	133.82	137.13	140.40	143.94	147.20	149.98	152.70	155.40
8–9	117.08	121.96	126.38	130.34	133.11	136.40	140.08	143.48	146.60	149.37	152.08
9–10	111.96	117.04	121.72	125.91	129.65	132.40	136.21	139.76	143.02	146.00	148.76
10–11	101.00	111.54	117.00	121.48	125.44	129.00	132.35	136.02	139.44	142.56	145.44
11–12	98.60	100.62	111.28	116.96	121.24	125.00	128.82	132.30	135.84	139.12	142.12
12–13	96.60	98.23	100.24	110.71	116.92	121.00	124.83	128.64	132.25	135.66	138.80
13–14	94.10	96.24	97.86	99.87	110.30	116.90	120.84	124.66	128.47	132.20	135.48
14–15	92.70	93.75	95.88	97.49	99.50	109.90	116.74	120.68	124.49	128.30	132.16

Age Intervals	Year									
	11	12	13	14	15	16	17	18	19	20
5–6	165.80	169.52	173.24	176.96	180.68	186.72	191.53	196.30	201.07	205.84
6–7	161.93	165.68	169.40	173.12	176.84	180.54	186.58	191.38	196.15	200.92
7–8	158.50	161.82	165.56	169.28	173.00	176.74	180.40	186.44	191.23	196.00
8–9	155.08	158.28	161.71	165.44	169.16	172.76	176.64	180.26	186.30	191.08
9–10	151.65	154.76	158.06	161.60	165.32	168.60	172.52	176.54	180.12	186.16
10–11	148.22	151.22	154.44	157.84	161.48	164.64	168.04	172.28	176.44	180.00
11–12	144.92	147.69	150.79	154.12	157.64	160.81	163.96	167.48	172.04	176.32
12–13	141.61	144.40	147.16	150.36	153.80	156.99	160.15	163.28	166.93	171.82
13–14	138.30	141.10	143.88	146.63	149.96	153.16	156.34	159.49	162.61	166.40
14–15	134.99	137.80	140.59	143.36	146.12	149.34	152.53	155.69	158.83	161.96

With the population projections and the rates of participation, we are ready to proceed. Let us assume that we want to know the number of male workers between 20 and 24 in year 20. We multiply the rate of participation by the number of persons in that age and sex interval as shown in the population projection. Without employing the detailed projections of the labor force by sex and age and merely using the total figures, Table 2-9 below shows the projections of the total labor force in Planiland.

At a later stage, we will make a detailed examination of the methods used to obtain projections of the educational structure of the labor force.

Table 2-9. Planiland: Total Labor Force Projections (thousands)

Year t	Labor Force L_t
5	1,764
10	2,050
15	2,387
20	2,764

References

More complete elementary discussions of demographic methods appear in:

Barclay, G. W., *Techniques of Population Analysis.* New York: Wiley, 1958.

Davis, R. C., *Planning Human Resource Development.* Chicago. Rand McNally, 1966.

Methods for Population Projections by Sex and Age. New York: United Nations Population Studies No. 25, 1956.

Pressat, R., *L'Analyse Démographique.* Paris: Presses Universitaires de France, 1961.

chapter 3

Economics

3-1   Content of This Chapter

The past several years have witnessed an increased interest in economics generally and in economic development in particular. Economic development has become one of the main objectives of every government in the world—and of the revolutions that sometimes overthrow these governments. Even laymen are vitally interested in the fluctuations of per capita income.

This does not mean that economic problems are more deserving of attention now than in the past. It has always been true to say that nothing can be obtained without economic means and nothing of real value can be obtained with economic means alone; this will doubtless hold true for the future. Thus education, which virtually everyone agrees has great value, requires more than merely money; but nonetheless educational officials must ultimately solicit the help of the financial authorities. This is a fact of life which, as a realist, the educational planner must recognize from the outset.

But if education requires economic support, the economy in turn requires educated people. The educator is not obliged to beg for funds in order to satisfy an abstract right to education; he is in a position to "sell" valuable, qualified personnel to the economy. As a result, economic officials have had to come to terms with educators. Discussions are now conducted on a basis of reciprocal interests.

Every discussion, however, calls for a common language. While economists may have become familiar with educational terminology, educational planners must become familiar with economic terms. To bring about this familiarity is one of the objectives of the present chapter. Another objective, more important than the first, is to explain the role of education in economic development. Actually, since the content of this chapter occupies such a fundamental position in the intellectual preparation of the educational planner, no further introduction is necessary.

3-2 National Accounts

3-2.1 Definition of Gross Domestic Product

National accounts, social accounts, national income accounts, etc., mean exactly the same thing. They bear the same relation to a country as do business accounts to a commercial enterprise. Just as the latter enable the owner of a firm to see the value of goods and services produced by his firm and the costs of this production so the national accounts reveal the total amount of goods and services produced and the main production costs for the country as a whole.

At first glance, it would seem that one need only add up production of all the firms within a country in order to obtain the national accounts. In fact, however, while it is relatively easy to establish the *value* of each good and service produced, it is less easy to determine how much of each good and service is being produced.

To begin with, it is impossible to talk of production as a momentary thing. Whereas population figures refer to a given moment, production figures refer to a flow over a period of time. Hence we must think in terms of production per month, production per year, and so on. National production is usually considered over a period of one year.

Let us now examine the case of a Planiland business which produces 2,200 items in the course of a year. If we assume these items sell for $5 each, the firm received $11,000 for its annual output. From this sum, $6,000 is spent on the purchase of materials, $3,000 on salaries, $500 as interest on loans and $500 on factory rent (for the sake of simplicity, we ignore depreciation of capital). In other words, $10,000 is paid out in the course of producing output worth $11,000 on the market. The owner's profit is the difference between total receipts and total payments to all others who have contributed to the production of the output (those receiving salaries, interest and rent, and those selling materials used in production).

How much of the value of yearly output of the firm can be counted as addition to national output? Since the raw materials purchased from outside were obviously not produced by the firm itself, the amount involved is necessarily excluded from the value of the firm's net contribution to national production. No other category of costs need be excluded and hence one can say that the firm's net contribution to national output is equal to the value of total sales (in this case, $11,000) less the amount paid to other firms for raw materials (in this case, $6,000). Thus we obtain a figure of $5,000 for the firm's contributions to national output. This figure is equal to the sum of the firm's yearly payments for salaries, interest and rent plus the firm's profit.

If only the values added by the firms as defined above are considered, we avoid the danger of counting any firm's production twice, a problem which would arise if the total sales of all the firms were to be added together.

In order to evaluate the national production of Planiland, all that is needed is to add up the contributions of each individual firm, i.e., their value added. This sum is equal to the total of profits, salaries, rents, and interest paid out throughout the country. It should be noted that in order for the above to be true, one must count all producing units in the country including the government as a "firm."

Since profits, salaries, interest, and rents are paid to someone, it follows that *national production and total personal income are equal.* Total production and total income, in other words, are two sides of a single coin: the production process.

In the analysis above, we have not paid attention to the fact that some goods and services are bought from foreign countries and sold to them. This fact does not introduce any modification in the method outlined to evaluate national production. However, *the transactions with foreign countries are usually presented separately from the internal transactions in the national accounts.* The national production is evaluated in the following way: First, the value added in "internal transactions" is computed; that is, for each firm, the value of all goods sold for consumption or further processing in the economy minus the value of all the raw materials and semiprocessed goods bought in the economy is computed. Then these values for all firms are added. Second, the value of all the goods and services sold to foreign countries minus the value of all goods and services bought from other countries is computed. National production is equal to the sum of the two components described above.

Economists, of course, would distinguish between net and gross values, domestic and national production, production and income, and the like, but these differences are not particularly important for our purposes. From our point of view it is important to use just one concept. Hence in all that follows we will be using a type of national output measure called "gross domestic product." Table 3-1 shows the values of the gross domestic product of Planiland from year − 12 to year 0.

One reason for studying national accounts is to make the concept of national production less vague. Annual national production, whether large or small, is a fixed quantity confronting all planners with definite limitations. It is essential to stress an obvious fact but one whose full implications are not always recognized: *resources are limited.* They must be distributed among a variety of users. Resources used for one purpose cannot be used for another.

These considerations bring us to the crux of the discussions between

Table 3-1.   Planiland: Values at Current Prices of
Gross Domestic Product from Year −12 to
Year 0 (millions of dollars)

Year	GDP
−12	5,458
−11	5,997
−10	6,511
− 9	7,032
− 8	7,746
− 7	8,135
− 6	8,383
− 5	9,236
− 4	10,240
− 3	11,165
− 2	12,027
− 1	12,834
− 0	13,932

educators and economists. The former contend that education is a right and must be guaranteed. The latter argue that several rights must be safeguarded out of limited resources—the rights to shelter, to food, to health, to employment, or to education. To increase expenditure on education means decreasing expenditure on safeguarding other rights. Hence, expenditure on education out of limited national output must be held within certain bounds.

3-2.2   Disaggregations of the National Accounts

In the study of the economic conditions of a country, in economic planning and its integration with educational planning, in addition to the total value of national production, several subdivisions are used. Some of these are considered below.

In Table 3-2 the distribution of gross domestic product in years −12, −6, and 0 between *public and private* resources is presented. These data will be used when dealing with public and private funds used in education.

In actual uses of the national accounts, total production is subdivided according to its *industrial origin*. In this case, the value added by firms,

Table 3-2.   Planiland: Distribution of Gross Domestic
Product Between Public and Private Resources
(millions of dollars at current prices)

Year	GDP	Public	Private
−12	5,458	958	4,500
− 6	8,383	1,510	6,873
0	13,932	2,492	11,440

for example, in agriculture, manufacturing and services, is presented. If it is necessary, more refined subdivisions can be used.

3-3 Comparison of National Accounts for Different Years

3-3.1 Price Changes and Real Changes in National Accounts

Educational planners, accustomed to dealing with figures showing the number of students, the number of teachers, and so on, may feel that, since there is no special problem in comparing those figures for different periods, it is unnecessary to devote particular attention to the comparison of national accounts for different years.

The number of students during a given period can be compared with the number during another period because a student is a student, irrespective of the time element; that is, the same unit of measurement is employed at all points in time. Such is not the case when dealing with national accounts: accounts for different periods are measured in different units.

Table 3-1 shows the gross domestic product of Planiland year after year in Planiland dollars, but a dollar in year -10 is not the same thing as a dollar in year -5. The fact is that the value of money steadily deteriorates. A household budget, for example, which was adequate six months previously, is found to be no longer sufficient because the prices of bread and meat have risen; the value of money in terms of bread and meat has declined. The dollar which bought four loaves in year -10 buys only three in year -5. In other words, the dollar is worth only three-fourths as much.

This, of course, is crucial in dealing with national accounts. Comparing the values for years -10 and -5 as shown in Table 3-1, it is impossible to say whether or not Planiland production has really increased. Production may not have risen but prices may have risen so that a reduced volume of goods is represented by an increased monetary value. Unless the effects of price changes are eliminated, changes in production, the *real* changes, cannot be seen.

3-3.2 Price Indices

In order to eliminate price changes, these changes must first be measured by means of *price indices*.

Let us examine a hypothetical family which in year -10 consumed 700 loaves of bread and 500 pounds of meat. Assuming one loaf to cost one dollar and one pound of meat two dollars, food expenses amounted to

$$700 \times 1 + 500 \times 2 = \$1,700$$

In year −5, the price of one loaf has risen to 1.2 dollars and the price of a pound of meat to 2.3 dollars, so that the hypothetical Planiland family must spend

$$700 \times 1.2 + 500 \times 2.3 = \$1,990$$

to consume in year −5 what it consumed in year −10. In other words, $1,700 in year −10 represented the same amount of bread and meat as did $1,990 in year −5. A simple division

$$\frac{1,990}{1,700} = 1.17$$

indicates that one dollar in year −10 is the equivalent of 1.17 dollars in year −5. Or, to put it another way, on the average an item carrying a price of 1 in year −10 carries a price of 1.17 in year −5. These are the index numbers for the Planiland family.

Index numbers usually refer not to one monetary unit but to one hundred, so that prices are said to have risen not from 1 to 1.17 but from 100 to 117. All that has been done is to multiply the component elements of the index by 100.

Index numbers, therefore, reveal the change in price from one year to another. The year taken as a point of reference (−10 in the example used here) is known as the *base year*. If the base year is changed, it follows that the index numbers also change. For example, the index number for prices in −5 would probably not be 1.17 if we were to take year −7 as the base year.

Index numbers for the whole society can be calculated in the same way as for a single family although all goods, and not merely food as in our simplified example, must be included. In Table 3-3, which shows Planiland price indices, year 0, when planning begins, has been selected as the base year. Accustomed as we are to seeing prices rise rather than fall, we may be surprised that all index numbers are below 100. These, however, refer to the past; e.g., four years earlier, in year −4, $91.4 was required to buy the same amount of goods that in year 0 can be bought with $100.

It is clear that index numbers are subject to a number of limitations. The index in the case of our hypothetical family, for instance, could be computed only because they ate bread and meat in both year −10 and year −5. If they had replaced bread with vegetables in the interval, an insoluble problem would have arisen. If a new product is introduced into the consumption pattern or if the quality of old products alters, there is no way of measuring price changes.

Since new products come on to the market every day, since qualities

Table 3-3.   Planiland:
Price Indices

Year	Index
−12	80.2
−11	80.8
−10	81.7
− 9	82.0
− 8	83.1
− 7	84.3
− 6	85.7
− 5	86.4
− 4	91.4
− 3	94.3
− 2	98.9
− 1	99.3
0	100.0

are continually changing and since index numbers cannot allow for such developments, how can index numbers be used significantly to measure changes in prices? Economists are well aware of the limitations involved. If they continue to use index numbers, it is because these are better than nothing at all. They provide only a very rough measurement of changes in prices, and this is duly recognized. For that matter, almost all economic figures are only rough measurements of real phenomena.

3-3.3   Use of Price Indices: Gross Domestic Product in Real Terms

Table 3-1 shows the values at current prices of Planiland's gross domestic product from year −12 to 0; Table 3-3 gives the index numbers of Planiland prices. How are we to eliminate the effect of price changes from the figures for the gross domestic product?

The point of departure is the base year (year 0 in Table 3-3). The first problem is to discover how many dollars in year 0 are equivalent to one dollar in year −1. Table 3-3 shows that goods costing $99.3 in year −1 cost $100 in year 0, so that $100 in the latter year is equivalent to $99.3 in the former. The simple division

$$\frac{100}{99.3} = 1.007$$

gives the year 0 equivalent of one dollar in year −1.

Table 3-1 shows that the value produced in year −1 was $12,834 million, measured in the prices prevailing in that year. Since one dollar in year −1 is equivalent to $1.007 in year 0, what is the equivalent of 12,834 million year −1 dollars in year 0 dollars? The answer is

$$1.007 \times 12,834 \text{ million} = 12,924 \text{ million}$$

representing the value which the goods produced in year -1 would have had if the prices prevailing had been those of year 0.

The same computation can be made for year -2. The ratio of year 0 dollars to year -2 dollars is determined as follows:

$$\frac{100}{98.9} = 1.01112$$

Thus we are able to obtain the value of year -2 production at year 0 prices:

$$1.01112 \times 12{,}027 \text{ million} = 12{,}161 \text{ million}$$

The same operation can be used to obtain the real values for the gross domestic product for all years between -12 and 0 as well as for public and private resources. Results are shown in Table 3-4. The notation Y_t represents gross domestic product at constant prices in year t. For instance, in Table 3-4 we see that

$$Y_{-5} = 10{,}690$$

Table 3-4. Planiland: Real Values of Gross Domestic Product (millions of dollars at year 0 prices)

Year	Gross Domestic Product	Rate of Growth	Public	Private
-12	6,805		1,194	5,611
		0.090		
-11	7,422			
		0.073		
-10	7,969			
		0.076		
-9	8,576			
		0.087		
-8	9,321			
		0.035		
-7	9,650			
		0.014		
-6	9,782		1,762	8,020
		0.092		
-5	10,690			
		0.048		
-4	11,204			
		0.057		
-3	11,840			
		0.027		
-2	12,161			
		0.063		
-1	12,924			
		0.080		
0	13,932		2,492	11,440
	Average rate of growth	0.062		

3-3.4 Comparison of the Gross Domestic Product in Different Years

Rate of growth of the gross domestic product

It now becomes possible to compare the values of gross domestic product, Y_t, since the dollar value for one year is the same as the dollar value for another year. A useful index for this comparison is the rate of growth defined by the following equation:

$$\frac{Y_t - Y_{t-1}}{Y_{t-1}}$$

For instance, the rate of growth between years -10 and -9 is

$$\frac{Y_{-9} - Y_{-10}}{Y_{-10}} = \frac{8,576 - 7,969}{7,969} = 0.076$$

This means that 0.076 dollar was added to each dollar of output in year -10, or that 7.6 dollars were added to each 100 dollars. (This latter figure of 7.6 is the percent rate of growth of gross domestic product, a figure of great interest to those concerned with measuring and comparing economic growth.) A similar calculation can be made for any two consecutive years; the results are shown in Table 3-4.

The year-to-year rates of growth in Table 3-3 do not, however, give any idea of conditions over the whole period. This can be obtained from the *average of the rates of growth* which indicates what the growth rate would have been from one year to the next if approximately the same rate had prevailed in each year. For the rates of growth in Table 3-4, the average is 0.062.

3-4   Economic Growth and Investment in Education

3-4.1   The Concept of Economic Growth

Economic growth is simply another phrase for the *increase in national production*. For example, the economic growth of Planiland between years -12 and 0 may be seen in Table 3-4, for it gives the real values of the gross domestic product for those years. To keep a record of a country's economic growth, of course, requires that the real values of national production be used. Changes in values at current prices show not only changes in real production levels but also changes in the price level.

Economists are not interested solely in keeping a record of economic growth. They are also anxious to discover its causes so as to be able to promote such growth.

3-4.2   Factors Outside Enterprises Which Influence Economic Growth

In the case of individual businesses, it is obvious that where one enterprise increases its production, the total production of the country will also increase unless another enterprise is simultaneously reducing production.

It is equally obvious that the decision to raise production within a given firm will depend on external institutional, political, and economic factors. These factors are normally beyond the control of individual enterprises. They include the laws of the country concerned and especially those laws dealing with economic matters such as taxation. Also, the degree of political stability has an impact on economic growth since firms will be much less interested in producing if there seems to be danger that the fruits of their efforts will be destroyed by political action.

As to general economic conditions, it is scarcely necessary to point out that enterprises will not increase their output unless they are reasonably sure of being able to sell profitably what they produce. Without going into the question of why people buy things, it is clear that people must have money in order to make purchases, and, for most people, this means that they must be employed. In other words, production is dependent on whether or not potential consumers are employed.

3-4.3 Factors Within Enterprises Which Influence Economic Growth

Turning back to the hypothetical business discussed earlier, we will assume that during the previous year this firm used machinery worth $5,000, buildings worth $4,500 (a fixed investment not included in the current expenditures already listed), plus money from the owner's bank for the purchase of raw materials and the payment of workers plus, finally, eight workers. What does this firm require in order to produce 4,400 items per year—that is, twice as many as before?

To begin with, it does *not*, as might be thought, need exactly twice as many machines, buildings and workers; nor does it need exactly twice as much money.

In order to decide what new production factors are needed, we must first see what use is being made of the already existing factors. It is possible, for instance, that some of the workers and machines might be able to produce more if additional raw materials were forthcoming; similarly, it might be possible to install additional machinery in the existing buildings, and so on. We will assume, however, that all the contributing factors are being utilized to the full. Does this mean simply that twice as many factors are needed to produce twice as much? Not necessarily. We can merely say that what is needed is more machines, more buildings, more money and more workers. The fact that it is not necessarily the case that *twice* as much is required is a vital consideration in economic growth.

At this point, two important items should be noted. First, when production factors are fully utilized and more machinery and buildings are required in order to increase production, part of the output of the country may be used to meet the firm's needs for equipment and factory space. But, for economic growth the firm cannot purchase already existing equipment or factory space from other firms, because, if this is done, the production of the firm will increase, but not that of the country as a whole. This operation of using part of a country's output to increase the stock of machinery and buildings is known as *investment*. Since the volume of goods that can be invested must be taken from national production and since most of national output must be in the form of consumer's goods and services, investment will always be only a small fraction (normally at most $\frac{1}{5}$) of the gross domestic product.

The second point to be noted is that the additional workers required in order to increase production must have certain skills and abilities, the possession of which is usually the direct or indirect result of previous formal education and on-the-job training. The size of the labor force is not all that sets a limit to output in the economy; the quality of that labor force is also a determinant of maximum possible output. It is thus true to say that resources applied to education in one period will enable the economy to produce more than would otherwise be possible in subsequent periods. This is one sense in which *education may be considered an investment*. This point is obviously vital as far as educational planners are concerned.

Economic growth with a proportional increase in the utilization of production factors

One way in which our hypothetical firm might double production is by using twice as many workers and machines. In such a case, the increment in the utilization of the factors is proportional to the increment in production; but, as will be seen below, this is not an example of much practical importance.

Economic growth and substitution of machines for workers

The firm might also double production by using more than twice as many machines and less than twice as many workers—that is, by substituting machines for workers. An example of such substitution is given in Table 3-5.

This table is based on data supplied by the firm itself, total production, number of workers and number of machines. Production per worker and per machine (*productivity per worker* or *per machine*) may be calculated by dividing total production by the number of workers or machines.

Table 3-5.   *Substitution of Machines for*
Workers in Shoe Factory

	Before	After
Value of total production	11,000	22,000
Number of workers	10	15
Production per worker	1,100	1,466.66
Number of machines	10	30
Production per machine	1,100	733.33

In the present example, productivity per worker is obtained as follows:

$$\frac{11,000}{10} = 1,100$$

The table indicates that, when machines are substituted for workers, productivity per machine is reduced while productivity per worker rises. This is normally the case.

This increment in labor productivity again involves formal education or on-the-job training in that the additional workers will need at least as much education as those previously engaged. That additional workers with a certain level of qualification are required does not, however, necessarily imply that expenditure on education or training must be increased. Just as a firm may increase production without investment if it has some underutilized resources, so there may be workers whose qualifications are higher than those needed for the work they perform. If a more exacting position becomes available, one of them would be able to fill it without any additional education. This is a case where the educational equipment of the human resources available is underutilized. We will assume, however, that such educational equipment is fully utilized and this means that some expenditure on education is required in order to increase the number of qualified workers, a specific example of the way in which education contributes to production.

Economic growth and increased productivity of workers and machines

Another way of increasing production consists of using not more, but better, machines. This method is normally adopted. With better machines, productivity per worker increases as does productivity per machine. Better-educated workers are usually required to operate the more complicated machines. Hence part of this increased labor productivity must be viewed as a return on previous investments in education.

Education, moreover, makes a contribution through the machines themselves insofar as scientific knowledge is applied to their construction. Thus at least part of the productivity increase attributable to the use of better machines can be looked upon as a return on earlier education investments.

To sum up: There are various methods of increasing production and, in all of them, the education of the workers plays a very important part.

3-5   *Economic Growth and Welfare*

Increments in production are an essential prerequisite for increments in consumption and welfare. *Per capita income is one very rough measure of such welfare.* It is calculated by dividing total production or total income by total population, revealing the amount of output available per person; if y_t denotes per capita income in year t, we have

$$y_t = \frac{Y_t}{P_t}$$

where Y_t denotes total income in year t and P_t total population in year t. Figures for per capita income in Planiland appear in Table 3-6.

Table 3-6.   Planiland: Per Capita Income
for Several Years (year 0 prices)

Year	Per Capita Income
−12	2,299
−11	2,409
−10	2,525
− 9	2,646
− 8	2,800
− 7	2,821
− 6	2,783
− 5	2,958
− 4	3,016
− 3	3,097
− 2	3,092
− 1	3,195
0	3,349

An analysis of per capita income figures for a period of years indicates whether the population's welfare is increasing or decreasing on the average, and it also demonstrates that *economic growth does not necessarily secure welfare growth.* Only if the rate of growth of production is greater than the rate of growth of population will there be an improvement in the welfare of the individual as measured by per capita income figures. The achievement of welfare growth may be compared to rowing upstream, with increments in production as oarstrokes and population as the current moving downstream. A good deal of effort is required just to remain stationary, and great effort is necessary to move very rapidly upstream.

Welfare growth measured by per capita income can be related to increments in labor productivity, but, for this purpose, we must review the concepts involved. Labor productivity is production per worker, figures for which are obtained by dividing total production by the total number of workers. Per capita income is obtained by dividing total production by total population. Tables 2-4 and 2-5 show that in year 0 the total labor force is 1,532 thousand (1.532 million) and the total population is 4,160 thousand (4.160 million). Thus there is one worker for each 2.72 persons in the population. We made the simplifying assumption that each worker is the head of a family (hence there are on the average 2.72 persons in each family). Thus the number of families in the population is the same as the number of workers. Productivity per worker and income per family, hence, are equal. Knowing the income per family, we need only divide that figure by the average number of persons in each family (2.72) in order to find the income per person. Thus, assuming that there is no change in the number of persons in each family, the rate of growth of labor productivity and that of per capita income will be the same.

This is of the greatest importance since it enables us to relate welfare growth, as measured by increments in per capita income, to the education of the labor force, since increments in the productivity of the labor force are made possible in part by previous investments in education.

3-6   Economic and Employment Planning

In both economic and educational planning, the first step consists of determining goals. In neither type of planning is there any scientific method of fixing the goals. Policy-makers usually determine goals for economic development without particular regard for economic theory; it is then up to the planners to decide whether these goals can be achieved. If it is decided that they are not feasible, they must be revised accordingly. Most of the technical aspects of economic planning are related to this verification of feasibility. When it is verified that the goals can be attained they are called targets.

Goals for economic development are usually expressed as, or can be reduced to, a rate of growth of per capita income (used as an index of welfare). These goals for Planiland's economic plans are in Table 3-7. By using population data and projections, the planners can convert per capita income goals into total production goals.

Once the total production targets are established, the economic planners must determine the capital and labor required to reach these goals.

Table 3-7.   Planiland: Goals for Per Capita Income

Year	Per Capita Income y_t
0	3,349
5	3,945
6	4,075
10	4,655
12	4,967
15	5,492
18	6,052
20	6,469

As regards capital, the problem is a simple one: on the basis of the current level of production and the current stock of capital, a reasonable determination can be made as to the total amount of capital required to achieve a given future level of production. The problem with respect to labor is more complex because workers must be considered both as factors of production and as consumers. The economic planner must bear this dual aspect in mind when determining the number of workers required for achieving a certain rate of economic development.

The results obtained with respect to future capital and labor requirements must be checked against estimates of probable future supplies of capital and labor to see whether the production factors needed to reach the economic growth goals can possibly be made available. Special attention must be paid to the availability of labor since economic plans must not only achieve production goals but also ensure full employment for the force if at all possible.

As already mentioned, goals must be revised and a further analysis must be made should it be found that the goals set by the policy-makers cannot be reached. If on the other hand it is found that enough capital is available and that there will be enough jobs for the labor force, then the goals are definitely adopted. When this stage is reached the goals can be called *targets of the plan*.

This is the stage that has been reached in Planiland. The target for the rate of growth of the gross domestic product has been set at 0.062 per year; in other words, production is to increase at a rate of 6.2 percent per annum. Since full employment is to be achieved, the number of workers employed will be equal to the number available according to the demographic projections. Table 3-8 shows the target values for gross domestic product, employment and productivity per worker.

The data given in Table 3-8 on future labor productivity are of particular interest to educational planners since the education of the labor force is one determinant of labor productivity. Thus when the targets are set for the labor force's productivity, implicitly the targets with respect to that force's education are also set.

Table 3-8.   Planiland: Target Values for Gross Domestic Product, Labor Force and Productivity per Worker

Year t	GDP (millions of dollars) y_t	Labor Force L_t	Productivity per Worker (dollars)
0	13,932	1,531,540	9,097
5	18,822	1,763,509	10,673
10	25,428	2,049,624	12,406
15	34,354	2,386,816	14,393
20	46,412	2,764,249	16,790

The first stage in preparing a plan for economic development ends with tables similar to Table 3-8. Thereafter, the economic planners must move in several different directions.

The figures shown in Table 3-8 do not specify the amount of physical and human resources to be used in, say, agriculture, manufacturing or services. The economic planner must disaggregate the total target figures; in other words, he must establish the best way of distributing the total increment in production among the different sectors of the economy. A distribution of future production of interest for educational planners is that between public and private sectors (see Table 3-9).

Further planning puts economic and educational planners in direct contact. From this point on, it is impossible to draw up socioeconomic plans without the collaboration of educational planners. The reason for this has already been mentioned: *the productivity of the labor force depends in part upon the education of its members.* Hence, economic and educational planners must work together to determine the educational structure of the labor force required to reach the productivity goals set up. The methods used to make this determination are discussed in Chapter 7.

Table 3-9. *Planiland: Planned Future Growth of Total, Public and Private Resources (thousands of year 0 dollars)*

Year	Total	Public	Private
0	13,932	2,480	11,452
5	18,823	3,435	15,387
6	19,782	3,620	16,162
10	25,428	4,679	20,749
12	28,098	5,226	22,872
15	34,354	6,527	27,827
18	39,885	7,658	32,227
20	46,412	9,004	37,408

References

The main concepts used in *National Accounting* are presented in all standard textbooks on economics. The reader may consult
Samuelson, P. A., *Economics: An Introductory Analysis.* 6th ed. New York: McGraw-Hill, 1964.

A more complete presentation appears in
A System of National Accounts and Supporting Tables. ("United Nations Studies and Methods," Series F, No. 2.) New York, 1964.

Basic references on economic development are
Bruton, H. J., *Principles of Development Economics.* Englewood Cliffs, N.J.: Prentice-Hall, 1965.

Lewis, A. W., *The Theory of Economic Growth.* Homewood, Ill.: Irwin, 1955.

On the economics of education and related topics, see

Correa, H., "Measuring Education's Contribution to Economic Growth," in S. Elam, and W. P, McLurr, (eds) *Educational Requirements for the 1970's.* New York: Frederick A. Praeger, 1967.

Schultz, T. W., *The Economic Value of Education.* New York: Columbia U.P., 1963.

Vaizey, J., *The Economics of Education.* London: Faber and Faber, 1961.

chapter 4

Basis for the Quantitative Analysis of the Educational System

4-1   Content of This Chapter

This chapter does not deal directly with the preparation of an educational plan. Rather, it provides the educational background needed for such tasks. In this sense, it is the educational counterpart of Chapters 2 and 3.

The first step in the analysis of an educational system is to determine its main elements. Perhaps the most important among these elements are:

(a) Timetables comprising two elements: time allotted to direct interaction between teachers and students; and educational content, i.e., the subjects taught

(b) Teachers and administrative personnel

(c) Buildings and other facilities

(d) Students

(e) Graduates and dropouts, which do not form part of the educational system itself, but are its output

Several attempts have been made to establish accounting relationships among these elements. Examples of these are student-teacher ratios, student-classroom ratios, and the like. Another example is the statistical data related to the number of students in the educational system. All of these elements measure different aspects of the same system. As a consequence, they must be defined with respect to each other. Actually, the elements of the educational system must give rise to systems of quantitative indices.

The object of this chapter is to present one such system of indices that places emphasis on the interrelations of the elements of the educational system.

In Sec. 4-2 weighted student-teacher and student-classroom ratios are introduced. For example, let us compare a class of 40 students with one teacher teaching all the subjects with a second class, also composed of 40 students, but with two teachers, each teaching half of the subjects. The student-teacher ratio for the first class is 40:1, while it is 20:1 for the second. From the knowledge of these ratios, a planner might suggest that the number of students per teacher be increased in the second class. However, the teacher of the first class as well as the two teachers of the second class face a group of 40 students, evaluate homework and examinations for 40 students, etc. This means that the number of students per class should not, perhaps, be changed.

The reason for the misinterpretation is that the student-teacher ratios do not take into consideration the number of hours that, according to the timetables, teachers must face students. The three elements mentioned: timetables, teachers, and students, are considered in the weighted ratios.

An analysis similar to the above could be made with reference to classrooms. Such an analysis would permit us to explain the need and the main characteristics of the student-classroom ratios.

In Sec. 4-3, the *flows of students* are considered. The starting point for this analysis is the equation:

$$\text{Students flowing in} = \text{Students flowing out}$$

The students flowing into the educational system can be classified as new entrants, reentrants and repeaters. Those flowing out can be classified as graduates, repeaters going through the same grade during the next school year, dropouts and deaths. In Sec. 4-3 precise mathematical expressions are constructed using these elements. These expressions are the basic building blocks with which we may construct indices to evaluate the characteristics of an educational system. We also have available the instruments to study the future development of the number of student dropouts, graduates, and others. The use of these indices and instruments is explained mainly in Chapter 5.

Once the instruments for the analysis of the flows of students are available, it is possible to begin to describe the *output of the educational system*. In this description, it must be remembered that the output is not only the students successfully finishing their studies but also those dropping out. A precise definition of the output is the instrument by which we can relate the educational system to the educational structure of the population and the labor force.

4-2 Quantitative Relations between Students, Teachers, and Physical Facilities

4-2.1 Basic Definitions

In this section, perhaps the most important in this book, the basic definitions and main relations among the following are presented.

S = total number of students

H = number of periods of education offered for unit of time (say a week)

N = number of periods of education received by all the students

s_h = average size of a class

h_s = average number of periods of education received by each student

To introduce these concepts, the timetable of Central High School and the number of students per grade are presented in Table 4-1. Such information can be obtained only through direct observation, which is a simple task in the case of a single school but a much more difficult undertaking where an entire educational system is concerned. For an entire educational system, a census or sample survey of schools would be needed to obtain such information.

It will be noted that the high school level is divided into six grades, some of which are further subdivided. All sections within the first two grades are taught the same subjects. For example, the three sections comprising the first grade have exactly the same curriculum; hence, all students could be grouped together or taught by a single instructional television series. The situation, however, is more complex in the case of the sixth grade, where curricula are not identical for all three sections. Students in 6A, for instance, do not study the same subjects as students in 6B, nor with the same intensity. The situation is rendered still more complex by the fact that subjects 7, 8, 17, 19, 21, and 24 are taught to all sixth-grade students together.

To introduce the basic definitions mentioned above, let us consider the case of a single grade first, say 1A, and one subject, say National language. According to Table 4-1, National language is offered five periods per week to the fifty students in grade 1A. The total number of periods received by the students is

$$5 \times 50 = 250$$

$$\begin{matrix} \text{Number of periods} \\ \text{education offered} \end{matrix} \times \text{Size of class} = \begin{matrix} \text{Number of periods} \\ \text{education received} \end{matrix}$$

An alternative way of expressing this equation is

$$50 = \frac{250}{5}$$

$$\text{Size of class} = \frac{\text{Number of periods of education received}}{\text{Number of periods of education offered}}$$

A second alternative is

$$5 = \frac{250}{50}$$

$$\begin{matrix} \text{Number of periods} \\ \text{education offered} \end{matrix} = \frac{\text{Number of periods of education received}}{\text{Size of class}}$$

Table 4-1.   Timetable for Central High School (periods per week)

Subject	Grade													
	1A	1B	1C	2A	2B	2C	3A	3B	4A	4B	5	6A	6B	6C
1 National language	5	5	5	5	5	5	—	—	—	—	—	4	—	—
2 National literature	—	—	—	—	—	—	—	—	—	—	—	5	—	—
3 World literature	—	5	5	5	5	5	5	5	5	5	5	2	3	3
4 Mathematics	5	5	5	5	5	5	5	5	5	5	5	—	5	3
5 National history	5	5	5	5	5	5	—	—	—	—	—	—	—	—
6 Continental history	—	—	—	—	—	—	—	—	—	—	—	—	—	—
7 World history	—	—	—	—	—	—	3	3	3	3	3	—	3	—
8 National geography	5	5	5	5	5	5	—	—	—	—	—	—	3	—
9 Continental geography	—	—	—	—	—	—	—	—	—	—	—	—	—	—
10 World geography	—	—	—	—	—	—	3	3	3	3	3	—	—	—
11 Economic and political geography	—	—	—	—	—	—	—	—	—	—	—	—	—	—
12 Nature study	5	5	5	5	5	5	—	—	—	—	—	—	—	—
13 Physics	—	—	—	—	—	—	3	3	4	4	4	—	5	4
14 Chemistry	—	—	—	—	—	—	3	3	4	4	3	—	1	—
15 Anatomy, physiology, hygiene	—	—	—	—	—	—	3	3	—	—	—	—	—	—
16 Biology	—	—	—	—	—	—	—	—	3	3	2	—	—	4
17 Civics	—	—	—	—	—	—	—	—	—	—	—	—	—	2
18 Philosophy	—	—	—	—	—	—	—	—	—	—	—	5	2	—
19 Psychology	—	—	—	—	—	—	—	—	—	—	—	—	3	—
20 Logic and ethics	—	—	—	—	—	—	—	—	—	—	3	—	—	—
21 Foreign language	3	3	3	3	3	3	3	3	3	3	2	—	2	—
22 Art	—	—	—	—	—	—	—	—	—	—	—	—	—	—
23 Social education	2	2	2	2	2	2	2	2	—	—	—	—	—	—
24 Physical training	2	2	2	2	2	2	2	2	2	2	2	—	2	—
Total number of periods per week offered each class	32	32	32	32	32	32	32	32	32	32	32	32	32	32
Number of students in each class	50	50	43	45	40	40	52	50	39	39	55	16	18	18

The same relationship can be demonstrated if, instead of considering only National language, all the subjects taught to the students in grade 1A or in any other grade are considered. This can be expressed in the following formula:

$$s_i N_i = H_i \qquad (4\text{-}1)$$

when $i = 1A$, $s_{1A} = 50$. H_i is the number of periods of education offered to class i. For instance, $H_i = 32$ for any i—that is, any grade in Central High School. N_i is the number of periods of education received by all the students in class i—that is, in the case of the students in class 1A, $N_{1A} = 50 \times 32 = 1,600$.

From Eq. 4-1 it follows that the size of the class is

$$s_i = \frac{N_i}{H_i} \qquad (4\text{-}2)$$

and the number of periods received per student is

$$H_i = \frac{N_i}{s_i} \qquad (4\text{-}3)$$

Suppose now that several classes are considered, for example, all the grades in Central High School. In this case, the *total number of students* S is obtained from the last row of Table 4-1.

$$S = S_{1A} + S_{1B} + S_{1C} + \cdots + S_{6A} + S_{6B} + S_{6C}$$
$$= 50 + 50 + 43 + \cdots + 16 + 18 + 18 = 555$$

The total number of periods of education offered per week H is the sum of periods offered to each class. A summary of the periods per week offered to each class appears in Table 4-2, which shows that each of the

Table 4-2. Central High School: Total Number of Class Periods per Week

Grades and Sections	Number of Grades and Sections	Periods per Week per Grade	Total Number of Periods
1A, 1B, 1C 2A, 2B, 2C 3A, 3B 4A, 4B 5	11	32	352
6A, 6B, 6C (separate)	3	16	48
6A, 6B, 6C (together)	1	16	16
Total			416

eleven grade sections from 1A to 5 receives 32 periods per week, making a total of

$$11 \times 32 = 352 \text{ periods per week}$$

Each of the three sixth-grade sections receives separately 16 periods per week, a total of

$$3 \times 16 = 48 \text{ periods per week}$$

In addition, the sixth grade taken as one section receives 16 periods per week. The sum of the three quantities gives a grand total of

$$H = 352 + 48 + 16 = 416 \text{ periods per week}$$

Schematically, the total periods of education offered is

$$H = H_{1A} + H_{1B} + H_{1C} + \cdots + H_{6A} + H_{6B} + H_{6C} + H_6$$

If data for all the schools of a given educational level in a particular country can be obtained, the value of H for that country can be determined.

In a similar way, the *total number of periods of education received by all the students* in Central High School is the sum of the periods received by the students in each class; i.e., using the figures in the last two rows of Table 4-1:

$$N = N_{1A} + N_{1B} + N_{1C} + \cdots + N_{6A} + N_{6B} + N_{6C} + N_6$$
$$= 1600 + 1600 + 1376 + \cdots + 256 + 282 + 288 + 832 = 17,760$$

From Eq. 4-2, it follows that the *average size of a class*, s_h, is

$$s_h = \frac{N}{H}$$
$$= \frac{17,760}{416} = 42.69 \tag{4-4}$$

Further, from Eq. 4-3, it follows that the *average number of periods received by each student*, h_s, is

$$h_s = \frac{N}{S}$$
$$= \frac{17,760}{555} = 32 \tag{4-5}$$

What is the meaning of this figure for the average number of students attending each period? Two meanings can be given: one if it is related to teachers and another if it is related to physical facilities. Let us examine these two interpretations.

4-2.2 Number of Teachers and Average Size of the Class

In order to relate the number of teachers to the average size of the class, the following equivalence is used: the *number of periods of education offered is equal to the total number of periods taught by all the teachers.* This is so because, by definition, a period of education in which a teacher teaches is a period of education offered.

Central High School's teachers, the subjects they teach, the grades in which they teach and the number of periods per week they teach are listed in Table 4-3 where the equivalence stated above can be observed—that is,

Table 4-3.   Teachers in Central High School

Teacher	Subject	Grade	Periods per Week
1	1	1A, 1B, 1C	15
2	1	2A, 2B, 2C	15
3	2	3A, 3B, 4A, 4B, 6A	24
4	3	5, 6A, 6B, 6C	16
5	4	1A, 2A, 3A, 4A	20
6	4	1B, 2B, 3B, 4B	20
7	4	1C, 2C, 5, 6A	17
8	4	6B, 6C	8
9	5, 6, 7	1A, 1B, 2B, 4A	18
10	5, 6	1C, 2A, 2C	15
11	7	3A, 3B, 4B, 5, 6	15
12	8	1A, 1B, 1C, 6	18
13	9	2A, 2B, 2C	15
14	10, 11	3A, 3B, 4A, 4B, 5	15
15	12	1A, 1B, 1C, 2A, 2B, 2C	30
16	13	3A, 3B, 4A, 4B, 5, 6B	23
17	14	3A, 3B, 4A, 4B, 5, 6B, 6C	22
18	15, 16	3A, 3B, 4A, 4B, 5, 6C	18
19	17, 23	1A, 1B, 1C, 6A, 6B, 6C	9
20	18, 19, 20	5, 6A, 6B, 6C	15
21	21	1A, 1B, 1C, 2A, 2B, 2C	18
22	21	3A, 3B, 4A, 4B, 5, 6	16
23	22	2A, 2B, 2C, 3A, 3B	10
24	24	1A, 1B, . . . , 6C	24
Total			416

the total number of periods taught each week by all the teachers (416) is the same figure as the number of periods offered per week (416). In other words, the same figure may be obtained by two different approaches.

We can now establish the following relationship between the total number of periods offered per week and teachers:

$$H = h_c T \qquad (4\text{-}6)$$

where T = number of teachers (24 in Central High School)

h_c = average number of periods taught by each teacher per week

The average number of periods per week per teacher in Central High School is

$$h_c = \frac{H}{T} = \frac{\text{Total number of periods offered per week}}{\text{Total number of teachers}}$$

$$= \frac{416}{24} = 17.33$$

As related to the number of teachers and average teaching hours per week, s_h, the average size of the class has the following precise meaning:

$$s_h = \frac{N}{H} = \frac{h_s \times S}{h_c \times T} \qquad (4\text{-}7)$$

This equation is derived by substitution in Eq. 4-4 of equivalent expressions for N and H which are given in Eqs. 4-5 and 4-6. This equation tells us that the number of students per period is the student-teacher ratio weighted by the ratio of periods per student to periods per teacher. Put in another way, the average number of students per period is the average number of students that a teacher faces per period. The ratio in Eq. 4-7 is more meaningful as an index of quality of education than the unweighted student-teacher ratio since the quality of the system, if related at all to the number of students per teacher, must be related to the average number of students a teacher faces each hour in the classroom.

Equation 4-7 is useful in considering possible alternative reactions to an increase in the number of students. Solving Eq. 4-7 for T, we find that

$$T = S \frac{h_s}{h_c \times s_h}$$

This equation shows that to hold the number (s_h) of pupils per period constant with rising student numbers (S), one must increase the number h_c of periods taught per teacher per week and/or the number T of teachers, or one must decrease the number h_s of periods of education received per student per week. Thus we see that a school system confronted with a rising student population has some flexibility in meeting the increase in student numbers without allowing quality (measured by class size—that is, s_h) to decline. Hence, an increase in student population may not necessarily require an increase in the number of teachers, especially if the number h_c of periods taught per teacher per week can be increased.

The equation above also reveals the different elements that should be considered in the estimation of the number of teachers required to teach a known number of students. If the number of students S to be taught is known and desired values for h_s, h_c, and s_h are established, then the number of teachers needed for the students can easily be determined. Since the estimation of the number of teachers required for a known number of students is one of the central problems in educational planning, the value of Eq. 4-7 to educational planners is apparent.

Equation 4-7 can be modified to consider several different teaching situations such as the cases in which each teacher has several teacher assistants or closed television circuits are used. In addition equations similar to Eq. 4-7 can be used to relate students and teachers with personnel in administrative and supervisory positions.

4-2.3 Physical Facilities: Number of Classrooms and Average Size of Class

The following classification will prove useful in studying the physical facilities involved in the educational process:

Plant consists of school buildings, areas set aside as playgrounds, sports fields, outdoor equipment and buildings for the housing of teachers and students. The various elements may be grouped under the general headings *School Areas* and *Housing Areas*. Elements under the former heading, primarily classrooms and laboratories, are common to all schools.

Instruments consist of books, furniture, indoor or laboratory equipment, audio-visual aids, and other teaching devices.

Central High School provides no living accommodations for teachers or students so we will not be concerned with Housing Area. The School Area is described in Table 4-4.

Table 4-4. Central High School: Characteristics of the School Area

Use of Space	Characteristics	
	mt^2 per Student	Number
Buildings		
Teaching		
Classrooms.	3.25	14
Laboratories	1.30	6
Administration	0.20	3
Auxiliary		
Library.	0.90	1
Auditorium	1.10	1
Storage.	0.15	4
Sanitary area	0.18	1
Gymnasium	0.50	1
Internal movement area	0.70	1
Multipurpose.	0.10	1
Open Space		
Playgrounds.	1.20	1
Sports fields	1.05	1
Parking	—	—

The School Area may be subdivided into Buildings and Open Space, a further distinction being drawn in the case of Buildings between premises used directly for teaching and administration and those used for auxiliary purposes. The Open Space consists of playgrounds, sports fields and parking lots. All these analytical subdivisions may be modified should it seem desirable to do so.

Since our present aim is to relate the space available to its employment for teaching proper, we will concentrate primarily on classrooms and laboratories. Table 4-5 shows the use made of these in terms of periods per week. It also indicates that, for most periods, each classroom or laboratory is occupied by only one grade section, although this does not apply to the Language (B) laboratory nor to the Psychology laboratory, nor to classroom 14, each of which is occupied by all sixth-grade sections together for several periods each week.

By totaling the number of periods for each laboratory and classroom given in the last line of Table 4-5—that is, by adding:

$$18 + 16 + 23 + \cdots + 16 + 10 + 19$$

we obtain a value of 416. (This is necessarily the same as the total number of periods shown in the timetable.) Since each period lasts one hour, this means that Central High School classrooms and laboratories are in use for a total of 416 hours per week.

We can now establish the following relationship between the total number of periods per week H and the number of classrooms and laboratories:

$$H = h_r R \qquad (4\text{-}8)$$

where R = number of classrooms and laboratories

h_r = average number of periods each room is used per week

The average number of periods during which each classroom and laboratory in Central High School is in use is found as follows:

$$h_r = \frac{H}{R} = \frac{\text{Total number of periods per week}}{\text{Total number of classrooms and laboratories}}$$

$$= \frac{416}{20} = 20.80 \text{ periods per week}$$

Now we can consider from the point of view of classrooms and laboratories the meaning to be attached to the number of students taking each period, s_h.

From Eqs. 4-4, 4-5, and 4-8 we obtain

$$s_h = \frac{N}{H} = \frac{h_s \times S}{h_r \times R} \qquad (4\text{-}9)$$

Table 4-5. Central High School: Use of Classrooms and Laboratories (periods per week)

User's Grade	Laboratories						Classrooms														Total
	Languages A	Languages B	Physics	Chemistry	Anatomy Biology	Psychology	1	2	3	4	5	6	7	8	9	10	11	12	13	14	
1A	3	—	—	—	—	—	29	—	—	—	—	—	—	—	—	—	—	—	—	—	29
1B	3	—	—	—	—	—	—	29	—	—	—	—	—	—	—	—	—	—	—	—	29
1C	3	—	—	—	—	—	—	—	29	—	—	—	—	—	—	—	—	—	—	—	29
2A	3	—	—	—	—	—	—	—	—	29	—	—	—	—	—	—	—	—	—	—	29
2B	3	—	—	—	—	—	—	—	—	—	29	—	—	—	—	—	—	—	—	—	29
2C	3	—	—	—	—	—	—	—	—	—	—	29	—	—	—	—	—	—	—	—	29
3A	—	3	3	3	3	—	—	—	—	—	—	—	20	—	—	—	—	—	—	—	20
3B	—	3	3	3	3	—	—	—	—	—	—	—	—	20	—	—	—	—	—	—	20
4A	—	3	4	4	3	—	—	—	—	—	—	—	—	—	18	—	—	—	—	—	18
4B	—	3	4	4	3	—	—	—	—	—	—	—	—	—	—	18	—	—	—	—	18
5	—	2	4	3	2	—	—	—	—	—	—	—	—	—	—	—	21	—	—	—	21
6A	—	—	—	—	—	—	—	—	—	—	—	—	—	—	—	—	—	16	—	—	16
6B	—	2	5	1	—	3	—	—	—	—	—	—	—	—	—	—	—	—	10	11	10
6C	—	—	—	4	4	—	—	—	—	—	—	—	—	—	—	—	—	—	—	—(+8)	19
Total	18	16	23	22	18	3	29	29	29	29	29	29	20	20	18	18	21	16	10	19	

i.e., the number of students per period is the student-room ratio weighted by the ratio of the number of periods per student per week to number of periods per room per week. The fact that the weighted ratios 4-7 and 4-9 are equivalent bears out our intuition. It is obvious that the average number of students that a teacher faces must be equal to the average number of students in the classroom when all classrooms have teachers and no classroom has more than one teacher in a given period.

Observations similar to those made with respect to the weighted student-teacher ratio can be made with respect to the ratio in Eq. 4-9.

Transforming eq. 4-9, we obtain

$$R = S \frac{h_s}{h_r \times s_h}$$

Hence if the number of students S to be taught increases, and one wants to hold the size of a class s_h constant so as to prevent deterioration in the quality of education, then either the number of periods per week h_r and/or the number of classrooms R must be increased; or the number of periods of education received per student per week h_s must be decreased.

Thus we see that a school system confronted with a rising·student population has, in the case of classrooms as in the case of teachers, some flexibility in meeting the increase in student numbers without allowing quality (measured by class size) to decline. An increase in student population may not necessarily require an increase in the number of classrooms and laboratories, especially if the number of periods a classroom is used per week can be increased.

The equivalence between ratios 4-7 and 4-9 shows us another fact: it is impossible to change the weighted student-teacher ratio without also changing the weighted student-room ratio. This is a necessary consequence of the relationships between different factors in education. These relationships should also be considered in educational planning.

In the derivation of the relationship between the number of classrooms and laboratories and the size of the class, no mention has been made of implements such as closed television circuits, teaching machines, etc. The basic equations can be modified to take into consideration cases such as the ones mentioned, but these modifications will not be presented here.

4-3   Flows of Students

4-3.1   Basic Equations for the Analysis of Flows of Students

Let us consider as before one grade in Central High School in a given year, say grade 1 in year 0 (Table 4-6). A basic equation can be estab-

Table 4-6.   Central High School: Structure 0

Grades	Years											
	−5	−4	−3	−2	−1	0	1	2	3	4	5	6
Total −1	115	121	126	130	135	143						
New	108	112	112	111	112	115						
Repeaters	7	9	14	19	23	28	32					
Total −2		105	110	115	120	125	133					
New		96	97	99	101	100	103					
Repeaters		10	13	17	19	25	30	36				
Total −3			80	87	95	102	108	118				
New			74	77	81	82	85	91				
Repeaters			6	10	14	20	23	27	31			
Total −4				66	71	78	89	97	110			
New				59	62	63	69	73	81			
Repeaters				7	9	15	20	24	29	34		
Total −5					53	55	64	73	79	91		
New					46	47	54	60	65	74		
Repeaters					7	8	10	13	14	17	21	
Total −6						52	57	66	75	83	91	
New						40	43	49	55	60	65	
Repeaters						12	14	17	20	23	26	30

Total enrollment year 0 = 555

lished with respect to these students in the period under consideration:

Students flowing in = Students flowing out

The students flowing into a school grade at the beginning of a school period in a given year can be classified as new entrants, reentrants and repeaters coming from the previous school year; those flowing out during and at the end of the school period can be classified as graduates of the grade, dropouts, repeaters going to the same grade next school year, and deaths. This relation can be written in the following way:

New entrants + reentrants   Graduates + dropouts
+ repeaters coming from = + deaths + repeaters
previous School year   staying next school year

Taking into consideration the values for grade 1 in year 0 (Tables 4-6 and 4-7), the equation above has the following form:

$$115 + 0 + 28 = 103 + 7 + 1 + 32$$

This equation is represented in Fig. 4-1. The two main lines in this figure are the lower horizontal one and the oblique line above it. The

Table 4-7.   *Central High School: Dropouts, Graduates, and Deaths from Structure 0*

Grades	Years										
	−5	−4	−3	−2	−1	0	1	2	3	4	5
Total −1	10	10	8	6	6	8					
Dropouts	8	7	6	5	5	7					
Deaths	2	3	2	1	2	1					
Total −2		19	16	16	13	10	6				
Dropouts		19	14	14	12	10	4				
Deaths		0	2	2	1	0	2				
Total −3			11	11	12	10	8	6			
Dropouts			11	11	10	9	8	5			
Deaths			0	0	2	1	0	1			
Total −4				11	9	4	5	3	2		
Dropouts				11	7	4	4	3	2		
Deaths				0	2	0	1	0	0		
Total −5					5	2	2	4	2	5	
Dropouts					5	2	2	3	2	5	
Deaths					0	0	0	1	0	0	
Total −6						38	40	46	52	57	61
Graduates						38	40	45	52	56	61
Deaths						0	0	1	1	1	0
Total	10	29	35	44	46	72	61	59	56	62	61
Dropouts	8	26	31	41	39	32	18	11	4	5	
Graduates						38	40	45	52	56	61
Deaths	2	3	4	3	7	2	3	3	0	1	0

time period between the beginning and the end of the school period is represented by the horizontal line, and the number of students at any time is measured by the distance between the horizontal and the oblique lines. The largest number of students appears at the beginning of the school period, and this number declines to its minimum at the end of the period. The difference between the number of students at the beginning of the school year minus those in it at time t appears in the shaded area, representing dropouts and deaths.

In the analysis made above, the time of reference has been the beginning of the period; however, there is no reason why the equation representing the students flowing in and flowing out could not be established with reference to any time between the beginning and the end of the period. Figure 4-2 is a graphical representation of the basic equation when the beginning of the school year is not taken as the time of reference. In this case, the number of students at time t can be expressed in

FIGURE 4-1

Graphical Representation of the Basic Equation
for Student Flows when the Beginning of the
School Year Is the Time of Reference

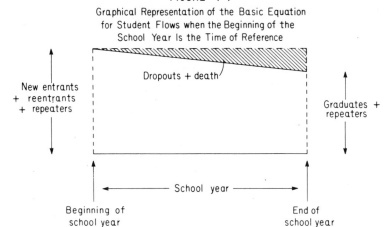

FIGURE 4-2

Graphical Representation of the Basic Equation
for Student Flows when the Beginning of the
School Year Is Not the Time of Reference

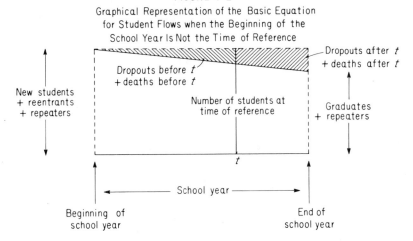

either of two ways: in terms of the students at the beginning of the period minus dropouts and deaths before t; or in terms of the graduates and repeaters at the end of the period plus dropouts and deaths after t.

These two ways to express the number of students at time t take the following form when mathematical symbols are used:

$$S_t = n_t + r_t - b_t - d_t^1 \qquad (4\text{-}10)$$

$$S_t = g_t + a_t + r_{t+1} + d_t^2 \qquad (4\text{-}11)$$

where S_t = number of students at time t
   n_t = number of new entrants

r_t = number of repeaters coming from the previous school period
b_t = dropouts before time t
d_t^1 = deaths before time t
g_t = graduates
a_t = dropouts after time t
r_{t+1} = repeaters going to the same grade next school period
d_t^2 = deaths after time t

In the equations above, no attention has been paid to reentrants because it is considered that their number is small, and we will work with this assumption in this book.

The equations above are particularly useful in educational planning because they serve as a frame of reference for the simultaneous consideration of several grades of the educational system, a level or several levels together, or even the whole system.

In considering the flow of students in an individual school or educational system, we will use the analytical framework illustrated in Table 4-6. This table shows Central High School enrollment (divided into new entrants and repeaters) for the six grades in year 0 and for those grades in years before and after year 0 whose enrollments influence or are influenced by the enrollments in year 0. We shall consider the enrollment figures in the table as one unit which we shall call a *structure*. The year about which the structure is centered will be called the *pivotal year*; in Table 4-6 the pivotal year is year 0. Each structure carries the name of its pivotal year; hence, the structure in Table 4-6 is called structure 0.

The whole history of an educational system or school can be analyzed in terms of a series of contiguous but nonoverlapping structures such as the structure shown in this table. Figure 4-3 represents several structures

FIGURE 4–3

Planiland High School Level Structures,
Grades 6 Through 12

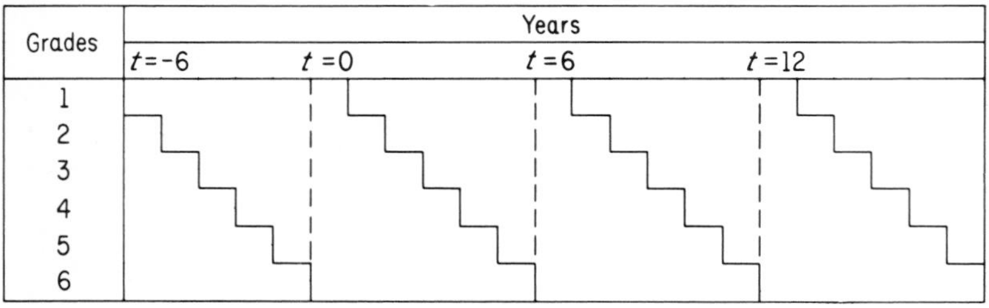

for one level of education which lasts six years. The steps going down to the right show the boundaries between structures. The pivotal years of these structures are separated by six years—the number of years that a student normally spends in high school in Planiland. Statistical data for contiguous structures are presented in Table 5-1. In the general case, if a level of education (primary, secondary, or tertiary) lasts k years and a pivotal year is t, then the preceding pivotal year for that level of education is $t - k$ and the succeeding pivotal year is $t + k$.

The numerical characteristics of the structure in Table 4-6 can be described by equations quite similar to those in Eqs. 4-10 and 4-11. It is required to modify only the meaning of the variables used in Eqs. 4-10 and 4-11. Below only these modified meanings will be used, so there is no risk of confusion. The modified interpretations of the variables given to the symbols are as follows:

S_t = total enrollment at the beginning of pivotal year t

n_t = new entrants in structure t

r_t = repeaters coming to structure t from structure $t - k$

b_t = dropouts from structure t before pivotal year t

a_t = dropouts from structure t during and after pivotal year t

g_t = graduates from structure t

d_t^i = deaths among the students in structure t

i = 1 before the pivotal year

i = 2 during and after the pivotal year

Let us clarify the meaning of "repeaters coming to structure t from structure $t - k$." For this, data in Table 4-6 will be used; we will refer to structure 0 and structure -6, which looks like structure 0 except that it extends from the first grade in year -11 to the sixth grade in year -1. The whole left flank of structure 0 between years -5 and 0 is open to the right flank structure -6. The students in the first grade in year -6 might repeat in year -5, thus becoming an input as regards structure 0. The same would apply to second grade repeaters in year -4, and so on. All these repeaters are accounted for under the heading "repeaters coming from structure -6."

By using the notation introduced above, the following equations can be established:

$$S_t = n_t + r_t - b_t - d_t^1 \tag{4-12}$$

$$S_t = g_t + a_t + r_{t+k} + d_t^2 \tag{4-13}$$

Let us consider Eq. 4-12 as it applies to the structure shown in Table 4-6, i.e., with $t = 0$.

To begin with, it is obvious that the number S_0 of students in the different grades at the beginning of year 0 is equal to the number entering the structure (new enrollments, n_0, plus repeaters, r_0) minus the number which left the structure prior to year 0 (dropouts, b_0, and deaths, d_0^1.

In Table 4-6 new entrants in the structure appear in the row for new entrants in the first grade for years -5 through 0. Their number is

$$n_0 = 108 + 112 + 112 + 111 + 112 + 115 = 670$$

The figure for the number of repeaters coming from structure -6 is obtained by adding together the figures for repeaters in the first grade for year -5, repeaters in the second grade for year -4, and so on up to repeaters in the sixth grade for year 0. Thus the number of repeaters entering structure 0 from structure -6 is

$$r_0 = 7 + 10 + 6 + 7 + 7 + 12 = 49$$

The students leaving the educational system are not shown in Table 4-6 but appear in Table 4-7. However, the number of students leaving the school may be obtained from the data in Table 4-6. In the first grade for year -5, for example, there are 115 students. Of these, 9 become repeaters in year -4 first grade and 96 go on to the second grade in year -4. The number of students leaving the first grade between years -5 and -4 is the number not accounted for by new entrants in the second grade or repeaters in the first grade for year -4:

$$115 - 9 - 96 = 10$$

The results of a similar analysis with respect to all the remaining figures in Table 4-6 are set out in Table 4-7. In addition, this table presents a breakdown (dropouts and deaths) of the students leaving the educational system. To estimate the number of deaths, the appropriate death rate was multiplied by the number of students at the beginning of the period. By adding the totals for dropouts and deaths for year -5 to -1 given in the last rows of Table 4-7, we obtain the figures for total dropouts and deaths from the structure 0 prior to pivotal year 0:

$$b_0 = \text{dropouts} = 145$$
$$d_0^1 = \text{deaths} \quad = \quad 19$$

Equation 4-12 takes the following form for structure 0:

$$555 = 670 + 49 - 145 - 19$$

The possible destinations of the students in a pivotal year are given in Eq. 4-13. The students in pivotal year 0 can graduate, drop out, pass to the next structure as repeaters or die.

The data found in Tables 4-6 and 4-7 can be used to quantify relationship for structure 0. Enrollment in year 0, as mentioned already in connection with relationship 4-12, is equal to 555 (Table 4-6). The total number of dropouts between years 0 and 5 as shown in Table 4-7 is

$$a_0 = 32 + 36 + 31 + 34 + 21 + 30 = 184$$

In order to obtain the figures relating to graduates which appear in Table 4-7, we have assumed that all those leaving school after beginning the sixth grade either die or graduate. Actually, there are dropouts in the sixth grade also, but their number may be assumed to be negligible.

Hence, we ignore the complicating factor of sixth-grade dropouts. If it is required, this assumption can be dropped and a more realistic point of view adopted. To obtain the number leaving the sixth grade in a given year, the number of sixth-grade repeaters for the next year must be subtracted from the total sixth-grade enrollment for the year considered. Thus the number leaving the sixth grade at the end of year 0 is

$$52 - 14 = 38$$

The number of those leaving after having begun sixth grade includes both graduates and deaths; figures for each category are shown in the sixth-grade row of Table 4-7. The total number of graduates for structure 0 is the sum of the numbers of graduates for years 0 through 5.

$$g_0 = 38 + 40 + 45 + 52 + 56 + 61 = 292$$

The number of deaths between year 0 and year 5 among those enrolled in year 0 is the sum of the figures for deaths given in the last row of Table 4-7 for years 0 to 5.

$$d_0^2 = 2 + 3 + 3 + 0 + 1 + 0 = 9$$

With the values obtained, relationship 4-13 for structure 0 becomes:

$$555 = 70 + 184 + 292 + 9$$

A summary of the analysis made above appears in Table 4-8.

Table 4-8. Central High School: Relationships 4-12 and 4-13 for Structure 0

Before Pivotal Year, Relationship 4-12				Total Enrollment, Pivotal Year 0	During and After Pivotal Year, Relationship 4-13			
New Entrants $+ n_0$	Repeaters $+ r_0$	Dropouts $- b_0$	Deaths $- d_0^1$	S_0	Dropouts $+ a_0$	Repeaters $+ r_6$	Graduates $+ g_0$	Deaths $+ d_0^2$
670	49	145	19	555	70	184	292	9

4-3.2 Indices for the Analysis of Flows of Students

Taking the basic relationships just defined as a starting point, several indices for the analysis of the student flows in a school or educational system can be defined. Some of these and their values for structure 0 of Planiland Central High School are presented in Table 4-9. Such indices can be used for the comparison of schools or educational systems.

4-3.3 Use of the Basic Equations for the Analysis of the Educational System as a Whole

In order to study an educational system as a whole, it is not enough to have an instrument to describe one of its levels. In this section the ex-

Table 4-9.   Central High School: Indices for the Analysis of
Student Flows Structure 0

Definition	Value
$\dfrac{\text{Repeaters}}{\text{Total inputs*}} = \dfrac{r_t}{n_t + r_t}$	$\dfrac{49}{670 + 49} = 0.068$
$\dfrac{\text{Dropouts before pivotal year}}{\text{Total inputs*}} = \dfrac{b_t}{n_t + r_t}$	$\dfrac{145}{670 + 49} = 0.202$
$\dfrac{\text{Deaths before pivotal year}}{\text{Total inputs*}} = \dfrac{d_t^1}{n_t + r_t}$	$\dfrac{19}{670 + 49} = 0.021$
$\dfrac{\text{Dropouts during and after pivotal year}}{\text{Enrollment pivotal year}} = \dfrac{a_t}{S_t}$	$\dfrac{70}{555} = 0.133$
$\dfrac{\text{Repeaters going to next structure}}{\text{Enrollment pivotal year}} = \dfrac{r_{t+6}}{S_t}$	$\dfrac{184}{555} = 0.332$
$\dfrac{\text{Deaths during and after pivotal year}}{\text{Enrollment pivotal year}} = \dfrac{d_t^2}{S_t}$	$\dfrac{9}{555} = 0.016$
$\dfrac{\text{Graduates}}{\text{Enrollment pivotal year}} = \dfrac{g_t}{S_t}$	$\dfrac{292}{555} = 0.526$

*Total inputs = new entrants + repeaters.

tensions required to use Eqs. 4-12 and 4-13 for the analysis of a complete educational system will be described.

In this book we shall assume that the educational system is divided into two basic branches: general education and teacher education. Two types of subdivisions of these branches will be considered: the usual subdivision of levels of education and a subdivision in qualitative strata. In this section we will consider only the problem of the adaptation of Eqs. 4-12 and 4-13 for the study of the different levels of the educational system. In Chapter 5 the use of these equations in the case when the educational system is divided in qualitative strata will be considered. Finally, in Chapter 10 the use of the equations for the study of teachers' education is presented.

In the analysis below we shall note that the educational system of Planiland is divided into three basic levels: elementary, high school, and college, and that the division into branches appears in high school and college. If for the time being no attention is paid to the division in branches, Eqs. 4-12 and 4-13 above should be distinguished only for each level. In this case they will be written as follows, with superscripts denoting educational level:

$$S_t^j = n_t^j + r_t^j - b_t^j - d_t^{1j} \qquad [4\text{-}12]$$

$$S_t^j = g_t^j + a_t^j + r_{t+k}^j + d_t^{2j} \qquad [4\text{-}13]$$

where j = 1, elementary level
     = 2, high school level
     = 3, college level

Already in Fig. 4-3 we have seen how the successive structures of one educational level are related. In Fig. 4-4, we see schematically how the

FIGURE 4-4

Structures −6 Through 12 for Elementary, High School, and College Levels

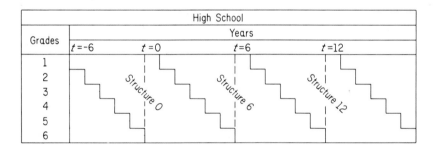

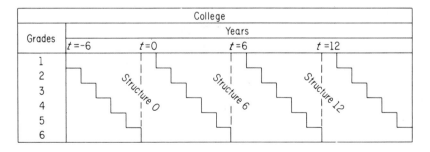

structures for the various levels of an educational system are related to each other. It is assumed in this figure that each level of education lasts six years; hence, pivotal years for all the education levels are six years apart and pivotal years for the different levels coincide. If levels within the system are of different lengths, the relations between the structures of the different levels are somewhat more complex but no conceptual change is required. We can see in the figure that, where all educational levels are the same length, new entrants in the high school and college levels (i.e., n_t^2 and n_t^3) are the graduates of the previous lower-level structure centered on the preceding pivotal year (i.e., g_{t-k}^1 and g_{t-k}^2). For instance, new entrants in structure 0 at the secondary level (i.e., n_0^2) are the graduates of primary level structure -6 (i.e., g_{-6}^1).

The procedure described above can be summarized as follows: First, construct a set of basic equations, 4-12 and 4-13, for each one of the subdivisions of the educational system to be considered; second, establish the proper relationship between new entrants of one subdivision and graduates from the others. Following these rules, it is possible to use the basic equations to study any subdivision of the educational system. To mention just a few of the most important subdivisions in practical application: subdivisions by sex of the students; subdivisions in public and private institutions; subdivisions in general and vocational education; and subdivisions according to type of vocational school.

It should be observed that the basic equations can be used also for the study of on-the-job training and adult education wherever some form of institutionalization exists. However, types of education without any formal structure (such as the mass media) cannot be studied with Eqs. 4-12 and 4-13.

4-4   Output of the Educational System

Perhaps the most important application of relationships 4-12 and 4-13 just introduced is that they permit definition in simple terms of the output of an educational system.

Here we will consider the output of two educational levels, high school and college, denoted by the superscripts 2 and 3 respectively. Let
0_t^j = output of the educational system of persons with education level
     $j = 2, 3$ between pivotal years $t - k$ and t

Then

$$0_{t+k}^2 = g_t^2 + (1 - \gamma^2)a_t^2 + (1 - \eta^2)b_{t+k}^2 \qquad (4\text{-}14)$$
$$+ \gamma^3 a_t^3 + \eta^3 b_{t+k}^3 - n_{t+k}^3$$

and

$$0_{t+k}^3 = g_t^3 + (1 - \gamma^3)a_t^3 + (1 - \eta^3)b_{t+k}^3 \qquad (4\text{-}15)$$

where η^j = proportion of dropouts from level j before the pivotal year
       that are considered a part of the output of the previous level
    γ^j = proportion of dropouts from level j during and after the pivotal year that are considered a part of the output of the previous level

The coefficients η^j and γ^j must be included, because it is a matter of definition whether a dropout from, say, the third year of high school will be considered an output of the high school or the elementary school level. The coefficient may be used to express all the possible alternative judgments as to what part of a levels' dropouts should not be counted as output of that level.

In Eq. 4-14 the output of high school between pivotal years t and $t + k\,(0_{t+k}^2)$ is equal to

g_t^2, i.e., graduates from high school between pivotal years t and $t + k$,

plus

$(1 - \gamma^2)a^2$, i.e., those dropouts from high school structure t during and after the pivotal year t which are considered as output from high school

plus

$(1 - \eta^2)b_{t+k}^2$, i.e., the dropouts from structure $t + k$ before year $t + k$ which are considered as output from high school

plus

$\gamma^3 a_t^3 + \eta^3 b_{t+1}^3$, i.e., those dropouts from college which are considered only high school output

minus

n_{t+k}^3, i.e., the number of high school graduates from structure t entering college in structure $t + k$

Similarly, Eq. 4-15 tells us that output from college between pivotal years t and $t + k\,(0_{t+k}^3)$ is equal to the sum of:

g_t^3, i.e., graduates from college between pivotal years t and $t + k$

$(1 - \gamma^3)a_t^3$, those dropouts from college structure t during and after pivotal year t that are considered as output from college

and

$(1 - \eta^3)b_{t+k}^3$, those dropouts from structure $t + k$ before pivotal year $t + k$ which are considered as output from college

References

This chapter is an elaboration of

Correa, H., "Basis for the Quantitative Analysis of the Educational System," *Journal of Experimental Education*, Vol. 35, No. 1 (Fall 1966).

A mathematically more sophisticated version of this chapter appears in
Correa, H., "A Survey of Mathematical Models in Educational Planning," *Mathematical Models in Educational Planning*. Paris: O.E.C.D., 1967.

A comparison of the model in this chapter with other models appear in
Davis, R. C., *Planning Human Resource Development*. Chicago: Rand McNally, 1966.

Glossary of Symbols

H number of periods offered per unit of time
N number of periods received by all students
R number of classrooms and laboratories
S number of students
T number of teachers
h_r average number of periods that each room is used per week
h_s average number of periods per week per student
h_c average number of periods per week per teacher
s_h average number of students per period; weighted student-teacher ratio; weighted student-room ratio
a_t dropouts from structure t during and after pivotal year t
b_t dropouts from structure t before pivotal year t
d_t^i deaths of students in structure t;

$$i = 1 \text{ before pivotal year } t$$
$$i = 2 \text{ during and after pivotal year } t$$

g_t graduates from structure t
k number of years that an educational level lasts
n_t number of new entrants in structure t
r_t number of repeaters entering structure t from structure $t - k$
0_t output of persons with education level, between pivotal years $t - k$ and t
η^j proportion of the dropouts from level j before the pivotal year which are considered a part of the output of the previous level
γ^j proportion of dropouts from level j during and after the pivotal year which are considered a part of the output of the previous level

Superscripts are used to designate education level (1 = elementary; 2 = high school; 3 = college).

chapter 5

Flows of Students

5-1   Content of This Chapter

A basic problem in planning is the forecasting of the future evolution of student flows. We find the basic information for such forecasts in the analysis of past and present characteristics and trends. Sec. 5-3.1 (Tables 5-1 and 5-2) contains the raw data required. Using the method introduced in Chapter 4, these data are summarized in Table 5-3.

Once the basic data are put into manageable form, it is possible to predict the future flows of students. Several methods can be used for this prediction. Two of them are presented in this chapter.

The first method considers only the influence of population growth on the flows of students. The information concerning the growth of the school-age population is provided by demographers using the methods outlined in Chapter 2. In the first method it is assumed that the proportion of school-age children entering the educational system will be the same as it has been in the past, and consideration is given to the persons who have never enrolled in the educational system, distinguishing them from the dropouts. When simpler approaches are used, it is likely that the number of children enrolling in the educational system will be overestimated.

The next step is to forecast the number of children continuing in the educational system and the number leaving it. In the first approach it is assumed that fixed proportions of those entering will become dropouts, graduates, or deaths.

The details of the first approach are presented in Sec. 5-4.2. The results obtained appear in Tables 5-14, 5-15, and 5-16.

One limitation of the first method is that it does not take into consideration the fact that as economic development takes place, the proportions of children entering and remaining in the educational system will tend to increase. This limitation is eliminated in *the second method, because this method takes into account the influence of per capita income growth on those proportions.* As a first step, the increase in the proportion of children entering the educational system due to increments in per capita income is evaluated. Next, a similar evaluation is made with respect to the proportions of those dropping out and graduating. These computations give the information needed to forecast the flows of students. The details of the method appear in Sec. 5-4.3, the results in Tables 5-25 and 5-28.

A brief comparison of the results obtained by the two methods shows that they are different, but not incompatible. The first forecast represents the minimum growth of the educational system while the second represents a more likely alternative.

5-2 Method

The instrument to be used in the analysis of the student flows was described in Sec. 4-3.1. There two basic equations were introduced:

$$S_t = n_t + r_t - b_t - d_t^1 \qquad [4\text{-}12]$$
$$S_t = g_t + a_t + r_{t+k} + d_t^2 \qquad [4\text{-}13]$$

where t = pivotal years, not calendar years

S_t = number of students at the beginning of pivotal year t

n_t = new entrants in educational structure t

r_t = repeaters in structure t coming from structure $t - k$

b_t = dropouts from structure t before pivotal year t

d_t^i = deaths among the students in structure t

$\qquad i = 1$ before pivotal year t

$\qquad i = 2$ during and after pivotal year t

g_t = graduates from structure t

a_t = dropouts from structure t during and after pivotal year t

These two equations will be used to study the student flows in the educational system of Planiland.

The analysis of the student flows is the analysis of the variables in Eqs. 4-12 and 4-13. Below we will obtain the values in the past of these variables using statistical data from Planiland's educational system, and we will study the development of these values.

5-3 Past and Present Characteristics of the Student Flows

5-3.1 Study of the Student Flows in the Different Levels of the Educational System

The educational system in Planiland is divided into three levels: elementary school, high school, and college. Each level lasts six years. Below, the variables in Eq. 4-12 and 4-13 will be evaluated for each one of these three levels.

In Table 5-1 appear the statistical data required for elementary school

Table 5-1. Planiland: Total Enrollment, New Entrants, and Repeaters in Elementary School (thousands)

Grades	Years													
	−13	−12	−11	−10	−9	−8	−7	−6	−5	−4	−3	−2	−1	0
Total 1	123.8	128.8	133.6	141.6	143.6	142.7	154.6	162.1	157.7	184.7	188.7	196.9	208.9	217.9
Repeaters		45.1	45.4	46.7	45.9	44.2	46.4	47.0	49.2	49.9	49.1	49.2	50.1	50.1
New		83.7	88.2	94.9	97.7	98.5	108.2	115.1	126.5	134.8	139.6	147.7	158.8	167.8
Total 2	63.0	65.8	68.4	72.9	76.3	78.1	87.3	91.6	100.3	105.0	106.4	111.1	117.9	123.2
Repeaters		17.8	18.0	18.6	18.8	18.7	20.2	20.5	21.7	21.9	21.4	21.4	21.8	21.8
New		48.0	50.4	54.3	57.5	59.4	67.1	71.1	78.6	83.1	85.0	89.7	96.1	101.4
Total 3	48.8	50.4	52.0	54.8	57.6	59.1	66.3	70.1	77.4	82.9	84.2	87.4	93.9	99.4
Repeaters		12.5	12.6	12.9	13.1	13.1	14.1	14.4	15.4	15.9	15.6	15.6	16.1	16.2
New		37.9	39.4	41.9	44.5	46.0	52.2	55.7	62.0	67.0	68.6	71.8	77.8	83.2
Total 4	29.3	30.8	32.3	34.7	36.4	37.2	41.7	44.7	50.2	54.4	56.9	60.8	65.9	70.5
Repeaters		7.3	7.4	7.7	7.9	7.8	8.5	8.8	9.5	9.9	10.0	10.3	10.7	10.9
New		23.5	24.9	27.0	28.5	29.4	33.2	35.9	40.7	44.5	46.9	50.5	55.2	59.6
Total 5	16.8	18.2	19.6	21.7	22.1	23.4	26.9	29.1	32.7	35.7	37.8	40.9	44.9	46.6
Repeaters		3.3	3.5	3.7	3.7	3.8	4.2	4.4	4.7	5.0	5.1	5.3	5.6	5.5
New		14.9	16.1	18.0	18.4	19.6	22.7	24.7	28.0	30.7	32.7	35.6	39.3	41.1
Total 6	14.0	14.5	15.0	16.0	16.4	16.4	20.2	22.0	25.0	27.6	29.4	32.1	35.2	38.2
Repeaters		2.1	2.1	2.2	2.2	2.1	2.5	2.6	2.9	3.1	3.2	3.3	3.5	3.6
New		12.4	12.9	13.8	14.2	14.3	17.7	19.4	22.1	24.5	26.2	28.8	31.7	34.6
Total	295.7	308.5	320.9	341.7	352.4	356.9	397.0	419.6	461.3	490.3	503.4	529.2	566.7	595.8

in Planiland from year -13 up to year 0. Since the plan is being prepared for years $1, 2, \ldots$, our last pivotal year before the plan must be year 0; the previous pivotal year is -6, then -12, etc.

In Table 5-1 structure -6 is delineated by a heavy steplike line. This structure has a shape identical to the structure in Table 4-7. Structure -6 is the only one that is complete in Table 5-1. However, data concerning the variables after pivotal year -12 and before pivotal 0 also appear in Table 5-1.

In order to separate structure -6 in Table 5-1 from the flow of students enrolling, repeating, or dropping out in elementary school, all students affecting enrollment in year -6 as well as all those affected by enrollment in the same year were considered.

Let us now evaluate relationships 4-12 and 4-13 for structure -6. Equation 4-12 in this case (the superscript 1 representing elementary school) will be

$$S^1_{-6} = n^1_{-6} + r^1_{-6} - b^1_{-6} - d^{11}_{-6}$$

The values corresponding to the terms used in relationship 4-12 are obtained as follows:

New enrollment in the first grade appears among the data corresponding to first grade in Table 5-1. The value is

$$n^1_{-6} = 602.6 = 88.2 + 94.9 + 97.7 + 98.5 + 108.2 + 115.1$$

Repeaters coming from structure -12 are obtained by adding together the repeaters in the first grade for year -11 plus repeaters in the second grade for year -10, and so on up to repeaters in the sixth grade for year -6. This means that the number of repeaters from structure -12 will be

$$r^1_{-6} = 91.7 = 45.4 + 18.6 + 13.1 + 7.8 + 4.2 + 2.6$$

Dropouts and deaths are not shown in Table 5-1 but appear in Table 5-2 with respect to structure -6. The number of students leaving the educational system may be obtained from the data in Table 5-1. In the first grade for year -11, for example, there are 133.6 thousand students. Of these, 46.7 thousand are repeaters (in year -10, first grade) and 54.3 thousand go on to the second grade, year -10. The number of students leaving the first grade between years -11 and -10 is therefore

$$133.6 - 46.7 - 54.30 = 32.6$$

The leaving students are divided into two groups in Table 5-2, representing dropouts and deaths respectively. Information concerning the latter was obtained with the aid of a death rate.

Table 5-2. Planiland: Dropouts, Graduates, and Deaths Corresponding to Structure −6 for Elementary School (units)

Grades		−11	−10	−9	−8	−7	−6	−5	−4	−3	−2	−1
1	Dropouts	32,066	37,634	39,426	28,629	35,882	33,652					
	Deaths	534	566	574	571	618	648					
2	Dropouts		9,308	11,295	5,388	10,751	7,534	10,999				
	Deaths		292	305	312	349	366	401				
3	Dropouts			14,870	11,564	15,735	13,634	16,690	20,068			
	Deaths			230	236	265	280	310	332			
4	Dropouts				5,851	8,033	7,021	9,399	11,482	10,772		
	Deaths				149	167	179	201	218	228		
5	Dropouts					2,992	2,184	3,069	4,257	3,549	3,436	
	Deaths					108	116	131	143	151	164	
6	Graduates						19,012	21,800	24,290	25,982	28,472	31,459
	Deaths						88	100	110	118	128	141
Total Dropouts		32,066	46,942	65,591	51,432	73,393	64,025	40,157	35,807	14,321	3,436	
Total Deaths		534	858	1,109	1,268	1,507	1,677	1,143	803	497	292	141

The results of a similar analysis with respect to all the remaining figures in Table 5-1 are set out in Table 5-2.

By adding the totals of the columns from year -11 to year -7, we obtain the dropouts and deaths prior to pivotal year -6:

$$b^1_{-6} = \text{dropouts} = 269.4$$
$$d^{11}_{-6} = \text{deaths} \quad = \quad 5.3$$

with the preceding values, relationship 4-12 takes the following form:

$$419.6 = 602.6 + 91.7 - 269.4 - 5.3$$

The destination of students in a pivotal year constitutes relationship 4-13 which, for structure -6, takes the following form, with the superscript 1 representing elementary school:

$$S^1_{-6} = g^1_{-6} + a^1_{-6} + r^1_0 + d^{21}_{-6}$$

The data appearing in Tables 5-1 and 5-2 can be used to quantify this relationship. To begin with, enrollment in year -6, as mentioned already in connection with relationship 4-12, is equal to 419.6. Dropouts between years -6 and -1 are shown in Table 5-2. The total number of dropouts (between years -6 and -1) is

$$a^1_{-6} = 157{,}746 = 64{,}025 + 40{,}157 + 35{,}807 + 14{,}321 + 3{,}436$$

Repeaters going to structure 0 are shown in Table 5-1. The total number is

$$r^1_0 = 106.2 = 49.2 + 21.9 + 15.6 + 10.3 + 5.6 + 3.6$$

In order to obtain the figure relating to graduates which appear in Table 5-2, we have assumed that all those leaving school after beginning sixth grade are graduates. Actually, however, there are dropouts in the sixth grade although their number may be assumed to be negligible. To obtain the number of sixth grade leavers in the total enrolled in a given year, the number of repeaters must be subtracted. At the end of year -6, for example, the number is

$$22.0 - 2.9 = 19.1$$

The number of those leaving after having begun sixth grade includes graduates and deaths; figures for these are shown in Table 5-2.

The total number of graduates is

$$g^1_{-6} = 151{,}015 = 19{,}012 + 21{,}800 + 24{,}290 + 25{,}982 + 28{,}472 + 31{,}449$$

The number of deaths between year -6 and year -1 among those enrolled in year -6 is

$$d^{21}_{-6} = 4{,}553 = 1{,}677 + 1{,}143 + 803 + 497 + 292 + 141$$

With the values obtained, relationship 4-13 assumes the following form:

$$419.6 = 151.0 + 157.8 + 106.2 + 4.6$$

Similar evaluations were made for Eq. 4-13 for structure -12 and for Eq. 4-12 for structure 0. The results appear in Table 5-3. In this table results obtained for high school and college are also presented.

In Chapter 4 several indices based on the variables of Eq. 4-12 and 4-13 were defined. By studying these indices, it is possible for us to obtain a better idea of the development of the educational system. Besides, these indices will be used later for the study of the future development of the student flows. The values of the indices are presented in Table 5-4.

5-3.2 Qualitative Subdivision of the Student Flows in Different Levels of the Educational System

The analysis of the past and present data with respect to the different levels of the educational system is not enough. Additional information is required which can be obtained by studying qualitative strata of the different levels of the educational system, as shown for Planiland's elementary and high school levels in Table 5-5.

The reason for describing these subdivisions as "qualitative" is evident in Table 5-6 which shows the ratios between the different variables. These reveal that stratum A represents the lowest ratios (2), (3), (5), and (6) and the highest ratio (8), which means that the proportion of repeaters and dropouts is very low in this stratum and that of graduates very high. The reverse is true of stratum D while strata B and C reveal changes ranging from the most satisfactory conditions of A to the least satisfactory conditions of D.

5-4 Projections of Student Flows

5-4.1 Basic Considerations with Respect to Projections of Student Flows

The method used in making projections of future student flows is similar to that used for projections in any science, whether natural or social. In the case of student flows, projection involves the following steps.

(a) A clear definition of the elements in student flows. Such a definition is given in relationships 4-12 and 4-13.

(b) Specification of factors influencing changes in the values of the variables in 4-12 and 4-13 and of the nature of these influences. Population growth and per capita income growth are the most important factors which systematically influence the value of the variables; the nature of the influence of these factors is considered in the following sections of this chapter.

Table 5-3. Planiland: Relationships 4-12 and 4-13 for the Three Levels of Education (thousands)

Pivotal Year t	Before Pivotal Year, Relationship 4-12				Total Enrollment, Pivotal Year S_t^j	During and After Pivotal Year, Relationship 4-13			
	New Enrollment n_t^j	Repeaters r_t^j	Dropouts b_t^j	Deaths $\overline{d}_t^{1j}$		Dropouts a_t^j	Repeaters r_{t+6}^j	Graduates g_t^j	Deaths d_t^{2j}
					Elementary School			$j = 1$	
−12					308.5				
−6	602.6	91.7	269.4	5.3	419.6	129.4	91.7	84.4	3.0
0	875.2	106.2	378.3	7.3	595.8	157.8	106.2	151.0	4.6
					High School			$j = 2$	
−12					24.5				
−6	54.2	5.1	18.0	0.8	40.5	7.8	5.1	11.1	0.5
0	87.4	6.5	23.6	1.3	69.0	13.1	6.5	20.1	0.8
					College			$j = 3$	
−12					3.7				
−6	7.7	0.5	3.0	0.1	5.1	1.4	0.51	1.72	0.08
0	12.8	0.7	4.4	0.17	8.9	2.5	0.70	1.8	0.1

Table 5-4. Planiland: Indices for the Analysis of the Student Flows

	Definition	Pivotal Year −12	Pivotal Year −6	Pivotal Year 0
			Elementary School	
(1)	$\dfrac{\text{New enrollment}}{\text{School age population}}$			
(2)	$\dfrac{\text{Repeaters}}{\text{Total inputs*}}$		$\dfrac{91.7}{602.6 + 91.7} = 0.132$	$\dfrac{106.2}{875.2 + 106.2} = 0.108$
(3)	$\dfrac{\text{Dropouts before pivotal year}}{\text{Total inputs*}}$		$\dfrac{269.4}{602.6 + 91.7} = 0.388$	$\dfrac{378.3}{875.2 + 106.2} = 0.385$
(4)	$\dfrac{\text{Deaths before pivotal year}}{\text{Total inputs*}}$		$\dfrac{5.3}{602.6 + 91.7} = 0.007$	$\dfrac{7.3}{875.2 + 106.2} = 0.007$
(5)	$\dfrac{\text{Dropouts during and after pivotal year}}{\text{Enrollment pivotal year}}$	$\dfrac{129.4}{308.5} = 0.419$	$\dfrac{157.8}{419.6} = 0.376$	
(6)	$\dfrac{\text{Repeaters passing to next structure}}{\text{Enrollment pivotal year}}$	$\dfrac{91.7}{308.5} = 0.297$	$\dfrac{106.2}{419.6} = 0.253$	
(7)	$\dfrac{\text{Deaths during and after pivotal year}}{\text{Enrollment pivotal year}}$	$\dfrac{3.0}{308.5} = 0.009$	$\dfrac{4.6}{419.6} = 0.011$	
(8)	$\dfrac{\text{Graduates}}{\text{Enrollment pivotal year}}$	$\dfrac{84.4}{308.5} = 0.274$	$\dfrac{151.0}{419.6} = 0.360$	

*Total inputs = new entrants + repeaters.

Table 5-4   (Continued)

	Definition	Pivotal Year −12	Pivotal Year −6	Pivotal Year 0
			High School	
(1)	$\dfrac{\text{New enrollment}}{\text{Graduates elementary school}}$		$\dfrac{54.2}{84.4} = 0.642$	$\dfrac{87.4}{151.0} = 0.579$
(2)	$\dfrac{\text{Repeaters}}{\text{Total inputs*}}$		$\dfrac{5.1}{54.2 + 5.1} = 0.086$	$\dfrac{6.5}{87.4 + 6.5} = 0.069$
(3)	$\dfrac{\text{Dropouts before pivotal year}}{\text{Total inputs*}}$		$\dfrac{18.0}{54.2 + 5.1} = 0.304$	$\dfrac{23.6}{87.4 + 6.5} = 0.251$
(4)	$\dfrac{\text{Deaths before pivotal year}}{\text{Total inputs*}}$		$\dfrac{.08}{54.2 + 5.1} = 0.013$	$\dfrac{1.3}{87.4 + 6.5} = 0.014$
(5)	$\dfrac{\text{Dropouts during and after pivotal year}}{\text{Enrollment pivotal year}}$	$\dfrac{7.8}{24.5} = 0.318$	$\dfrac{13.1}{40.5} = 0.323$	
(6)	$\dfrac{\text{Repeaters passing to next structure}}{\text{Enrollment pivotal year}}$	$\dfrac{5.1}{24.5} = 0.208$	$\dfrac{6.5}{40.5} = 0.160$	
(7)	$\dfrac{\text{Deaths during and after pivotal year}}{\text{Enrollment pivotal year}}$	$\dfrac{0.5}{24.5} = 0.020$	$\dfrac{0.8}{40.5} = 0.020$	
(8)	$\dfrac{\text{Graduates}}{\text{Enrollment pivotal year}}$	$\dfrac{11.1}{24.5} = .453$	$\dfrac{20.1}{40.5} = .496$	

*Total inputs = new entrants + repeaters.

Table 5-4 (Continued)

College

	Definition	Pivotal Year −12	Pivotal Year −6	Pivotal Year 0
(1)	$\dfrac{\text{New enrollment}}{\text{Graduates high school}}$		$\dfrac{7.7}{11.1} = 0.694$	$\dfrac{12.8}{20.1} = 0.637$
(2)	$\dfrac{\text{Repeaters}}{\text{Total inputs*}}$		$\dfrac{0.5}{7.7 + 0.3} = 0.061$	$\dfrac{0.7}{12.8 + 0.7} = 0.052$
(3)	$\dfrac{\text{Dropouts before pivotal year}}{\text{Total inputs*}}$		$\dfrac{3.0}{7.7 + 0.5} = 0.366$	$\dfrac{4.4}{12.8 + 0.7} = 0.326$
(4)	$\dfrac{\text{Deaths before pivotal year}}{\text{Total inputs*}}$		$\dfrac{0.1}{7.7 + 0.5} = 0.012$	$\dfrac{0.2}{7.7 + 0.5} = 0.015$
(5)	$\dfrac{\text{Dropouts during and after pivotal year}}{\text{Enrollment pivotal year}}$	$\dfrac{1.4}{3.7} = 0.378$	$\dfrac{2.5}{5.1} = 0.490$	
(6)	$\dfrac{\text{Repeaters passing to next structure}}{\text{Enrollment pivotal year}}$	$\dfrac{0.5}{3.7} = 0.135$	$\dfrac{0.7}{5.1} = 0.137$	
(7)	$\dfrac{\text{Deaths during and after pivotal year}}{\text{Enrollment pivotal year}}$	$\dfrac{0.08}{3.7} = 0.022$	$\dfrac{0.1}{5.1} = 0.020$	
(8)	$\dfrac{\text{Graduates}}{\text{Enrollment pivotal year}}$	$\dfrac{1.72}{3.7} = 0.465$	$\dfrac{1.8}{5.1} = 0.353$	

*Total inputs = new entrants + repeaters.

Table 5-5. Planiland: Qualitative Subdivision of Elementary and High School Levels Structure −6 (thousands)

Elementary School

Type	Before Pivotal Year				Enrollment, Pivotal Year S_{-6}^{1i}	After Pivotal Year			
	New Entrants n_{-6}^{1i}	Repeaters r_{-6}^{1i}	Dropouts b_{-6}^{1i}	Deaths d_{-6}^{11i}		Dropouts a_{-6}^{1i}	Repeaters r_0^{1i}	Graduates g_{-6}^{1i}	Deaths d_{-6}^{21i}
i = A	42.72	0.93	1.3	0.35	42.0	1.36	1.0	39.18	.460
i = B	116.34	19.33	29.83	0.83	105.0	21.05	20.18	62.62	1.150
i = C	120.8	28.33	42.94	1.19	105.0	40.21	30.81	32.83	1.150
i = D	322.74	43.11	195.33	2.93	167.6	95.18	54.21	16.37	1.840
Total	602.6	91.70	269.40	5.30	419.6	157.8	106.2	151.0	4.600

High School

Type	Before Pivotal Year				Enrollment, Pivotal Year S_{-6}^{2i}	After Pivotal Year			
	New Entrants n_{-6}^{2i}	Repeaters r_{-6}^{2i}	Dropouts b_{-6}^{2i}	Deaths d_{-6}^{12i}		Dropouts a_{-6}^{2i}	Repeaters r_{-6}^{2i}	Graduates g_{-6}^{2i}	Deaths d_{-6}^{22i}
i = A	4.16	0.10	0.21	0.05	4.0	0.10	0.11	3.71	0.08
i = B	12.70	1.0	1.72	0.18	11.8	4.31	1.75	5.51	0.24
i = C	31.79	2.9	12.14	0.45	22.1	7.19	4.04	10.43	0.44
i = D	5.55	1.1	3.94	0.09	2.6	1.50	0.00	0.45	0.05
Total	54.2	5.1	18.0	0.8	40.5	13.1	6.5	20.1	0.80

Table 5-6. Planiland: Indices for the Qualitative Subdivisions of Elementary School and High School Structure −6

Index	i = 1 Elementary School					i = 2 High School				
	Total	j = A	j = B	j = C	j = D	Total	j = A	j = B	j = C	j = D
(2) Repeaters / Total inputs	0.1321	0.0213	0.1425	0.1900	0.1178	0.0860	0.0235	0.0730	0.0836	0.1654
(3) Deaths before pivotal year / Total inputs	0.3880	0.0298	0.2199	0.2879	0.5339	0.3035	0.0493	0.1255	0.3500	0.5925
(4) Deaths before pivotal year / Total inputs	0.0080	0.0061	0.0080	0.0080	0.0076	0.0135	0.0117	0.0131	0.0130	0.0135
(5) Dropouts during and after pivotal year / Enrollment pivotal year	0.3761	0.0324	0.2005	0.3830	0.5679	0.3235	0.0250	0.3653	0.3253	0.5769
(6) Repeaters passing to next structure / Enrollment pivotal year	0.2531	0.0238	0.1922	0.2934	0.3235	0.1605	0.0275	0.1483	0.1828	0.2308
(7) Deaths during and after pivotal year / Enrollment pivotal year	0.01096	0.01096	0.01096	0.01096	0.01096	0.1975	0.1975	0.1975	0.1975	0.1975
(8) Graduates / Enrollment pivotal year	0.3599	0.9329	0.5964	0.3127	0.0977	0.4963	0.9275	0.4665	0.4720	0.1731
(9) New entrants in higher level / Graduates elementary school	0.5788	0.8984	0.6915	0.2559	0.0305	0.6368	0.9083	0.7350	0.5062	0.2222

(c) Collection of data on past and present values of the variables in 4-12 and 4-13 and of the influencing factors mentioned in (b). Such data for Planiland is presented in Chapter 2 (about population) and Chapter 3 (about per capita income).

(d) Evaluation of the future development of the influencing factors. This development might be spontaneous, as in the case of population, or planned, as in the case of per capita income. Such data for Planiland is also presented in Chapters 2 and 3.

(e) Calculation of the future quantities in the basic relationships. These calculations will be based on the data collected in steps (b), (c), and (d). If, for instance, we know that a 10 percent increase in per capita income over a previous five-year period was accompanied by a 5 percent increase in the number of new entrants, and further, if we estimate that there will be a 10 percent increase in per capita income over the next five years, we can reasonably project an increase for the next five years of about 5 percent in the number of new entrants.

Two examples of the method for projecting student flows outlined above are presented below. In Sec. 5-4.2 we assume that the only determinant of future changes in the flows is population growth; in Sec. 5-4.3, per capita income is also taken into account as an influencing factor.

5-4.2   Projections of Student Flows Considering only Influence of Population Growth

The first step, definition of student flows, has already been completed and the second step, identification of the factors influencing the flows and the nature of that influence, has been partly completed since we have specified that we are only concerned with population growth.

In a discussion of the nature of the influence of population growth, a clear distinction can be made at the outset: population growth influences directly only the number of new entrants in elementary school and has no direct influence on the numbers of repeaters, dropouts, deaths, and graduates at elementary and higher levels or on the numbers of new entrants in high school and college. Of course, population growth influences these latter elements in the flows, but only indirectly through its effects on the number of new entrants at the elementary level.

The distinction is important since it means that we can concentrate on the impact of population growth on elementary level new entrants; we can then calculate the effects of changes in the number of elementary level new entrants on the other variables for all three levels.

In the following illustration we will begin by determining the nature of the influence of population growth on new entrants in elementary school and go on to a discussion of projections, based on estimated population growth of the elements in the student flows at the elementary level. We will then proceed to projections relating to the high school and college levels.

Relationship between population and new entrants in elementary school

Table 5-7 shows new entrants in the first grade of elementary school between years -12 and 0, classified according to age. An important aspect of the figures in Table 5-7 is revealed in Tables 5-8 and Fig. 5-1.

In Fig. 5-1 all the main elements that should be considered in the relationship between population and new entrants are included. The figure is divided into three parts. At the left appear the years to be considered, -12 and -11. Limitations of space do not permit us to extend the number of years considered, but the characteristics of the figure do not change. The part of Fig. 5-1 just described corresponds to the column "year of entrance" in Table 5-8. At the center appears the changing distribution of the population between new entrants and nonentrants, and at the right, the change of the age group of the population caused by mortality. Let us begin with a detailed study of the right-hand portion of the figure.

At the bottom of the right side appears the age group of age 6 in year -12; this is denoted by $P_{-12,6}$. In Table 5-8 it can be seen that $P_{-12,6}$ is equal to 87,770. In year -11 this group has become $P_{-11,7}$; that is, all the survivors are age 7. Their number is 87,100 in Table 5-8. The

FIGURE 5–1
Population and New Entrants in Elementary School

Year	Distribution of the Population Between New Entrants and Nonentrants	Population Change Caused by Mortality
-11	$n_{-12,6}^1(1-\nu)$ $n_{-11,7}^1$	$P_{-11,7}=P_{-12,6}(1-\nu)$
-12	$n_{-12,6}^1$	$P_{-12,6}$

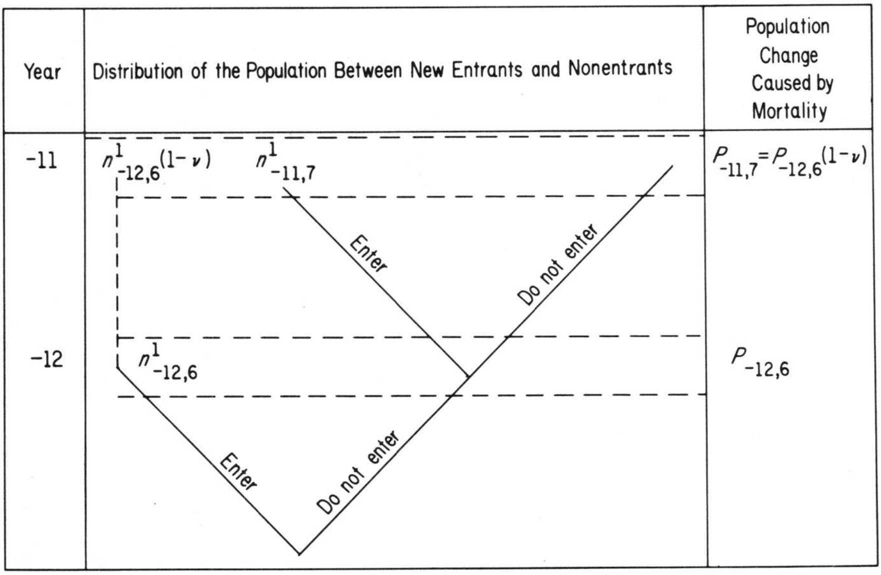

Table 5-7. *Planiland: Population of 6 Years of Age and New Entrants in First Grade of Elementary School by Age Groups (units)*

Age j							Year						
	$h=-12$	$h=-11$	$h=-10$	$h=-9$	$h=-8$	$h=-7$	$h=-6$	$h=-5$	$h=-4$	$h=-3$	$h=-2$	$h=-1$	$h=0$
Population of Six Years of Age P_{hj}													
	87,770	90,290	92,760	95,190	96,320	97,650	98,960	100,240	102,200	112,830	117,680	122,510	127,320
New Entrants n^1_{hj}													
6	—	—	—	—	—	—	—	—	8,590	27,282	38,222	46,358	50,151
7	—	—	—	—	—	—	6,085	19,306	32,860	35,066	35,439	36,963	38,481
8	—	—	5,420	12,470	18,838	27,897	36,014	39,166	34,499	28,520	26,562	29,376	30,640
9	21,864	28,659	34,628	34,612	32,231	32,328	29,245	26,608	23,428	19,393	18,024	18,385	20,332
10	28,878	27,763	25,486	23,476	22,022	22,162	20,108	18,389	16,167	13,345	12,436	12,652	12,918
11	16,223	15,625	14,368	13,261	12,440	12,654	11,516	10,507	9,327	7,698	7,136	7,288	7,415
12	10,126	9,773	9,004	8,317	7,810	7,994	7,325	6,736	5,943	4,919	4,569	4,630	4,733
13	4,149	4,005	3,694	3,421	3,217	3,274	3,018	2,820	2,491	2,064	1,921	1,952	1,976
14	2,463	2,377	2,193	2,032	1,915	1,948	1,795	1,673	1,504	1,246	1,342	1,186	1,205
Total	83,703	88,202	94,793	97,589	98,473	108,207	115,106	125,265	134,809	139,533	145,651	158,790	167,851

Table 5-8.   Relations Between Population and New Entrants in First Grade

Age of New Entrants j	Year of Entrance h	Number of New Entrants n^1_{hj} (a)	Total Population in Age Group P_{hj} (b)	$\tau = \dfrac{n^1_{hj}}{P_{hj}}$	Year of Entrance h	Number of New Entrants n^1_{hj} (a)	Total Population in Age Group P_{hj} (b)	$\tau = \dfrac{n^1_{hj}}{P_{hj}}$
6	−12	0	87,770	0.0	−8	0.0	96,320	0.0
7	−11	0	87,100	0.0	−7	0.0	95,580	0.0
8	−10	5,420	86,440	0.0627	−6	36,014	94,850	0.3797
9	−9	34,612	86,400	0.4006	−5	26,608	94,120	0.2827
10	−8	22,022	86,360	0.2550	−4	16,167	93,830	0.1723
11	−7	12,654	86,320	0.1466	−3	7,698	93,540	0.0823
12	−6	7,325	86,280	0.0849	−2	4,569	93,250	0.0490
13	−5	2,820	86,230	0.0327	−1	1,952	92,960	0.0210
14	−4	1,504	85,960	0.0175	0	1,205	92,700	0.0130
Totals		86,357		1.0000		94,213		1.0000

relationship between age 7 in year -11 and population of age 6 in year -12 is given by the formula

$$P_{-11,7} = P_{-12,6}(1 - \nu)$$

where ν is the mortality rate.

In the same way, the relationship (not shown in Fig. 5-1) of the population 8 years of age in year -10 to the population 7 years of age in year -11 is

$$P_{-10,8} = P_{-11,7}(1 - \nu)$$

which is equivalent to

$$P_{-10,8} = P_{-12,6}(1 - \nu)^2$$

Using the same method, the relationship between population $P_{-9,9}$ and $P_{-8,10}$ to $P_{-12,6}$ can be established. In the center part of Fig. 5-1, the changing distribution of the population between new entrants and non-entrants is presented. Since we are assuming that 6 years of age is the minimum required to enter school, the analysis begins with the age group of six years in year -12. This group is divided into those who enter the school system, represented by $n^1_{-12,6}$, equal to 0 in Table 5-8, and those who do not enter. The total of those entering plus those not entering is equal to the age group; or, to put it another way, the number of those entering is equal at most to the total population group. In symbols this is expressed by

$$n^1_{-12,6} \leq P_{-12,6}$$

In year -11 we should consider three things: First, the survivors of those entering in year -12. This is expressed by

$$n^1_{-12,6}(1 - \nu)$$

In addition, some persons enter school in year -11 at the age of 7 and are denoted by $n^1_{-11,7}$. Finally, a group of nonentrants might remain. Since all these three subgroups are part of the age group of 7 years of age in year -11 we can write

$$n^1_{-12,6}(1 - \nu) + n^1_{-11,7} \leq P_{-11,7}$$

with nonentrants excluded. In the same way, we can write

$$n^1_{-12,6}(1 - \nu)^2 + n^1_{-11,7}(1 - \nu) + n^1_{-10,8} \leq P_{-10,8}$$

and so on to year -4, in which

$$n^1_{-12,6}(1 - \nu)^8 + n^1_{-11,7}(1 - \nu)^7 + n^1_{-10,6}(1 - \nu)^6 + \cdots$$
$$+ n^1_{-5,13}(1 - \nu) + n^1_{-4,14} \leq P_{-4,14}$$

In the general case, let

$P_{h,j}$ = population of age j in year h (we use "h" here to denote year because our attention will not be restricted to pivotal years only, as in Chapters 4 and 5).

$n_{h,j}^1$ = new elementary school entrants of age j in year h.

Then the relationship between population and new entrants can be expressed by the formula

$$n_{h,6}^1(1 - \nu)^8 + n_{h+1,7}^1(1 - \nu)^7 + \cdots$$
$$+ n_{h+7,13}^1(1 - \nu) + n_{h+8,14}^1 \leq P_{h+8,14} \quad (5\text{-}1)$$

Observations about the total number of new entrants by age can be translated into ratios between the number of new entrants of a given age and the population of that age. These ratios are shown in Table 5-8, columns 5 and 9.

Let τ_{hj} be the proportion of persons of age j in year h becoming new entrants in elementary school; i.e.,

$$\tau_{hj} = \frac{n_{hj}^1}{P_{hj}} \quad (5\text{-}2)$$

The values of this ratio are presented in Table 5-8 for years -12 to 0 and ages 6 to 14. With the aid of equation (1), it will be shown below that $\tau_{-12,6} + \tau_{-11,7} + \tau_{-10,8} + \cdots + \tau_{-5,13} + \tau_{-4,14} \leq 1$; that is, the sum of τ's, the ratio of new entrants in different years to the population of the same age, must be less than or equal to one. The equation for the general case is

$$\tau_{h,6} + \tau_{h+1,7} + \tau_{h+2,8} + \cdots + \tau_{h+7,13} + \tau_{h+8,14} \leq 1 \quad (5\text{-}3)$$

This type of sum will be called a *diagonal sum* because the τ's are the proportions of new entrants corresponding to $n_{h,j}^1$ found in diagonals sloping down to the right in tables such as 5-7. Also, the τ's themselves are found in diagonals sloping down to the right in Table 5-9.

In order to verify Eq. 5-3 we observe that

$$n_{hj}^1 = \tau_{hj} P_{hj}$$

If this equality is used in Eq. 5-1, we obtain

$$\tau_{h,6} P_{h,6}(1 - \nu)^8 + \tau_{h+1,7} P_{h+1,7}(1 - \nu)^7 + \cdots$$
$$+ \tau_{h+7,13} P_{h+7,13}(1 - \nu) + \tau_{h+8,14} P_{h+8,14} \leq P_{h+8,14}$$

In addition, observe that (according to the right-hand side of Fig. 5-1) we have

$$P_{h,6}(1 - \nu)^8 = P_{h+8,14}$$
$$P_{h+1,7}(1 - \nu)^7 = P_{h+8,14}$$
$$P_{h+8,14} = P_{h+8,14};$$

that is, we have

$$\tau_{h,6} P_{h+8,14} + \tau_{h+1,7} P_{h+8,14} + \cdots + \tau_{h+7,13} P_{h+8,14} + \tau_{h+8,14} P_{h+8,14} \leq P_{h+8,14}$$

Table 5-9. Ratios τ_{hj} Between New Entrants and Population

j \ h	-12	-11	-10	-9	-8	-7	-6	-5	-4	-3	-2	-1	0
6	0.0	0.00	0.00	0.00	0.00	0.00	0.00	0.00	0.0842	0.2418	0.3248	0.3784	0.3939
7	0.0	0.00	0.00	0.00	0.00	0.00	0.0628	0.1966	0.3289	0.3446	0.3149	0.3149	0.3149
8	0.0	0.00	0.0627	0.1396	0.2053	0.2976	0.3797	0.4073	0.3525	0.2864	0.2617	0.2617	0.2617
9	0.2798	0.3550	0.4158	0.4006	0.3619	0.3542	0.3144	0.2827	0.2447	0.1988	0.1816	0.1816	0.1816
10	0.3854	0.3580	0.3181	0.2822	0.2550	0.2496	0.2215	0.1991	0.1723	0.1400	0.1279	0.1279	0.1279
11	0.2262	0.2101	0.1867	0.1657	0.1497	0.1466	0.1301	0.1170	0.1013	0.0823	0.0752	0.0752	0.0752
12	0.1478	0.1373	0.1220	0.1082	0.0977	0.0957	0.0849	0.0763	0.0660	0.0536	0.0490	0.0490	0.0490
13	0.0634	0.0589	0.0523	0.0464	0.0419	0.0410	0.0364	0.0327	0.0283	0.0230	0.0210	0.0210	0.0210
14	0.0394	0.0366	0.0325	0.0288	0.0260	0.0254	0.0225	0.0202	0.0175	0.0142	0.0130	0.0130	0.0130

Dividing both sides of the equation by $P_{h+8,14}$, the relationship 5-3 is obtained.

Equations 5-1 and 5-3 have a very clear interpretation: the number of new entrants in different years at the elementary school level from a given group of the population defined by age and year cannot be larger than the number of persons in the group of the population considered.

Projection of new entrants in elementary school

If population growth is the only factor influencing the number of new entrants, the ratios τ between entrants and population will remain constant; in other words, the number of new entrants will increase if the population increases and not otherwise.

This general principle of constant τ ratios may be used for projecting the numbers of new entrants in future years, when it is assumed that only population changes bring changes in the numbers of new entrants. However, if the values of the τ's over previous years have been changing due to influencing factors other than population changes, and if we were to maintain constant their past values, this might being about "diagonal sums" of τ's greater than one. Whenever this is the case, the past values for τ for the highest age levels must be sufficiently reduced (in many cases to 0) to avoid diagonal sums in excess of one.

Let us assume that we begin with the data in Table 5-9 for Planiland and make a projection of the values of τ in future years. Since we assume that only population changes affect the numbers of new entrants, we will assume the values of τ for future years to be equal to the values for the different age levels in year 0 so long as diagonal sums do not exceed one. Thus for year 1, we assume initially that the value of τ for six-year-olds in that year will be 0.3939, for seven-year-olds, 0.3149 and so on up to 0.0130 for fourteen-year-olds. We then check the diagonal sums and find that the diagonal sums ending at $\tau_{1,6}$, $\tau_{1,7}$ and $\tau_{1,8}$ are all under 1.0000. Thus for $\tau_{1,8}$, the diagonal sum is $\tau_{-1,6} + \tau_{0,7} + \tau_{1,8} = 0.3784 + 0.3149 + 0.2617 + 0.9550$. However, if 0.1816 (the value of $\tau_{0,9}$) is taken as the value of $\tau_{1,9}$, the diagonal sum ending at $\tau_{1,9}$ exceeds 1.0000.

$$\tau_{-2,6} + \tau_{-1,7} + \tau_{0,8} + \tau_{1,9} = 0.3248 + 0.3149 + 0.2617 + 0.1816$$
$$= 1.0830$$

Hence, the projected value of $\tau_{1,9}$ must be reduced to make the diagonal sum exactly equal to 1.0000. The amount of this reduction is the amount the diagonal sum exceeds 1.0000 (i.e., 0.0830); thus the final projected value for $\tau_{1,9}$ is $0.1816 - 0.0830 = 0.0986$. For all age levels above 9 in year 1, it will be found that τ must be assumed to be 0.0000 if all diagonal sums are to be 1.0000 or less.

For year 2, we take the values obtained for year 1 and perform the same operation as above to eliminate values for the higher age levels which take the diagonal sums over 1.0000. Values for ages 6, 7, and 8 from year 1 are acceptable for year 2, but the value of $\tau_{2,9}$ must be reduced from 0.0986 to 0.0450 to make the diagonal sum ending at $\tau_{2,9}$ (i.e., $\tau_{-1,6} + \tau_{-0,7} + \tau_{1,8} + \tau_{2,9}$) equal to 1.0000. As in year 1, the values for τ in year 2 for all age levels over 9 must be zero.

The same procedure can then be used in year 3 in which we must again reduce the value for age 9 this time to 0.0295. From year 4 on, the values for year 3 may be used for all age levels without having a diagonal sum exceed one. Projections for values of τ up to year 6 together with actual values of τ for years −9 to 0 are given in Table 5-10.

Once projections for the values of the ratios τ_{hj} for years $h = 1, 2, \ldots$ have been made, the number of new elementary school entrants can be projected with the formula

$$n^1_{hj} = \tau_{hj} P_{hj} \qquad (5\text{-}4)$$

This formula states that for year h, the number n^1_{hj} of new entrants of age j is equal to the proportion τ_{hj} of new entrants of that age in that year times the size P_{hj} of the population of the age level in question.

For example, one may obtain a projection for the number of new entrants age 9 in year 1 by means of the following multiplication:

$$n_{1,9} = \tau_{1,9} P_{1,9}$$
$$11.54 = .0986 \times 117.04$$

(We use the data for population by age presented in Table 2-8.)

The computations for new entrants of different ages in year 1 are presented in Table 5-11.

The sum of such products for different age levels in a given year is the projection for the total number of new entrants for that year. Table 5-11 indicates that for year 1 this figure is 135.29 thousands.

In order to use formulae 4-12 and 4-13 for future structures, we need to estimate the number of new entrants for periods of six years. The number of new entrants in educational structure 6 may be obtained by adding the figure for new entrants in year 1 to that for new entrants in year 2, and so on up to year 6. This operation is carried out in Table 5-12. Table 5-13 shows the number of new entrants in educational structures 6, 12, and 18.

Projection of graduates, dropouts, repeaters, and deaths in elementary school

In this section a method for estimating the numbers of graduates, dropouts, repeaters, and deaths—that is, variables other than new entrants in identities 4-12 and 4-13—will be presented. To estimate future

Table 5-10. Projection of Ratios τ_{hj} Between New Entrants in Elementary School and Population

h / j	-9	-8	-7	-6	-5	-4	-3	-2	-1	0	1	2	3	4	5	6
6	0.00	0.00	0.00	0.00	0.00	0.0842	0.2418	0.3248	0.3784	0.3939	0.3939	0.3939	0.3939	0.3939	0.3939	0.3939
7	0.00	0.00	0.00	0.0628	0.1966	0.3289	0.3446	0.3149	0.3149	0.3149	0.3149	0.3149	0.3149	0.3149	0.3149	0.3149
8	0.1396	0.2053	0.2976	0.3797	0.4073	0.3525	0.2864	0.2617	0.2617	0.2617	0.2617	0.2617	0.2617	0.2617	0.2617	0.2617
9	0.4006	0.3619	0.3542	0.3144	0.2827	0.2447	0.1988	0.1816	0.1816	0.1816	0.0986	0.0450	0.0295	0.0295	0.0295	0.0295
10	0.2822	0.2550	0.2496	0.2215	0.1991	0.1723	0.1400	0.1279	0.1279	0.1279	0.0000	0.0000	0.0000	0.0000	0.0000	0.0000
11	0.1657	0.1497	0.1466	0.1301	0.1170	0.1013	0.0823	0.0752	0.0752	0.0752	0.0000	0.0000	0.0000	0.0000	0.0000	0.0000
12	0.1082	0.0977	0.0957	0.0349	0.0763	0.0660	0.0536	0.0490	0.0490	0.0490	0.0000	0.0000	0.0000	0.0000	0.0000	0.0000
13	0.0464	0.0419	0.0410	0.0364	0.0327	0.0283	0.0230	0.0210	0.0210	0.0210	0.0000	0.0000	0.0000	0.0000	0.0000	0.0000
14	0.0288	0.0260	0.0254	0.0225	0.0202	0.0175	0.0142	0.0130	0.0130	0.0130	0.0000	0.0000	0.0000	0.0000	0.0000	0.0000

Table 5-11.   *Planiland: Estimation of the Number of New Entrants*
in Elementary School in Year 1 (thousands)

Age j	Population (Table 3-7) P_{1j}	Ratios (Table 5-10) τ_{1j}	New Entrants $n_{1j} = \tau_{1j}P_{1j}$
6	131.74	0.3939	51.89
7	126.85	0.3149	39.94
8	121.96	0.2617	31.92
9	117.04	0.0986	11.54
10	111.54	0.000	0.0
11	100.62	0.000	0.0
12	98.23	0.000	0.0
13	96.24	0.000	0.0
14	93.75	0.000	0.0

Total of new entrants in year 1 = 135.29

Table 5-12.   *Planiland: New Entrants in Elementary*
School in Structure 6 (thousands)

Year	New Entrants in Educational Structure 6
1	135.29
2	132.80
3	134.26
4	137.43
5	140.69
6	144.23

Total n_6^1 = 824.70

Table 5-13.   *Planiland: New Entrants in Elementary*
School in Structure 6, 12, and 18

Structure	New Entrants n_t^1
$t = 6$	824.79
$t = 12$	927.06
$t = 18$	1,056.00

values of these other variables, taking into account population changes and resulting changes in numbers of new entrants, we will assume that the ratios between the variables which were presented in Table 5-4 remain constant in the years after year 0. In each of the Eqs. 4-12 and 4-13, if we have or can estimate future values for four of the five variables, we can then use the equation itself to project a value for the fifth variable. Various combinations of four variables can be the object of initial projections in the case of each equation, but we will find it most convenient to proceed in the following manner: For Eq. 4-12, we have the number (n_t^1) of new entrants, and the number (r_t^1) of repeaters entering the structure. We will make projections of dropouts before the pivotal year (b_t^1) and deaths before the pivotal year (d_t^{11}), using the ratios from Table 5-4. Once these four have been determined, the future values of S_t^1 can be calculated by using Eq. 4-12. For Eq. 4-13, we have the value just obtained of S_t^1, and we make projections of the number of dropouts during and after pivotal years (a_t^1), the number of repeaters entering the next structure (r_{t+6}^1), and the number of deaths during and after the pivotal year (d_t^{21}) by means of the ratios from Table 5-4. Then the future values of g_t^1 can be calculated directly from Eq. 4-13.

For using this method of projection of the values of the variables, we will need the following equations, based on the ratios from Table 5-4:

$$b_t^1 = 0.385\,(n_t^1 + r_t^1) \tag{5-5}$$

$$d_t^{11} = 0.007\,(n_t^1 + r_t^1) \tag{5-6}$$

$$a_t^1 = 0.376\,S_t^1 \tag{5-7}$$

$$r_{t+6}^1 = 0.253\,S_t^1 \tag{5-8}$$

$$d_t^{21} = 0.011\,S_t^1 \tag{5-9}$$

We will now demonstrate the use of the procedures described above for Planiland Elementary School level structures 0, 6, 12, and 18. We begin with Eq. 4-13 for structure 0:

$$S_0^1 = g_0^1 + a_0^1 + r_6^1 + d_0^{21}$$

We already have the value of one of these five variables, namely, enrollment in year 0, (S_0^1), which amounts to 595.8 thousand. This value is shown in Table 5-3 and is reproduced in Table 5-14.

In order to estimate the number of dropouts from structure 0 during and after year 0 we must use Eq. 5-7:

$$
\begin{aligned}
a_0^1 &= 0.376\,S_0^1 \\
&= 0.376 \times 595.8 \\
&= 224.0 \quad \text{(all figures in thousands)}
\end{aligned}
$$

Equations 5-8 and 5-9 are used to estimate the numbers of repeaters (r_6^1) and deaths (d_0^{21}), 150.7 thousand and 6.5 thousand respectively (Table 5-14).

So far we have the values of four of the five variables in Eq. 4-13 for structure 0, namely S_0^1, a_0^1, r_6^1, and d_0^{21}. In order to estimate the value of the fifth variable, i.e., g_0^1, Eq. 4-13 itself must be used, in the following form:

$$
\begin{aligned}
g_0^1 &= S_0^1 - a_0^1 - r_6^1 - d_0^{21} \\
&= 595.8 - 224.0 - 150.7 - 6.5 \\
&= 214.6
\end{aligned}
$$

Table 5-14. Planiland: Projections of the Student Flows in Elementary School Level,
Considering Only the Influence of Population Growth (thousands)

Pivotal Year	Before Pivotal Year, Relationship 4-12				Total Enrollment, Pivotal Year	After Pivotal Year, Relationship 4-13			
	New Entrants	Repeaters	Dropouts	Deaths		Dropouts	Repeaters	Graduates	Deaths
0	875.2	106.2	378.3	7.3	595.8	224.0	150.7	214.6	6.5
6	824.7	150.7	375.5	6.8	593.1	223.0	150.0	213.6	6.5
12	927.1	150.0	414.7	7.5	654.9	246.2	165.7	235.8	7.2
18	1,056.0	165.7	470.3	8.5	742.9				

All these values are reproduced in the first row of Table 5-14.

All the variables in relationship 4-13 for structure 0 have now been estimated and we can proceed to relationship 4-12 for structure 6:

$$S_6^1 = n_6^1 + r_6^1 - b_6^1 - d_6^{11}$$

This also has five variables, two of which are already known: new entrants n_6^1 (824.7), estimated on the basis of population growth (see Table 5-13), and repeaters r_6^1 coming from structure 0 (150.7), estimated as one of the variables in relationship 4-13 for structure 0. All that remains, therefore, is to estimate the value of three variables.

To estimate dropouts before the pivotal year 6, i.e., b_6^1, we must use Eq. 5-5, which yields

$$
\begin{aligned}
b_6^1 &= 0.385 \, (n_6^1 + r_6^1) \\
&= 0.385 \, (824.7 + 150.7) \\
&= 375.5
\end{aligned}
$$

In a similar way Eq. 5-6 permits us to estimate the number of deaths before pivotal year 6, d_6^{11}, i.e., 6.8 thousand.

We now have the values for four of the five quantities in relationship 4-12 for structure 6. In order to estimate the value of the fifth variable—enrollment in pivotal year 6, S_6^1, we must make use of relationship 4-12 itself. The values so calculated for relation 4-12 for structure 6 are given in Table 5-14.

Having estimated total enrollment in year 6, we can use this figure together with Eqs. 4-12, 4-13, and 5-5 to 5-9 to compute the values of all the variables for pivotal years 6, 12, and 18. The method is the same as that used for structures 0 and 6 and need not be described again. The results of calculations for structures 6, 12, and 18 are presented in Table 5-14.

Projection of student flows at the high school level

The method to be used for the high school level is quite similar to the one used for the projections for the elementary school level. For the secondary level, we will use Eqs. 4-12 and 4-13 with superscript 2 denoting high school level:

$$S_t^2 = n_t^2 + r_t^2 - b_t^2 - d_t^{12} \qquad [4\text{-}12]$$

$$S_t^2 = g_t^2 + a_t^2 + r_{t+6}^2 + d_t^{22} \qquad [4\text{-}13]$$

and the following equations based on the ratios in Table 5-4:

$$n_t^2 = 0.642 \, g_{t-6}^1 \qquad (5\text{-}10)$$

$$b_t^2 = 0.251 \, (n_t^2 + r_t^2) \qquad (5\text{-}11)$$

$$d_t^{12} = 0.014 \, (n_t^2 + r_t^2) \qquad (5\text{-}12)$$

$$a_t^2 = 0.318 \, S_t^2 \qquad (5\text{-}13)$$
$$r_{t+6}^2 = 0.160 \, S_t^2 \qquad (5\text{-}14)$$
$$d_t^{22} = 0.020 \, S_t^2 \qquad (5\text{-}15)$$

Of Eqs. 5-10 to 5-15, all but Eq. 5-10 parallel Eqs. 5-5 through 5-9 for the elementary school level. Equation 5-10 takes the place of Eq. 5-4 used to make projections of elementary school new entrants. The reason for this change at the secondary level is that population growth as such has a direct influence only on new entrants in elementary school, while the number of graduates from the elementary level will influence the number of new entrants in high schools.

The process of estimation of the future values of variables for high school level structures is the same as that described above for elementary level structures; hence we will not undertake a detailed description of such estimation here. Projected values for the variables for Planiland high school level structures 0, 6, 12, and 18 are given in Table 5-15.

Projection of student flows at the college level

The equations used for college level projections take the following forms for Planiland:

$$S_t^3 = n_t^3 + r_t^3 - b_t^3 - d_t^{13} \qquad [4\text{-}12]$$
$$S_t^3 = g_t^3 + a_t^3 + r_{t+6}^3 + d_t^{23} \qquad [4\text{-}13]$$
$$n_t^3 = 0.694 \, g_{t-6}^2 \qquad (5\text{-}16)$$
$$b_t^3 = 0.326 \quad (n_t^3 = r_t^3) \qquad (5\text{-}17)$$
$$d_t^{13} = 0.015 \quad (n_t^3 + r_t^3) \qquad (5\text{-}18)$$
$$a_t^3 = 0.378 \, S_t^3 \qquad (5\text{-}19)$$
$$r_{t+6}^3 = 0.135 \, S_t^3 \qquad (5\text{-}20)$$
$$d_t^{23} = 0.020 \, S_t^3 \qquad (5\text{-}21)$$

Applying these equations, we obtain the results shown in Table 5-16 for Planiland college level structures 0, 6, 12, and 18.

5-4.3 Projections of Student Flows Considering the Influence of Population Growth and Change in Per Capita Income

The projections in Sec. 5-4.2 were made on the assumption that only population growth causes changes in student flows; hence, we could assume the indices in Tables 5-4 and 5-10 remain constant over the years. But in the real world there are other factors which influence the values of the variables in Eqs. 4-12 and 4-13. The existence of these other factors explains why the values of the indices needed to calculate the elements in future flows do not remain constant. Among the factors other than

Table 5-15. *Planiland: Projections of Student Flows at the High School Level, Considering Only the Influence of Population Growth (thousands)*

Pivotal Year	Before Pivotal Year, Relationship 4-12				Total Enrollment, Pivotal Year	After Pivotal Year, Relationship 4-13			
	New Entrants	Repeaters	Dropouts	Deaths		Dropouts	Repeaters	Graduates	Deaths
0	87.4	6.5	23.6	1.3	69.0	22.0	11.1	34.5	1.4
6	137.8	11.1	37.4	2.1	109.4	34.8	17.6	54.8	2.2
12	137.2	17.6	38.9	2.1	113.8	36.2	18.3	57.1	2.2
18	151.4	18.3	42.6	2.3	124.8				

Table 5-16. *Planiland: Projections of the Student Flows at the College Level Considering Only the Influence of Population Growth*

Pivotal Year	Before Pivotal Year, Relationship 4-12				Total Enrollment, Pivotal Year	After Pivotal Year, Relationship 4-13			
	New Entrants	Repeaters	Dropouts	Deaths		Dropouts	Repeaters	Graduates	Deaths
0	12.8	0.7	4.4	0.2	8.9	3.4	1.2	4.1	0.2
6	23.9	1.2	8.2	0.4	16.5	6.2	2.2	7.8	0.3
12	38.0	2.2	13.1	0.6	26.5	10.0	3.6	12.4	0.5
18	39.6	3.6	14.1	0.6	28.5				

population which influence student flows, the most important is probably change in per capita income.

Hence a more realistic method of projecting future student flows would take into consideration, in addition to the effects of population change, the effects of per capita income changes on the variables in relations 4-12 and 4-13. This more realistic method of estimating future flows is described in the remainder of this chapter. Essentially, this method follows the approach described in Sec. 5-4.2. First, we calculate the relationships existing over time between determining factors (population and per capita income growth) and elements determined by these factors (the elements in the student flows). We then estimate the change of the determining factors and finally calculate the changes in the determined factors caused by changes in the determining factors. We will use in the following projections the population data and forecasts presented in Chapter 2 and the economic development data and plans discussed in Chapter 3.

Relationship between numbers of new entrants at elementary school level and population and income changes

Over the long run, the key age level as far as new entrants are concerned is six years, since almost all systems attempt to enroll all children when they are six. Therefore, in this and the following sections we shall concentrate most of our attention on the new entrants of six years of age.

In most countries where less than 100 per cent of six-year-olds enter the school system, the proportion of six-year-olds entering school is increasing. Thus not only does the actual number of new entrants increase with growing population (which we saw in Sec. 5-4.2 where constant values for the τ's were assumed) but also there is a yearly increase in the *proportion* of six-year-olds entering the first grade. (This last development can be shown in terms of our symbols by a yearly increase in the value of τ for the six-year age level.) Although other factors may sometimes play an important part in influencing change in the value of τ, we will assume, to simplify the projection of future values of τ for six-year-olds, that the only factor which causes changes in the proportion of six-year-olds entering school is change in per capita income.

It is important for our purpose to quantify this relationship between increasing proportions of six-year-olds entering school and increasing per capita income. To do this we use a concept called "elasticity" which is simply the value of the ratio of the two rates of change. The elasticity of special interest to us here is the elasticity of τ with respect to per capita income. In symbols this elasticity, which we shall write ϵ_τ is represented by

$$\epsilon_\tau = \frac{\dfrac{\Delta \tau_{h6}}{\tau_{h6}}}{\dfrac{\Delta y_6}{y_6}} \tag{5-22}$$

where $\Delta \tau_{h6}$ = the change from year h to year $h + 1$ in the value of τ for six-year-olds; i.e.,

$$\Delta \tau_{h,6} = \tau_{h+1,6} - \tau_{h,6}$$

y_h = per capita income in year h (Chapter 3), and

Δy_h = the change from year h to year $h + 1$ in the value of per capita income; i.e.,

$$\Delta y_h = y_{h+1} - y_h$$

By way of example, let us see how this elasticity for the period between years -1 and 0 is computed. In Table 5-17 the rate of growth of

Table 5-17. *Planiland: Elasticities of the New Entrants Ratios τ_{h6} with Respect to Per Capita Income*

Years h	New Entrants Ratios (Table 5-9) τ_{h6}	Rate of Growth of the Ratios $\dfrac{\Delta \tau_{h6}}{\tau_{h6}}$	Per Capita Income (Ch. 3) y_h	Rate of Growth $\dfrac{\Delta y_h}{y_h}$	Elasticities $\epsilon_\tau = \dfrac{\dfrac{\Delta \tau_{h6}}{\tau_{h6}}}{\dfrac{\Delta y_h}{y_h}}$
0	0.3939		3,349		
		0.041		0.048	0.85
-1	0.3784		3,195		
		0.165		0.033	5.00
-2	0.3248		3,092		
		0.343		-0.017	-201.80
-3	0.2418		3,097		
		1.87		0.027	69.33
-4	0.0842		3,016		

Average elasticity for years -1 and 0 = 2.925

the new entrant ratio, amounting to 0.041 (4.1 percent), appears in the first line of the third column; the rate of growth of per capita income, amounting to 0.048 (4.8 percent), appears in the fifth column. The elasticity is thus

$$\frac{0.041}{0.048} = 0.85$$

This figure tells us that if the rate of growth of per capita income went up by one percentage point to 5.8 percent, the rate of increase in the value of new entrant ratio would go up by .85 percent to 4.95 percent.

Figures for elasticities for other pairs of years between year −4 and year −1 are presented in Table 5-17 along with the figures from which these elasticities are calculated. The elasticities for changes between years −4 and −3 and years −3 and −2 must not be used for projections since they involve an "abnormal" increase in the value of τ of nearly 200 percent in the first case and an "abnormal" decrease in per capita income in the second case.

This arbitrary decision is based on a sense of what is "normal" developed through a knowledge of the experiences of other countries. Only better statistics and better methods of estimation would give a scientific basis for deciding whether or not to use the elasticities between years −4 and −3 and years −3 and −2.

The elasticities for years −2 and −1 and years −1 and 0 can be used in projections since they are based on figures which do not appear abnormal and they are for the most recent years. To obtain a figure for use in projecting numbers of new entrants in the Planiland school system in future years, we take the average of the last two elasticities available— the average of 0.85 and 5.00 which is 2.925. We assume this elasticity remains constant for all rates of per capita income change.

Projection of the new entrant ratios for population of six years of age

Once we have estimated the value of ϵ_τ we can use such estimates together with projections of per capita income and population to estimate the future growth of new entrants in the Planiland first grade.

In order to see how the elasticities can be used for this purpose, we must bear in mind the definition of these elasticities in Eq. 5-22. For instance, the estimate of the elasticity made before permits us to write

$$\frac{\Delta \tau_{hj}}{\tau_{hj}} = 2.925 \frac{\Delta y_h}{y_h} \tag{5-23}$$

So, knowing the probable future of growth of per capita income, we can estimate the future rate of growth of the new entrant ratios.

An estimate for the future rate of growth of per capita income should be supplied by the economists preferably as part of a long-term plan for the economy. Where Planiland is concerned, its economic plan sets out the figures which are presented in Table 3-7.

We now have the two elements required to estimate the rate of growth of the new entrant ratios: the elasticity of 2.925 and the rate of growth of per capita income.

By way of example, let us take the rate of growth in the new entrant ratio between years 0 and 6. The elasticity being 2.925 and the rate of growth of per capita income being 0.218 per six years, the rate of growth per six years of the new entrant ratio is estimated to be

$$2.925 \times 0.218 = 0.638$$

The results of similar calculations for years 6 through 12 and 12 through 18 are given in Table 5-18.

Table 5-18.   Estimation of the Rate of Growth of the New Entrants Ratio

Years	Elasticity	Rate of Growth of Per Capita Income	Estimated Rate of Growth of New Entrants Ratios
0–6	2.925	0.218	0.638
6–12	2.925	0.220	0.644
12–18	2.925	0.218	0.638

We now use the results in Table 5-18 to estimate the future values of new entrant ratios. The rate of growth gives the increment in the new entrant ratio per unit of the ratio's values at the beginning of the period. For example, the rate of growth between year 0 and year 6 is estimated to be 0.638 which means that there will be an increment of 0.638 between year 0 and year 6 in respect to each unit of the new entrant ratio in year 0.

The initial value of the enrollment ratio in Table 5-19 is 0.3939, so that the total increment between years 0 and 6 will be

$$0.3939 \times 0.638 = 0.2513$$

To obtain the value of the new entrant ratio in year 6, we must add the increment to the initial value, i.e.,

$$0.3939 + 0.2513 = 0.6452$$

The procedure must be repeated in order to obtain the projections for year 12, this time taking the new entrant ratio for year 6 as a starting point. The projected new entrant ratios for years 6 and 12 are shown in Table 5-19.

Table 5-19.   Planiland: Projection of New Entrants Ratio for Six Years of Age

Year h	Ratio τ_{h6}
0	0.3939
6	0.6452
12	1.0607
18	

We have previously observed that the diagonal sums of the new entrant ratios can never be greater than one, since the ratios represent the number of new entrants per person in an age level of the population and the number of new entrants must be equal to or less than the total in the age interval. For year 12, Table 5-19 shows the projected ratio to be 1.0607. To avoid projecting an impossible value, we must reduce the projected ratio to 1.0000. This value is given to the ratio for year 12; we assume that the ratio will maintain this value in years after 12. After having estimated the value of τ_{h6} for years 6, 12, and 18, it is possible to obtain by interpolation the values for the ratios τ_{h6} for each year through 18. The results of the interpolation are presented in Table 5-20.

Table 5-20.   Planiland: Values for Each Year Between 0 and 18 of the New Entrants Ratio for Six Years of Age

Year h	Ratio τ_{h6}	Year h	Ratio τ_{h6}	Year h	Ratio τ_{h6}
0	0.3939				
1	0.4278	7	0.7010	13	1.000
2	0.4646	8	0.7614	14	1.000
3	0.5056	9	0.8270	15	1.000
4	0.5491	10	0.8982	16	1.000
5	0.5963	11	0.9756	17	1.000
6	0.6452	12	1.000	18	1.000

Projection of the new entrant ratios for age levels above six years

We have discussed the projection of future values of new entrant ratios for six-year-olds on the basis of the estimated future per capita income growth rate. We now turn to the question of projections of new entrant ratios for higher age levels. We will use as data for these projections the estimates of future new entrant ratios for six-year-olds which we have calculated, and the year 0 ratios for higher age levels. Making use of the principle that diagonal sums cannot be greater than one, we project the ratios for the higher age levels reducing their value if a diagonal sum otherwise would exceed one. The results are presented in Table 5-21.

If we compare the ratios in Table 5-21 with those in Table 5-10, we see the effect of the yearly increase in the value of new entrant ratios for six-year-olds. When these were constant, all ratios for higher age level were likewise constant from year 3 onward. The growth of the ratio for age 6 brings about a progressive reduction in all the other ratios until the ratio for age 6 equals 1 and the ratios for other age levels equal 0. When this point is reached, all children age 6 enter school and there are none left to be entrants at age 7 or more. From this point on, the number of new entrants grows at the same rate as the six-year-old population.

Projections of new entrants in elementary school

Once the future values of the new entrant ratios are known, Eq. 5-4 can be used to project numbers of new entrants in elementary school in future years. We simply multiply the new entrant ratios which hold for various age levels in a given year by the number of children in the various age levels and add the figures thus obtained.

Table 5-21.   Planiland: New Entrants Ratios for 6 up to 10 Years of Age

Age	\multicolumn{17}{c}{Year}																
	-4	-3	-2	-1	0	1	2	3	4	5	6	7	8	9	10	11	12
6	0.0842	0.2418	0.3248	0.3784	0.3939	0.4278	0.4646	0.5056	0.5491	0.5963	0.6452	0.7010	0.7614	0.8270	0.8982	0.9756	1.000
7	0.3289	0.3446	0.3149	0.3149	0.3149	0.3149	0.3149	0.3149	0.3149	0.3149	0.3149	0.3149	0.2990	0.2386	0.1730	0.1018	0.0244
8	0.3525	0.2864	0.2617	0.2617	0.2617	0.2617	0.2617	0.2573	0.2205	0.1795	0.1360	0.0888	0.0399	0.000	0.000	0.000	0.000
9	0.2447	0.1988	0.1816	0.1816	0.1816	0.0986	0.0450	0.0295	0.000	0.000	0.000	0.000	0.000	0.000	0.000	0.000	0.000
10	0.1723	0.1400	0.1279	0.1279	0.1279	0.000	0.000	0.000	0.000	0.000	0.000	0.000	0.000	0.000	0.000	0.000	0.000

Table 5-22.   Planiland: Total Number of New Entrants in Elementary School for Year 0 to Year 18 (thousands)

Year	New Entrants	Year	New Entrants	Year	New Entrants
(0)	(139.6)	7	164.7	13	169.4
1	139.8	8	167.4	14	173.1
2	142.3	9	165.5	15	176.8
3	149.1	10	169.4	16	180.5
4	150.0	11	174.1	17	186.6
5	154.8	12	169.6	18	191.4
6	159.7				
Total n_t^1	895.7		1,010.7		1,077.9

The totals of new entrants in years 0 to 18 and in structures 6, 12, and 18, appear in Table 5-22.

Projection of graduates, dropouts, repeaters, and deaths in elementary school

In Sec. 5-4.2 we used equations of the forms

$$S_t^1 = n_t^1 + r_t^1 - b_t^1 - d_t^{11} \tag{4-12}$$

$$S_t^1 = g_t^1 + a_t^1 + r_{t+6}^1 + d_t^{21} \tag{4-13}$$

$$b_t^1 = \beta^1(n_t^1 + r_t^1) \qquad \text{with } \beta^1 = 0.385 \tag{5-24}$$

$$d_t^{11} = \delta^{11}(n_t^1 + r_t^1) \qquad \text{with } \delta^{11} = 0.007 \tag{5-25}$$

$$a_t^1 = \alpha^1 S_t^1 \qquad \text{with } \alpha^1 = 0.376 \tag{5-26}$$

$$r_{t+k}^1 = \rho^1 S_t^1 \qquad \text{with } \rho^1 = 0.253 \tag{5-27}$$

$$d_t^{21} = \delta^{21} S_t^1 \qquad \text{with } \delta^{21} = 0.011 \tag{5-28}$$

Since we were considering only the influence of population changes on student flows, it was assumed that the parameters β^1, δ^{11}, ρ^1, δ^{21} were constant. When we take into account effects of per capita income growth, we must consider changes in the values of these parameters resulting from income changes. On the following pages, we will first project the values of the parameters for years 6, 12, and 18. Then these values will be used in Eqs. 5-24 through 5-28 to calculate the values of the variables for structures 6, 12, and 18.

Projection of the values of the parameters

The parameters δ^{11} and δ^{21} relating to deaths change relatively little from structure to structure, as can be seen in Table 5-4. In addition, such changes as do occur in these ratios do not seem to be meaningfully related to change in per capita income. We will therefore assume that these ratios for future structures will not change with changes in income. In projecting future student flows the values used for δ^{11} and δ^{21} will be those given in Eqs. 5-6 and 5-9.

For the projection of the values of the other three parameters, elasticities must be calculated and used. Calculations of elasticities of α^1, β^1, and ρ^1 with respect to per capita income are shown in Table 5-23.

The use of elasticities for the projection of the six-year-olds new entrant ratio is explained in detail above. The procedure is the same for the projection of the parameters α^1, β^1, and ρ^1. For instance, let us project the value for structure 0 of the parameter α. The elasticity of this parameter with respect to per capita income is -0.489 (Table 5-23).

The first step is to multiply the elasticity by 0.203, the rate of growth per six years of per capita income from pivotal year -6 to pivotal year 0; that is,

$$-0.489 \times 0.203 = -0.099$$

The figure -0.099 represents the six-year rate of growth of the value of the parameter α^1. Since this is a negative figure, we know that the value of α^1 is projected to decline by 9.9% from structure -6 to structure 0.

Table 5-23.   Elasticities for the Parameters in the Equations Referring to Elementary School Level

Pivotal Years	Past Values (Table 5-4)	Rate of Growth of the Parameters (a)	Per Capita Income	Rate of Growth of Per Capita Income (b)	Elasticities $\dfrac{a}{b}$
		Elasticity for Dropouts Before Pivotal Year, β^1			
-6	0.388	-0.008	2,783	0.203	-0.039
0	0.385		3,349		
		Elasticity for Dropouts After Pivotal Year, α^1			
-12	0.419	-0.103	2,299	0.210	-0.489
-6	0.376		2,783		
		Elasticity for Repeaters, ρ^1			
-12	0.297	-0.148	2,299	0.210	-0.705
-6	0.253		2,783		

Since the value of α^1 for structure -6 is 0.376, the value of α^1 for structure 0 is

$$0.376 + (0.376)(-0.099) = 0.339$$

The future values of the other parameters are estimated in the same way and are shown in Table 5-24.

With the values for the parameters of Eqs. 5-24 to 5-28 presented in Table 5-24, we can proceed to the *estimation of the values of the variables in these equations.*

Table 5-24.   Planiland: Projected Values of the Parameters α^1, β^1, δ^{11}, δ^{21}, and ρ^1

Parameter	Year			
	0	6	12	18
Dropouts before pivotal year, β^1		0.382	0.379	0.376
Deaths before pivotal year, δ^{11}		0.007	0.007	0.007
Dropouts after pivotal year, α^1	0.339	0.303	0.270	0.242
Repeaters, ρ^1	0.217	0.184	0.156	0.132
Deaths after pivotal year, δ^{21}	0.011	0.011	0.011	0.011

In Sec. 5-4.2, three basic sets of figures were used to prepare projections of student flows at the elementary school level taking population growth alone into account: (1) information on the pivotal year 0; (2) projections of new entrants in elementary school; and (3) values of the parameters for the elementary school level.

The same elements are required in order to project future student flows when taking both population and per capita income changes into account.

The method has already been explained in the above-mentioned section. We begin by estimating the values of the variables in relationship 4-13 for year 0. We first use Eqs. 5-26 to 5-28 and the parameter values of Table 5-24 to estimate the values for dropouts (a_0^1) during and after the pivotal year, repeaters (r_0^1) passing to the next structure and deaths (d_0^{21}) during and after the pivotal year. The results appear in Table 5-25.

Once these three values have been obtained, the number of graduates may be established by using the actual figure for student enrollment in year 0 and Eq. 4-13.

Having computed the values of the variables for relationship 4-13 for structure 0, we can proceed to estimate values for the variables in relationship 4-12 for structure 6. New entrants have already been estimated and, with this value together with that for repeaters coming from structure 0, the value of total inputs can be calculated.

We can use this value, the estimated values of parameters from Table 5-24 and Eqs. 5-24 and 5-25 to estimate the number of dropouts and deaths prior to pivotal year 6.

We are now in a position to use relationship 4-12 to calculate total enrollment in pivotal year 6.

At this point, we have the same information with respect to structure 6 as we had previously with respect to structure 0. By using the approach sketched above, we can obtain estimates for the variables in relationship 4-13 for structure 6. These enable us to compute the values for relationship 4-12 for structure 12, and so on. The results of such calculations are shown in Table 5-25.

Projection of student flows at high school and college levels

For this projection the following steps are required:

(a) Equations 5-10 through 5-15 for high school and 5-16 through 5-20 for college should be written, using in place of the constant indices the parameters α^i, β^i, δ^{1i}, δ^{2i}, ρ^i, and τ_i with $i = 2$ for high school and $i = 3$ for college. The parameter τ^i will be used in equations of the form corresponding to Eqs. 5-10 and 5-16.

$$n_t^i = \tau^i g_{t-6}^{i-1} \qquad i = 2, 3 \qquad (5\text{-}29)$$

Table 5-25. Planiland: Projections of Students Flows in Elementary School Considering the Influence of Population and Income Growth (thousands)

Year	New Entrants n_t^1	Before Pivotal Year, Relationship 4-12			Total Enrollment, Pivotal Year S_t^1	After Pivotal Year, Relationship 4-13			
		Repeaters r_t^1	Dropouts b_t^1	Deaths d_t^{11}		Dropouts a_t^1	Repeaters r_{t+6}^1	Graduates g_t^1	Deaths d_t^{21}
0	895.7	129.3	391.5	7.2	595.8	202.0	129.3	258.0	6.5
6	1,010.7	115.2	426.7	7.9	626.3	189.8	115.2	314.4	6.9
12	1,077.9	107.8	445.8	8.3	691.3	186.9	107.8	389.0	7.6
18					731.6				

Table 5-26.   Elasticities for the Parameters in the Equations Referring to High School and College Levels

HIGH SCHOOL

Pivotal Years	Past Values	Rate of Growth of the Parameter a	Per Capita Income	Rate of Growth of Per Capita Income b	Elasticities $\dfrac{a}{b}$
Elasticity for New Entrants					
−6	0.642	−0.109	2,783	0.203	−0.537
0	0.579		3,349		
Elasticity for Dropouts before Pivotal Year, β^2					
−6	0.303	−0.172	2,783	0.203	−0.847
0	0.251		3,349		
Elasticity for Dropouts after Pivotal Year, α^2					
−12	0.318	0.016	2,299	0.210	0.075
−6	0.323		2,783		
Elasticity for Repeaters, ρ^2					
−12	0.208	−0.231	2,299	0.210	−1.100
−6	0.160		2,783		

COLLEGE

Pivotal Years	Past Values (Table 7-4)	Rate of Growth of the Parameter a	Per Capita Income	Rate of Growth of Per Capita Income b	Elasticities $\dfrac{a}{b}$
Elasticity for New Entrants					
−6	0.694	−0.089	2,783	0.203	−0.438
0	0.637		3,349		
Elasticity for Dropouts before Pivotal Year, β^3					
−6	0.366	−0.109	2,783	0.203	−0.537
0	0.326		3,349		
Elasticity for Dropouts after Pivotal Year, α^3					
−12	0.378	0.296	2,299	0.210	1.404
−6	0.490		2,783		
Elasticity for Repeaters, ρ^3					
−12	0.135	0.016	2,299	0.210	0.074
−6	0.137		2,783		

(b) Estimates should be made of the elasticities with respect to per capita income changes of the parameters named in step (a). The values of these and the figures of which they are based are presented in Table 5-26.

(c) Using the elasticities, we should estimate the rates of growth of the parameters and the future values of the parameters themselves. These values are given in Table 5-27.

An analysis of these values suggests that they are reasonable for high school, but not for college. In this level proportion α^3 of dropouts after the pivotal year is larger than one, which would indicate that the number of dropouts is larger than the number of students enrolled. Since this is obviously absurd, α^3 cannot be used.

(d) With the projected values of the parameters, Eqs. 4-12, 4-13 and 5-10 through 5-21, and the modifications introduced because of the unacceptable value of α^3, the values of the variables refering to students flows can be obtained.

The modifications used to accommodate the rapid increase in college dropouts at the expense of graduates are as follows. Values for the numbers of repeaters and deaths are estimated using Eqs. 5-19 and 5-20 with the projected values for ρ^3 and δ^{23}. The number of college graduates from structures 6 and 12 is assumed to be zero. Then, it is possible to estimate the number of dropouts, using Eq. 4-13 for the college level. The results for high school and college are shown in Table 5-28.

The assumption that there will be no graduates from structures 6 and 12, despite its being consistent with the trends observed in the past, is obviously unrealistic. In reality, before reaching this point, the parameter

Table 5-27. Planiland: Projected Values of the Parameters α^i, β^i, δ^{1i}, δ^{2i}, ρ^i, and τ^i

Parameter	Year 0	Year 6	Year 12	Year 18
High School $i = 2$				
New entrants, τ^2		0.642	0.642	0.642
Dropouts before pivotal year, β^2		0.205	0.167	0.136
Deaths before pivotal year, δ^{12}		0.014	0.014	0.014
Dropouts after pivotal year, α^2	0.328	0.333	0.338	0.343
Repeaters, ρ^2	0.124	0.094	0.071	0.054
Deaths after pivotal year, δ^{22}	0.020	0.020	0.020	0.020
College $i = 3$				
New entrants, τ^3		0.694	0.694	0.694
Dropouts before pivotal year, β^3		0.288	0.254	0.224
Deaths before pivotal year, δ^{13}		0.015	0.015	0.015
Dropouts after pivotal year, α^3	0.630	0.822	1.075	
Repeaters, ρ^3	0.139	0.141	0.143	0.145
Deaths after pivotal year, δ^{23}	0.020	0.020	0.020	0.020

Table 5-28. *Planiland: Projections of Students Flows in High School and College Considering the Influences of Population and Income Growth (thousands)*

Year	Before Pivotal Year, Relationship 4-12				Total Enrollment, Pivotal Year S_t^i	After Pivotal Year, Relationship 4-13			
	New Entrants n_t^i	Repeaters r_t^i	Dropouts b_t^i	Deaths d_t^{1i}		Dropouts a_t^i	Repeaters r_{t+6}^i	Graduates g_t^i	Deaths d_t^{2i}
High School $i = 2$									
0	165.6	8.6	35.7	2.4	69.0	22.6	8.6	36.4	1.4
6	201.8	12.8	35.8	3.0	136.1	45.3	12.8	75.3	2.7
12	249.7	12.5	35.7	3.7	175.8	59.4	12.5	100.4	3.5
18					222.8				
College $i = 3$									
0	25.3	1.2	7.6	0.4	8.9	5.6	1.2	1.9	0.2
6	52.3	2.6	13.9	0.8	18.5	15.5	2.6	0.0	0.4
12	69.7	5.7	16.9	1.1	40.2	33.7	5.7	0.0	0.8
18					57.4				

α^3 will become constant, or will begin reducing its value. Unfortunately there is no statistical data relevant to this question. Only with such information could a more realistic projection of the students flows in college be made.

In summary, projections of student flows are identical in form regardless of whether income changes are considered. Where population growth is the only influence taken into account, the parameters used in calculations are constant.

When the influence of per capita income is added, the parameters used are assumed to vary with changes in per capita income. These changing values for the parameters can be calculated using past elasticities of the parameters with respect to per capita income.

References

A more detailed analysis of the factors influencing student flows is given in
Correa, H., *The Economics of Human Resources*. Amsterdam: North Holland Publishing Co., 1963, Chapter 7.

A computerized application of the previous model is presented in
Correa, H., and E. Reimer, *A Simulation Model for Educational Planning in Puerto Rico*. San Juan: Department of Public Instruction (Mimeographed), 1969.

Another mathematical model for the study of the educational system is given in
Stone, R., "A Model of the Educational System," *Minerva*, Winter 1965.

chapter 6

The Educational Structure of the Population

6-1 Content of This Chapter

In this chapter we introduce the methods to forecast the educational structure of the population. These methods actually are simpler than those used to study the future development of the flows of students. The reason for this is that, excluding emigration, the only determinants of changes in the educational structure of the population are the output of the educational system and deaths. In fact, the basic accounting equation is the following: Present number of persons with, for example, a college education, plus the output from college, minus deaths equal the future number of persons in the same category of education.

The elements that should be included in the output of the educational system were mentioned in Sec. 4-4. The forecasts of flows of students provide the main data required to evaluate these outputs. The only thing that remains is the detailed accounting work.

6-2 Method to Be Used

In Sec. 2-2.3, data on the distribution of the population by level of education were presented. We call this distribution the *educational structure* of the population. Our purpose in this chapter is to study the changes in time of that educational structure. The principle involved is quite simple: Take the structure in any given year, add to it the output of the educational system during a related period; subtract the number of deaths during that period; the result will be the educational structure at the end of that period. This can be expressed in formulas. Let

Pe_t^i = number of persons other than students with educational level i in year t

O_t^i = output of the educational system of persons of level $i = 1, 2, 3$ between pivotal years $t - 6$ and t

The interpretation of the above statement is as follows:

$$Pe^i_{t+6} = Pe^i_t + O^i_{t+6} - \text{deaths} \qquad (6\text{-}1)$$

Let us study in more detail Eq. 6-1. In Chapter 2, all persons who had received any elementary schooling at all were considered part of the population with some elementary education. Similarly, figures for those with some high school or college education include all those who have received education of the relevant level whether for one day or through graduation. This means that the output Eqs. 4-14 and 4-15 will be reduced to

$$O^i_{t+6} = g^i_t + a^i_t + b^i_{t+6} - n^{i+1}_{t+6} \qquad i = 1 \text{ and } 2 \qquad (6\text{-}2)$$

and

$$O^3_{t+6} = g^3_t + a^3_t + b^3_{t+6} \qquad (6\text{-}3)$$

For instance, for the period between -12 and -6, the output of elementary school, according to the data in Table 5-3 is

$$\begin{aligned} O^1_{-6} &= g^1_{-12} + a^1_{-12} + b^1_{-6} - n^2_{-6} \\ &= 84.4 + 129.4 + 269.4 - 54.2 \\ &= 429.0 \end{aligned}$$

It is easy to see that Eq. 6-2 above is a particular case of the general output equation

$$O^i_{t+k} = g^i_t + (1 - \gamma^1)a^i_t + (1 - \eta^1)b^1_{t+k} + \gamma^2 a^2_t + \eta^2 b^2_{t+k} - n^2_{t+k}$$

In Eq. 6-2, η^1, η^2, γ^1, and γ^2 equal zero because dropouts from a level are counted as output from that level.

Any other treatment of dropouts that was deemed useful could be handled without difficulty. An alternative treatment, for instance, would be to include only those having graduated from a particular level in the stratum corresponding to that level; e.g., the elementary educational stratum would include all graduates from that level plus all those who had received some high school education but had dropped out before graduating. In this case, η^i and γ^i in the general output equation would both have values of one.

The third element in Eq. 6-1, i.e., "deaths," is more difficult to handle. There are two types of deaths that should be considered: first, those among the persons Pe^i_t already included in the stratum at date t; second, deaths among persons O^i_{t+6} in the output of a given level between year t and year $t + 6$. To see why this second group has to be considered we should remember that Pe^i_t represents the persons with educational level i at *instant* t, while O^i_{t+6} represents the output of education between t and $t + 6$. But some of those leaving school during this period die before date $t + 6$, so they should be subtracted from the total added to Pe^i_t to obtain Pe^i_{t+6}.

The method described can be used equally well to study the past changes or to project the future changes of the educational structure of the population. Both uses will be considered below. First, we examine in some detail the application of the method to a study of the past changes of the educational structure of the population.

6-3   Past Evolution of the Educational Structure of the Population

As an example, we will estimate the educational structure of the Planiland population in year -6 using the data on the educational structure in year -12 (Table 2-3) and figures for the output of the educational system (Table 5-3). The steps required with respect to the population with elementary school education appear in Table 6-1.

Table 6-1.   Planiland: Changes of the Population with Elementary Education from Year -12 to Year -6 (thousands)

	Sign	Variables	Values
1	+	Total population with elementary education year -12 (Table 2-3)	1,077.6
2	−	Enrollment in elementary school year -12, S^2_{-12} (Table 5-3)	308.5
3		Population with elementary schooling outside the system year -12, Pe^1_{-12}	769.1
4	+	Survivors in year -6 of those in $Pe^1_{-12} = 0.9289\ Pe^1_{-12}$	714.4
5	+	Graduates from structure -12, g^1_{-12} (Table 5-3)	84.4
6	−	New entrants in high school, n^2_{-6} (Table 5-3)	54.2
7	−	Deaths of graduates after they left school, i.e., among $(g^1_{-12} - n^2_{-6})$	.5
8	+	Dropouts, a^1_{-12} (Table 5-3)	129.4
9	−	Deaths among a^1_{-12}	2.2
10	+	Dropouts, b^1_{-6} (Table 5-3)	269.4
11	−	Deaths among b^1_{-6}	2.9
12		Population outside the educational system year -6, Pe^1_{-6}	1,137.8
13		Enrollment in elementary school year -6, S^1_{-6} (Table 5-3)	419.6
14		Total population with elementary school year -6 (Table 2-3)	1,557.4

The figure in the first line of Table 6-1 (1,077.6) represents the number of persons in the population with elementary education in year -12. From this we subtract the number of those enrolled in elementary school (308.5) in that year, thereby obtaining the number of those outside elementary school with some elementary schooling but no higher education (Pe^1_{-12}), (769.1).

The survival rate for the period between -12 and -6 represents the number of persons surviving in year -6 per person alive in year -12; in other words, for each person alive in year -12, 0.9289 will be alive in year -6. Since 769.1 thousand persons with some elementary education were alive in year -12,

$$769.1 \text{ thousand} \times .9289 = 714.4 \text{ thousand}$$

will be alive in year -6. This number is shown in line 4 of Table 6-1.

Let us consider now the output of the educational system. The total number of graduates (g^1_{-12}) and dropouts (a^1_{-12} and b^1_{-6}) must not be used without modification in estimating the number added to the elementary level stratum between years -12 and -6. Several modifications must be introduced: First, not all graduates from elementary school leave the educational system; some of them enroll in high school and these must not be included in the net addition to the elementary level stratum of the population. This analysis explains why the number of new entrants in high school (54.2) is accompanied by a minus sign in line 6 of Table 6-1. Secondly, after leaving school between years -12 and -6, some dropouts and graduates die.

Table 6-2 shows the method to estimate the number of deaths from year -12 to year -6 among dropouts (a^1_{-12}) and graduates (g^1_{-12}) after they leave school. In the first part of this table, figures for the total number of dropouts and graduates for each year from -12 to -7 are given. To calculate the number of these persons leaving the school system who survive until year -6, we use yearly survival rates (Table 2-6) as many

Table 6-2.   Planiland: Survivals Among Dropouts and Graduates from Structure −12 After They Left School (units)

	Elementary School						
	Year in Which the School Is Left						
	-12	-11	-10	-9	-8	-7	-6
Graduates	12,342	12,740	13,736	14,234	13,834	17,519	
Dropouts	62,224	28,011	24,766	1,406			
	Survivors in Year						
	-12	-11	-10	-9	-8	-7	-6
	74,566	74,268	73,971	73,675	73,380	73,086	72,794
		40,751	40,588	40,426	40,264	40,103	39,943
			38,691	38,536	38,382	38,228	38,075
				27,000	26,892	26,784	26,677
					15,240	15,179	15,118
						17,519	17,449

Total survivors year -6 210,056

Total dropouts + graduates including deaths 213,767

Number of deaths . . . . 3,711 times as there are years between the time of leaving the educational system and the next pivotal year. Thus with a yearly survival rate of 0.996, the number of those leaving the school system in -12 as dropouts and graduates (74,566 from Table 6-2) who are still alive in year -6 is

$$74,566 \times 0.996 \times 0.996 \times 0.996 \times 0.996 \times 0.996 \times 0.996$$
$$= 74,566 \times (0.996)^6 = 72,784$$

For those leaving in year -8, the number surviving in year -6 is

$$15,240 \times 0.996 \times 0.996 = 15,240 \times (0.996)^2 = 15,118$$

The last column of Table 6-2 shows the survivors in year -6 from among those leaving structure -12 from year -12 to year -7, the total being 210,056.

The total number of those leaving school in the six-year period, not taking into account subsequent deaths, is obtained by adding the number of those leaving each year:

$$74,566 + 40,751 + 38,691 + 27,000 + 15,240 + 17,519 = 213,767$$

The number of deaths may then be calculated:

$$213,767 - 210,056 = 3,711$$

Similar computations were made for elementary school, high school and college levels for dropouts (b_t^i and a_t^i) and for graduates (g_t^i) for all the years for which data were available. The results are shown in Table 6-3.

With the figures for the total number of dropouts and graduates and the number of deaths among them, it becomes possible to calculate the death rates for these groups. The values obtained for the death rates are shown in the last column of Table 6-3. With these rates the estimated number of deaths shown in Table 6-1 were computed.

We have now analyzed all the figures shown in Table 6-1, together with the reasons for adding or subtracting them; the result of the indicated operations (1,137.8 thousand) appears in line 12. This figure represents those outside the educational system in year -6 who have received some elementary education but nothing more. In order to establish the total number in the elementary schooling strata, we must add the figure for those attending elementary school in year -6 (419.6 thousand). Thereby we obtain a figure of 1,557.4 thousand for the total number with only some elementary education in year -6.

The operations just described can be expressed in the following formula:

Table 6-3.　Planiland: Total Number of Dropouts and Graduates and Number of Their Deaths After They Have Left the Educational System and Before the Next Pivotal Year (thousands)

	Leavers			Deaths* Before Next Pivotal Year (4)	Rates $\dfrac{\text{Column (3)}}{\text{Column (4)}}$
	Graduates (1)	Dropouts (2)	Totals (3)		
Elementary School					
From structure − 12 during and after pivotal year	84.4	129.4	213.8	3.7	0.017
From structure − 6 before pivotal year		269.4	269.4	2.9	0.011
From structure − 6 during and after pivotal year	151.0	157.8	308.8	5.0	0.016
From structure 0 before pivotal year		378.3	378.3	3.9	0.010
High School					
From structure − 12 during and after pivotal year	11.1	7.8	18.9	0.5	0.027
From structure − 6 before pivotal year		18.0	18.0	0.3	0.017
From structure − 6 during and after pivotal year	20.1	13.1	33.2	0.89	0.027
From structure 0 before pivotal year		23.6	23.6	0.4	0.017
College					
From structure − 12 during and after pivotal year	1.7	1.4	3.1	0.1	0.27
From structure − 6 before pivotal year		3.0	3.0	0.1	0.17
From structure − 6 during and after pivotal year	1.8	2.5	4.3	0.1	0.28
From structure 0 before pivotal year		4.4	4.4	0.1	0.19

*There might be some difference between the values for the death rates and the values that can be computed with the figures for deaths appearing in this table. This difference is due to the rounding off of the figures in the table.

$$
\begin{aligned}
Pe^1_{-6} = {} & (1 - 0.0711)\, Pe^1_{-12} \\
& + (1 - 0.017)(g^1_{-12} - n^2_{-6}) \\
& + (1 - 0.017)\, a^1_{-12} \\
& + (1 - 0.011)\, b^1_{-6}
\end{aligned}
\tag{6-4}
$$

Formula 6-4 is the same as formula 6-1 with deaths:

$$0.0711 \, Pe^1_{-12} + 0.017 \, (g^1_{-12} - n^2_{-6}) + 0.017 \, a^1_{-12} + 0.011 \, b^1_{-6}.$$

For future reference it is useful to generalize formula 6-4 using Greek letters as parameters for all educational levels and periods in place of the numerical death ratios shown in formula 6-1. This is done in formula 6-5

$$
\begin{aligned}
Pe^i_{t+6} = \;& (1 - \nu^{i1}) \, Pe^i_t \\
+ \;& (1 - \nu^{i2})(g^i_t - n^{i+1}_{t+6}) \\
+ \;& (1 - \nu^{i3}) a^i_t \\
+ \;& (1 - \nu^{i4}) b^i_{t+6}
\end{aligned}
\tag{6-5}
$$

when ν represents the "death" rate.

Similar operations can be carried out to obtain all the other figures relating to the "educational structure of the population" in years -6 and 0. The number of persons over six years of age without education can be obtained for each year by subtracting the total number of people with some education from the total population over six years of age. The educational structure of the population over six years of age for years -12, -6, and 0 is presented in Table 6-4.

Table 6-4. *Planiland: Educational Structure of the Population of Six and More Years of Age (thousands)*

Educational Level	Years		
	-12	-6	0
Without education	1,152.8	1,012.1	744.5
Elementary	1,077.6	1,557.4	2,250.3
High school	165.2	199.8	260.9
College	18.4	24.7	35.8
Total	2,414.0	2,794.0	3,292.0

6-4 Future Changes of the Educational Structure of the Population

The method described in Sec. 6-2 may be used to project the educational structure of the population in future pivotal years. In this case we begin with the structure for year 0 (Table 6-4) and the projected output of the educational system between years 0 and 6. We may use either the output projections shown in Tables 5-14 to 5-16 (where only the influence of population growth is taken into account) or those shown in Tables 5-25 and 5-28 (where the influence of both population and income growth is taken into account). On the basis of these figures, we may estimate the structure in year 6 and then use this estimate to make a projec-

Table 6-5. Planiland: Projection of the Number of Persons with Some High School Education from Year 6 (thousands)

	Only Population Influences Considered (Tables 5-14 to 5-15)	Population and Economic Growth Influences Considered (Table 5-25, Table 5-28)
Total population six years and more, year 0	260.9	260.9
− Enrollment in pivotal year 0, S_0^2	− 69.0	− 69.0
Population outside the educational system year 0, Pe_0^2	191.9	191.9
Survivors in year 6 of population outside system	179.6	179.6
+ Graduates educational structure 0, g_0^2	+ 34.5	+ 36.4
− Graduates entering college structure year 6, n_6^3	− 23.9	− 25.3
+ Dropouts after pivotal year 0, a_0^2	+ 22.0	+ 22.6
− Deaths of graduates and dropouts from structure 0 after they left school, i.e., $g_0^2 + a_0^2 - n_6^3$	− 0.9	− 0.9
+ Dropouts from structure 6 before pivotal year, b_6^2	+ 37.4	+ 35.7
− Deaths among dropouts from structure 6 after they left school	− 0.6	− 0.6
Population outside the educational system year 6, Pe_6^2	248.1	247.5
+ Total enrollment in structure 6	+ 109.4	+ 136.1
Total population six year and more, year 6	357.5	383.6

Table 6-6. Planiland: Projections of the Educational Structure of the Population (thousands)

	Years			
Educational Level	0	6	12	18
Only the Influence of Population Growth Considered				
Without education	744.6	701.9	659.4	633.3
Elementary	2,250.8	2,809.8	3,470.4	4,219.5
High school	260.9	357.5	438.6	528.7
College	35.7	57.0	91.7	126.1
Total	3,292.0	3,926.2	4,660.1	5,507.7
Influence of Population and Income Growth Considered				
Without education	744.6	631.6	509.5	467.3
Elementary	2,250.8	2,852.6	3,530.6	4,202.5
High school	260.9	383.6	513.1	667.3
College	35.7	58.4	106.9	170.5
Total	3,292.0	3,926.0	4,660.1	5,507.6

tion of the structure to year 12, and so on. The process of projecting the number of persons in the high school strata in year 6 is shown in Table 6-5; this table might well be studied in relation to the explanations given in Sec. 6-3.

Projections for the three levels for years 6, 12, and 18 are given in Table 6-6.

References

Correa, H., "A Survey of Mathematical Models in Educational Planning," *Mathematical Models in Educational Planning.* Paris: O.E.C.D., 1967.

A computerized version of the model in this chapter appears in
Correa, H., and E. Reimer, *A Simulation Model for Educational Planning in Puerto Rico.* San Juan: Department of Public Instruction (Mimeographed), 1969.

chapter 7

Manpower Needs

7-1 Content of This Chapter

In Chapter 3 it was observed that in order to increase production in an economy over the long run, the level of education of the economy's labor force must be raised. This is particularly true with respect to increases in labor productivity.

In the description of economic planning in the same chapter, we noted that in order for a country to reach the targets of the economic plan, the labor force must have certain educational qualifications. *The object of this chapter is to estimate the educational structure of Planiland's labor force required to achieve the targets of the economic plan.*

The simple fundamental concepts involved in the method can be introduced with an example: Assume that in year 0 a production of 10 units is obtained by 20 workers with college education, and 30 with high school education. If the target of the plan is to produce 20 units in year 5, a first estimate of the number of workers required would be 40 with college education and 60 with high school education.

One of the limitations of this method is lack of attention to productivity changes. However, the method below considers the influence of productivity changes on the number of workers required and on their educational qualifications. Unfortunately, this is possible only through a somewhat more elaborate approach.

In its general form the method used to forecast the educational structure of the labor force is similar to the one introduced in Chapter 5 to estimate the future development of the flows of students. The first step in Chapter 5 was to study the relationship observed in the past between on the one hand flows of students and on the other population and per capita income. The first step in this chapter is to study the relationship observed in the past between productivity of the labor force and its educational structure. When this relationship is known, the targets of the economic plan will permit us to determine the educational structure required to attain these economic targets.

7-2   Past and Present Relationship between Educational Structure of the Labor Force and Productivity

In the study of the relationship between the educational structure of the labor force and productivity, it is possible to use two types of data: time-series and cross section. In the time series, the number of workers with different levels of education and the level of productivity in different time periods are considered. These data appear in Table 7-1 and will be used in this book.

Table 7-1.   Planiland: Educational Structure of the Labor Force and Gross Domestic Product

Labor Force (thousands)	Year		
	$t = -10$	$t = -5$	$t = 0$
Without education, L_t^0	523	537	580
With elementary education, L_t^1 (between 0 and 6 years)	580	686	781
With high school education, L_t^2 (between 6 and 12 years)	75	103	149
With college education, L_t^3 (more than 12 years)	11	15	22
Total labor force, L_t	1,189	1,341	1,532
Gross domestic product, Y_t (in millions of year 0 dollars)	7,969	10,690	13,932

The second type of data consists of information about the education of the labor force and productivity similar to that presented in Table 7-1. However, in this case the data do not refer to different years but to different industries, regions of a country or different countries.

The method to be described below can be used equally well with time-series or cross-sectional data. In actual planning, it is convenient to use both types of information. However, it should be observed that it is easier to obtain cross-sectional than time-series data.

In order to study the relationship between the output of the educational system and the educational structure of the labor force, the same classifications should be used in both the analysis of the educational system and the educational structure of the labor force. In actual planning, an educational classification that should be taken into consideration is on-the-job training. In order to simplify this presentation, on-the-job training is not considered here. However, the methodology introduced in Chapter 4 for the analysis of the educational system and in this chapter for the study of the labor force can be adapted to the analysis of on-the-job training.

In the type of data mentioned above, the occupational distribution of the labor force has not been taken into consideration since the purpose of this book does not require data on occupations. However, in actual planning, such data is required. This is so, because occupations are, while levels of education are not, natural subdivisions of the labor force in its relation to the economic process. From the occupational classification of the labor force, information about managers can be obtained, and managers are a crucial factor in economic development. From the study of the quantitative and qualitative aspects of managerial roles, some of the important characteristics of the content of education can be observed. What has been said with respect to managers is also true for other occupational classifications. The analysis of these can also provide information for an evaluation of the content of education. However, due to the influence of managers in the process of economic development, the managerial roles deserve special analysis.

7-2.1 Inverse Productivities

We will find it convenient in this chapter to use instead of normal productivity figures, "inverse productivity" figures. Just as productivity figures may be obtained by dividing total production by the number of workers, so inverse productivity figures may be obtained by dividing the number of workers by the value of production. In considering the relationship between the educational structure of the labor force and productivity, we will need to consider not only the inverse productivity of the total labor force but also the inverse productivities of the various educational strata in the labor force.

The following is the notation to be used. Let

L_t^i = number of workers with educational level i in year t

$i = 0$ without education

$i = 1$ with elementary education

$i = 2$ with high school education

$i = 3$ with college education

L_t = total number of workers

Y_t = gross domestic product in year t at constant prices

The inverse productivities (l_t^i and l_t) are defined

$$l_t^i = \frac{L_t^i}{Y_t} \qquad \text{for } i = 0, 1, 2, 3, \tag{7-1}$$

and

$$l_t = \frac{L_t}{Y_t}$$

The inverse productivities for years -10, -5, and 0 may be calculated on the basis of the figures in Table 7-1. For example, in order to obtain the inverse productivity for that part of the labor force with no education in year -10, the number of workers in that strata in year -10 (523 thousand) is divided by the gross domestic product in year -10:

$$l^0_{-10} = \frac{523{,}000}{7969} = 65.62 \text{ workers per million dollars of GDP}$$

The values obtained by applying this operation to the figures in Table 7-1 are shown in Table 7-2.

Table 7-2.   Planiland: Inverse Productivities of the Labor Force
Classified by Level of Education (workers per million dollars of production)

Inverse Productivities of the Labor Force by Level of Education	Year		
	$t = -10$	$t = -5$	$t = 0$
Without education, l^0_t	65.62	50.27	41.64
With elementary education, l^1_t	72.72	64.14	56.06
With high school education, l^2_t	9.35	9.65	10.67
With college education, l^3_t	1.417	1.446	1.54
Total labor force, l_t	149.11	125.53	109.91

It should be noted that the main characteristics of the labour force's educational structure are maintained in the table of inverse productivities. To begin with, the sum of the numbers in the various educational strata of the labor force is equal to the figure for the total labor force. Thus for year 0,

$$L^0_0 + L^1_0 + L^2_0 + L^3_0 = L_0$$
$$580 + 781 + 149 + 22 = 1532$$

The same applies to the inverse productivities for the strata and for the entire labor force. For year 0 in Table 7-2, for example, we have

$$l^0_0 + l^1_0 + l^2_0 + l^3_0 = l_0$$
$$41.64 + 56.06 + 10.67 + 1.54 = 109.91$$

In addition, the relationship between the total and any one of the components is the same for the structure and the table of inverse productivities. If, for instance, we consider the strata of those without education in year 0 in Table 7-1 and in Table 7-2, we find that

$$\frac{L^0_0}{L} = \frac{l^0_0}{l_0}$$

that is,

$$\frac{580}{1532} = \frac{41.64}{109.93} = 0.378$$

The same applies to all the strata and in all years.

It is worthwhile studying the figures in Table 7-2. They indicate that

Planiland experienced economic and welfare growth between years −10 and 0, made possible by increments in production per worker or (what amounts to the same thing) decreases in the number of workers per unit of output; i.e., decrease in the inverse productivity of the total labor force. The inverse productivity of the labor force as a whole dropped from 149 workers per million dollars of the GDP in year −10 to 109 in year 0. This reduction was made up of a reduction in the inverse productivities of workers with no education and those with only an elementary education and an increase in the inverse productivities of workers with high school or college education. These changes in inverse productivities indicate that over the years from year −10 to year 0 fewer workers with low educational qualifications were employed per unit of output but more workers with high school and college education were employed per unit of final output.

7-2.2   Relationship between Educational Structure and Productivity

We are interested in the relationships that hold between the educational structure of the labor force and its productivity. For this we will use the following elasticities:

$$\epsilon_I^i = \frac{\dfrac{\Delta l_t^i}{l_t^i}}{\dfrac{\Delta l_t}{l_t}} \qquad i = 0, 1, 2, 3 \qquad (7\text{-}2)$$

where l_t and l_t^i have the definition in Eq. 7-1, and

$$\Delta l_t^i = l_{t+k}^i - l_t^i$$
$$\Delta l_t = l_{t+k} - l_t$$

Since data on past educational structure in Planiland are available at five-year intervals, k will be 5 for Planiland.

As in the case of the elasticities used in Chapter 5, the elasticity in Eq. 7-2 is a quotient of two rates of growth. In the numerator appears

$$\frac{\Delta l_t^i}{l_t^i}$$

that is, the rate of growth of the inverse productivity of labor with educational level i; in the denominator appears $\Delta l_t/l_t$, that is, the rate of growth of the inverse productivity of the total labor force.

Let us consider an example. Table 7-2 indicates that the inverse productivity of workers without education changed from 65.62 workers per million dollars of production in year −10 to 50.27 workers per million dollars of production in year −5. This means the rate of growth of inverse productivity was

$$\frac{l^0_{-10}}{l^0_{-10}} = \frac{l^0_{-5} - l^0_{-10}}{l^0_{-10}} = \frac{50.27 - 65.62}{65.62} = -0.2339$$

Making similar calculations for all the educational strata for periods -10 to -5 and -5 to 0, we obtain the rates of growth shown in Table 7-3.

Table 7-3.   *Planiland: Rate of Growth of the Inverse Productivities of the Educational Strata of the Labor Force*

$$\frac{l^i_t - l^i_{t-5}}{l^i_{t-5}}$$

		Rates of Growth	
i	Educational Strata	Between Year -10 and Year -5	Between Year -5 and Year 0
0	Without education	-0.2339	-0.1717
1	With elementary education (from 0 to 6 years)	-0.110	-0.1260
2	With high school education (from 6 to 12 years)	0.0321	0.1057
3	With college education (more than 12 years)	0.0205	0.0650
	Total labor force	-0.1581	-0.1243

Let us now take the case of the stratum of workers with no education and see how the elasticities are computed. Table 7-3 shows that the rate of growth of inverse productivity for this stratum between years -10 and -5 is -0.2339. The rate of growth of the inverse productivity of all labor for the same period is -0.1581. The formula used to obtain the elasticity is the rate of growth of inverse productivity of the educational stratum divided by the rate of growth of the inverse productivity of the total labor force. We thus obtain a value for this elasticity of

$$\frac{-0.2339}{-0.1581} = 1.4794$$

The elasticity formula enables us to calculate the figures for elasticity shown in Table 7-4, columns 2 and 3. In column 4 appear the averages of these values for the two periods.

It would perhaps be worthwhile to try to clarify the meaning of the elasticity figures at this point. Let us consider the elasticity between years -5 and 0 for the stratum with elementary education which in Table 7-4 is shown to be equal to 1.0136. This means that a change of a unit in the inverse productivity of the total labor force will be accompanied by a change of 1.0136 units in the inverse productivity of the labor force with elementary education.

Table 7-4. Planiland: Elasticities of the Inverse Productivities of the Educational Strata of the Labor Force with Respect to the Inverse Productivities of the Total Labor Force

$$\epsilon_l^i$$

i	Labor Force	Elasticities		
		Between -10 and -5	Between -5 and 0	Average
0	Without education	1.4794	1.3814	1.4304
1	With elementary education (from 0 to 6 years)	0.7457	1.0136	0.8796
2	With high school education (from 6 to 12 years)	−0.2029	−0.8505	−0.5267
3	With college education (more than 12 years)	−0.1294	−0.5231	−0.3263

So far we have computed the elasticities of the inverse productivities without considering possible interrelations among the elasticities. Such interrelations do in fact exist because the larger the proportion of workers in one educational stratum the smaller can be the proportion of workers in the other strata. As a result of this interrelation, the elasticities must fulfill the following condition:

$$\epsilon_l^0 \frac{L_t^0}{L_t} + \epsilon_l^1 \frac{L_t^1}{L_t} + \epsilon_l^2 \frac{L_t^2}{L_t} + \epsilon_l^3 \frac{L_t^3}{L_t} = 1 \qquad (7\text{-}3)$$

That is, the weighted sum of the elasticities must be equal to one, the weight being the quotients L_0^i/L_0.

With the data in Tables 7-1 and 7-4 we can verify that the elasticities between years -5 and 0 fulfill condition 7-3:

$$1.3814 \frac{537}{1341} + 1.0136 \frac{686}{1341} - 0.8505 \frac{103}{1341} - 0.5231 \frac{15}{1341} = 1$$

However, it is easy to show that the average elasticities in Table 7-4 do not fulfill condition 7-3 with year 0 weights. We have for the average elasticities the following situation:

$$1.4304 \frac{580}{1532} + 0.8796 \frac{781}{1532} - 0.5267 \frac{149}{1532} - 0.3263 \frac{22}{1532} = 0.935$$

Therefore the average elasticities in Table 7-4 must be corrected. To do so, we will multiply them by a correction factor that will make both sides of the equation equal to one. This factor will be denoted by X. Performing this multiplication, we obtain

$$1.4304X \frac{580}{1532} + 0.8796X \frac{781}{1532} - 0.5267X \frac{149}{1532} - 0.3263X \frac{22}{1532}$$

$$= 0.935X = 1$$

From this we see that

$$0.935X = 1$$

$$X = \frac{1}{0.935} = 1.070$$

The average elasticities multiplied by the correction factor are presented (Table 7-5).

Table 7-5. *Corrected Average Elasticities*
Year −10 to Year −0

Educational Strata	Corrected Elasticities
Without education	1.5302
Elementary	0.9409
High school	−0.5673
College	−0.3489

7-3   *Estimation of the Educational Structure of the Labor Force Required to Achieve the Targets of the Economic Plan*

The target values for future gross domestic product and labor force are given in the economic plan. They are presented in Table 3-8 and are reproduced in Table 7-6. In the latter table, the target inverse productivities of the total labor force and the rate of growth of these inverse productivities also are given. These data and the elasticities in Table 7-5 will be used to estimate the educational structure of the labor force required to achieve the targets of the economic plan. To make these estimates, we will assume that the elasticities remain constant.

Table 7-6.   *Planiland: Target Values for Gross Domestic Product, Labor Force, Inverse Productivities, and Their Rates of Growth*

Year	GDP (millions of dollars) Y_t	Labor Force L_t	Inverse Productivities	
			Values l_t	Rates of Growth $\Delta l_t / l_t$
0	13,932	1,531	109.93	−0.1477
5	18,822	1,763	93.69	−0.1076
10	25,428	2,049	80.61	−0.1381
15	34,354	2,387	69.48	−0.1427
20	46,412	2,764	59.56	

The method to be used follows from the definition in Eq. 7-2 of the elasticities of the inverse productivities. An elasticity is the value of the rate of growth of the inverse productivity of a labor force educational stratum corresponding to a value of one unit of the rate of growth of the inverse productivity of the total labor force. In Table 7-5, for example, the elasticity for the labor force having a college education is -0.3489. This means that a value of one in the rate of growth of the inverse productivity of the total labor force corresponds to a value of -0.3489 of the rate of growth of the inverse productivity of the labor force having a college education. Table 7-6 indicates that the value of the rate of growth of the inverse productivity of the total labor force is estimated to be -0.1477 for the period between years 0 and 5. Hence the rate of growth of inverse productivity of the labor force with college education is estimated to be

$$-0.3489 \times - 0.1477 = 0.051$$

This is a single application of the following general formula for calculating future growth rates of inverse productivities of the individual strata.

$$\frac{\Delta l_t^i}{l_t^i} = \epsilon_i^i \frac{\Delta l_t}{l_t} \qquad (7\text{-}4)$$

This formula is used to calculate the other rates of growth for the period between year 0 and year 5 shown in Table 7-7.

Table 7-7.   Rates of Growth of the Inverse Productivities of the
Educational Strata of the Labor Force for the Period Between
Year 0 and Year 5

Educational Strata	Elasticities (Tables 7-5)	Rates of Growth
Without education	1.5302	-0.226
Elementary	0.9409	-0.139
High school	-0.5633	0.083
College	-0.3489	0.051

The projected rates of growth of the inverse productivities of the educational strata enable us to estimate the change in the inverse productivities over five years. The results of such estimation are presented in Table 7-8.

Table 7-8.   Estimated Changes in the Inverse Productivities from Year 0
to Year 5 and Estimated Inverse Productivities in Year 5

Educational Strata	Rate of Growth (Table 9-7)	Inverse Productivities (Table 9-2)	Change in Inverse Productivity between Year 0 and 5	Inverse Productivity (year 5)
Without education	-0.226	41.64	-9.410	32.230
Elementary	-0.139	56.06	-7.790	48.270
High school	0.083	10.67	0.887	11.557
College	0.051	1.54	0.079	1.619

Once the future inverse productivities have been estimated, it becomes possible to estimate the educational structure of the labor force required in year 5 to achieve the targets of the economic plan. For this purpose the following formula should be applied:

$$L_t^i = l_t^i Y_t \qquad (7\text{-}5)$$

This formula is obtained from the definition of inverse productivity introduced in Eq. 7-1.

As an example of the use of Eq. 7-5, let us estimate the number of workers with a high school education required by the economic plan in year 5:

$$L_5^2 = l_5^2 Y_5 = 11.557 \times 18,822$$
$$= 217.5 \text{ thousand}$$

The other values in column 4 of Table 7-9 were obtained by applying the same method; they show the educational structure of the labor force required in year 5 to achieve the targets of the economic plan.

An important point to be noted is that the sum of the number of workers in the various educational strata as shown in Table 7-9 is equal to the total labor force in Table 7-6 which we used as a starting point. This is a necessary consequence of using the corrected elasticities from Table 7-5.

The next step consists of estimating the educational structure of the labor force in year 10. It might seem reasonable to utilize the elasticities from Table 7-5 and apply the same method as was used going from year 0 to year 5. Unfortunately, the elasticities in Table 7-5 cannot be used as such for the period between years 5 and 10, for the elasticities in the table refer to the educational structure in year 0, which is not the same as the educational structure in year 5. Hence, *we must first adapt the elasticities in Table 7-5 to the educational structure of the labor force in year 5.*

The method is the same as that used for adapting the average elasticities of Table 7-4 to the educational structure in year 0. First the weighted sum

Table 7-9.   *Planiland: Educational Structure of the Labor Force in Year 5*

Educational Strata	Inverse Productivities (Table 9-8)	GDP Year 5 (millions of dollars)	Number of Workers in Each Interval of the Educational Strata (thousands)
Without education	32.230		607.0
Elementary	48.270	18,822	909.0
High school	11.560		217.5
College	1.619		30.0
Total			1,763.5

$$1.5302 \frac{607}{1763.5} + 0.9409 \frac{909}{1763.5}$$

$$- 0.5633 \frac{217.5}{1763.5} - 0.3489 \frac{30}{1763.5} = 0.936$$

is obtained. With this sum we can then calculate the correction factor

$$X = \frac{1}{0.936} = 1.068$$

Using this correction factor, we can obtain the corrected elasticities given in Table 7-10.

With these corrected elasticities, it becomes possible to project the educational structure of the labor force from year 5 to year 10, the method being the same as that used in projecting the structure from year 0 to year 5.

Projection of the structure from year 10 to year 15 involves the same process—correction of elasticities which are then used to obtain the structure for year 15. This projection is then used to correct the elasticities needed to estimate the required educational structure of the labor force in year 20; and so on.

The corrected elasticities and the required educational structure of the labor force for years 0, 5, 10, 15, and 20 are given in Table 7-10.

7-4   Limitations of the Method Used in Estimating the Manpower Needs

What are the *limitations of this method?* Like the strengths of the method, they lie in the nature of statistical data used. It is obviously desirable that our method should be based on actual observations but statistical data available do not exactly describe the phenomena in which we are primarily interested. We are concerned with the labor force *required* for production whereas we have statistics only on the labour force *being used*.

The method does not take into account the problems of underemployment of labor since the statistical data show no distinction between those who are fully employed and those who are underemployed. If the general level of underemployment were reduced, fewer workers in certain strata might be required to reach the economic targets than our estimates indicate.

A detailed study of the utilization of qualified manpower within a given country and comparisons of the educational structures of the labor forces in different countries would give some indication of the amount of underemployment in the country in question. There is, however, no method of solving the problem of underemployment in the projection of required educational structures of the labor force.

Table 7-10. Planiland: Educational Structure of the Labor Force and Elasticities for Years 0, 5, 10, and 20 (thousands of workers)

i	Educational Strata	Year 0		Year 5		Year 10		Year 15		Year 20	
		Structure	Elasticity	Structure	Elasticity	Structure	Elasticity	Structure	Elasticity	Structure	Elasticity
0	Without education	580	1.5302	607	1.6351	632	1.7758	636	2.0789	604	
1	Elementary	781	0.9409	909	1.0054	1,055	1.0192	1,220	1.1913	368	
2	High school	149	−0.5633	218	−0.6019	319	−0.6537	469	−0.7624	702	
3	College	22	−0.3489	30	−0.3728	43	−0.4048	61	−0.4731	89	
	Total	1,532		1,764		2,049		2,387		2,764	

7-5   Extensions of the Method Introduced in This Chapter

In the preparation of an educational plan integrated with an economic plan, it is likely that data much more disaggregated than those introduced in the present section will be used.

To begin with, the economic plan will provide information disaggregated by industrial sectors both for volume of production and for employment. With this data, it will be possible to observe the changes in the composition of national production and of the employment by the industrial sector. In addition, an economic plan is likely to be disaggregated by geographical regions.

The labor force will also be described in more detail than the one included in this chapter. For instance, the sex distribution of the labor force is one aspect that is usually considered in actual planning. Also, data about on the job training is likely to be included.

The important point that should be remembered is that the method described above for the estimation of the required educational structure of the labor force when only the level of education is considered needs no modification when being applied to more refined data.

Two basic steps were involved in the method to estimate the educational structure of the labor force required for economic growth: First, the relationship in the past between educational structure and productivity was studied and some basic relationships, such as the elasticities, were established. Next, these elasticities and the production target of the economic plan were used to determine the required educational structure of the labor force for future years. Similar steps must be taken whenever it is necessary to estimate future needs for a specific type of manpower. First, we note and quantify the past relationship between the number in the specific manpower group and some other variable (such as total production or population). We then estimate the future changes of the basic variable. By assuming that the past relationship between the basic variable and number in the manpower group will be the same in the future, we estimate the future need for the type of manpower in question.

Another example of this procedure is seen in Chapter 10 when the *estimation of teachers needed* to achieve the targets of the educational plan is presented. A further example is the estimation of the *qualified persons required to fill government posts.* Again the same steps described above can be applied to the female labor force in the textile industry. These examples show the main advantage of a mathematical model for planning: it can be widely applied.

In other cases, the method presented in this chapter requires some modifications. We can use at least two alternative approaches to estimate the number of *doctors and other qualified persons in health services* required in the future. One way is to relate the number of such persons to the need for them in terms of sickness. We would say that to care for 100 persons in the population, the number of doctors and nurses needed would be so much. This coefficient permits us to find the number of doctors and nurses required in the future. In the second approach, we would recognize that the actual demand for medical services is related to per capita income. In this case, economists could estimate the relationship between demand for medical services and income. The estimated future changes in income will permit evaluation of the future need for doctors and nurses. The first approach would be more useful when medical care is provided as a social service, and the second when it is obtained in the market for services. Appropriate mixtures of projection methods could also be used.

Detailed studies such as those described for teachers or doctors should be made as part of the planning process. These specific studies would clarify and complement the aggregate estimates described in the previous sections of this chapter.

References

An application of more sophisticated statistical techniques to the method of estimation of the elasticities of the inverse productivities is presented in

Correa, H., "¿ Ha prestado la Planificacion Economica atencion suficiente a la Education?" *El Trimestre Economico,* Mexico City, October–December 1964.

Other methods of estimating manpower needs are presented in
Correa, H., and J. Tinbergen, "Quantitative Adaptation of Education to Accelerated Growth," *Kyklos,* Vol. 15 (1962).
"Econometric Models of Education." Paris: O.E.C.D., 1965.

A model for the estimation of manpower needs, when several economic sectors are considered, is presented in
Correa, H., *The Economics of Human Resources.* Amsterdam: North Holland Publishing Co., 1922, Chapter 14.

Some of the limitations in the use of statistical data for the estimation of manpower needs are discussed in
Hollister, R. G., "The Economics of Manpower Forecasting," *International Labour Review,* April 1964.

A complete, nonmathematical discussion of the estimation of manpower needs is presented in
Parnes, H. S., "Forecasting Educational Needs for Economic and Social Development." Paris: O.E.C.D., 1962.

Enlightening examples can be found in
Folger, J. V., "The Balance between Supply and Demand for College Graduates," *The Journal of Human Resources,* Vol. 2, No. 2, Spring 1967.
Harbison, F., and C. Myers (eds.), *Manpower and Education.* New York: McGraw-Hill, 1965.

chapter 8

Student Flows Required
for Economic Growth

8-1   Content of This Chapter

Having determined the future educational structure of the labor
force required to ensure that economic growth targets are reached, we
now consider the problem of how the educational system should be
adapted to produce the output required to achieve these educational
structures.

In approaching this problem, it should be noted that the output of the
educational system and the labor force are not equivalent. The output
of the educational system is educated people, but not all educated people
are members of the labor force. As a consequence, the first step below is
to determine the required educational structure of the population as a
whole from which a labor force with the required educational structure
can be drawn.

The data concerning the educational structure necessary in the population permit us to determine the required output of the educational system. This method follows from the one used to forecast the educational
structure of the population in Chapter 6. To the number of persons with,
for example, college education in year 0, the output from college between
years zero and five was added and the number of deaths subtracted. In
the present case the number of persons with college education in years
zero and five is known. The difference between the two figures corrected
for deaths must be the output from college.

The final step is to evaluate the characteristics of the flows of students
necessary to bring about the desired output of the educational system for
the labor force and to provide enough entering students for higher educational levels. The relationship used in Chapter 6 between the flows of
students and the output of the system is used below, but in the opposite
direction.

8-2   Educational Structure of the Population Required in Order to Reach Economic Growth Targets

8-2.1   Statement of the Problem

Since the educational system produces educated people, some of whom do not become part of the labor force, the first essential is to calculate the future educational structure of the population as a whole from which the required labor force will emerge. For this purpose, we have three sets of data concerning educational structures: the educational structures of the labor force in years prior to year 0; the educational structures of the population as a whole in years prior to year 0; and the required educational structures of the labor force in years after year 0.

8-2.2   Data Concerning the Labor Force

Data concerning the past and the required future educational structures of the labor force are set out in Table 8-1.

The estimates of requirements may vary according to the particular assumptions used to make them. For this reason, educational planners must be carefully briefed by the economic planners who prepare the estimates of the educational structures required. Let us now review the characteristics of the data set out in Table 8-1, remembering that our remarks concern only these data.

Table 8-1.   Planiland: Past and Required Future Educational
Structures of the Labor Force (thousands)

Educational Level	Past Information (Table 2-4)			Requirements According to Targets of Economic Plan (Table 7-10)			
	Years			Years			
	−10	−5	0	5	10	15	20
Without education	523	537	580	607	632	636	604
Elementary	580	686	781	909	1,055	1,220	1,368
High school	75	103	149	218	319	469	702
College	11	15	22	30	43	61	89
Total	1,189	1,341	1,532	1,764	2,049	2,387	2,764

To begin with, laborers are placed in the educational strata corresponding to the highest education level which they attained. (A student is considered to have "attained" an educational level upon entrance rather than upon graduation.) In addition, the Table 8-1 estimates reflect the Planiland situation in years − 10, − 5, and 0 when there may have been an oversupply of certain types of labor with resulting underemployment for some types of manpower. The estimates would then show that still more such workers will be needed. A similar problem could arise in regard to past scarcities of certain types of skilled labor. Such considerations inevitably reduce the confidence which can be placed in the Table 8-1 figures.

Modifications of data required

Since our analysis of the output of an educational system has been in terms of six-year periods, it will be helpful to convert data and estimates on the educational structure of the labor force from five-year to six-year periods. This may be done most easily by interpolating or extrapolating (using rates of growth) from the five yearly figures in Table 8-1. The actual and the future required educational structures of the labor force for years − 12, − 6, 0, 6, 12, and 18 are presented in Table 8-2.

Table 8-2.   Planiland: Educational Structure of the Labor Force, Actual and Future Required (thousands)

Educational Level	Years					
	− 12	− 6	0	6	12	18
Without education	515	535	580	613.7	638.5	626.0
Elementary	542	663	781	936.5	1,117.9	1,306.5
High school	66	97	149	235.2	372.1	597.4
College	10	14	22	32.4	49.5	76.5
Total	1,133	1,309	1,532	1,817.8	2,178.0	2,606.4

8-2.3   Educational Structure of the Population as Related to that of the Labor Force

Table 2-3 set out the educational structure of the population for years − 12, 6, and 0 and these data are reproduced in Table 8-3.

It should be noted that these data refer to the population age 6 and up rather than to the total population since only those age 6 and above can belong to the labor force. The data could be improved also in other directions; for instance, the working age begins around 14 or 15 so the population between 6 and 14 years of age, outside the educational system, should also be eliminated, but no data are available. We must therefore rely on the information contained in Table 8-3.

The same table shows the number of those enrolled in the educational system in years − 12, 6, and 0. Total population over six minus the num-

Table 8-3. Planiland: Educational Structure of the Population of Six and More Years of Age (thousands)

| | | t = -12 | | t = -6 | | | t = 0 | |
| | | | | Years | | | | |
i	Educational Level	Total	Enrolled	Outside Educational System $P^i e_{-12}$	Total	Enrolled	Outside Educational System $P^i e_{-6}$	Total	Enrolled	Outside Educational System $P^i e_0$
0	Without education	1,152.8		1,152.8	1,012.1		1,012.1	744.6		744.6
1	Elementary	1,077.6	308.5	769.1	1,557.4	419.6	1,137.8	2,250.8	595.8	1,655.0
2	High school	165.2	24.5	140.7	199.8	40.5	159.3	260.9	69.0	191.9
3	College	18.4	3.7	14.7	24.7	5.1	19.6	35.7	8.9	26.8
	Totals Pe_t	2,414.0			2,794.0			3,292.0		

ber of students enrolled gives us the number of those in each educational stratum outside the system, i.e., Pe_t^i in the notation of Chapter 6. These figures must be compared with the numbers in the various educational strata of the labor force.

Certain problems arise when we compare the number of those with a given level of education outside the educational system, as estimated in Table 8-3, and the figures for the educational structure of the labor force because some people are simultaneously students and workers. In a more elaborate study, data on the number of such working students would be required; but, in the present instance, it can only be assumed that the error introduced by ignoring this factor is not of great importance.

8-2.4 Comparison of the Educational Structures of the Population and Labor Force

For this purpose, the most profitable index is the ratio between population outside the education system with a level of education and labor force with the same level of education. For instance, for the elementary education stratum in year -12 we have

$$\frac{Pe_{-12}^2}{L_{-12}^2} = \frac{769.1}{542} = 1.419$$

This ratio tells us that for each worker with elementary education in year -12, there were 1.419 persons with that level of education in the population. An equivalent statement is that for each 100 workers with some elementary schooling in year -12, there were 141.9 persons with that level of education in the population. The values of these ratios appear in Table 8-4.

8-2.5 Educational Structure of the Population Required to Reach Economic Growth Targets

We are now in a position to determine the educational structure of the population required in order to reach the economic growth targets; but before we do so it would be well to review the actual concept involved.

Not all of the population exercises a direct influence on production: if all those who have retired, for instance, were to die, the production capacity would be in no way affected. Why, then, must we concern ourselves with the educational structure of the total population when dealing with economic growth targets? The reason is, of course, that the output of the educational system affects directly the educational structure of the population as a whole and not just the educational structure of the labor force.

In order to make the transition from required labor force educational structures to required educational structures of the total population, the

Table 8-4. *Planiland: Comparison of the Educational Structures of the Population Outside the Educational System (Table 8-2) and of the Labor Force (Table 8-3)*

	Educational Level	Years								
		−12			−6			0		
i		Population over Six (Table 8-3) Pe^i_{-12}	Labor Force (Table 8-2) L^i_{-12}	$\dfrac{Pe^i_{-12}}{L^i_{-12}}$	Population over Six (Table 8-3) Pe^i_{-6}	Labor Force (Table 8-2) L^i_{-6}	$\dfrac{Pe^i_{-6}}{L^i_{-6}}$	Population over Six (Table 8-3) Pe^i_0	Labor Force (Table 8-2) L^i_0	$\dfrac{Pe^i_0}{L^i_0}$
0	Without education	1,152.8	515	2.238	1,012.1	535	1.892	744.6	580	1.284
1	Elementary	769.1	542	1.419	1,137.8	663	1.716	1,655.0	781	2.119
2	High school	140.7	66	2.132	159.3	97	1.642	191.9	149	1.288
3	College	14.7	10	1.47	19.6	14	1.4	26.8	22	1.218
	Totals	2,077.3	1,133.		2,328.8	1,309		2,618.3	1,532	

required number of workers in each stratum must be multiplied by the population labor force ratio for that stratum. Since the ratios for years −12 and −6 are not likely to be as relevant to the future as the ratios for year 0 we will use these latter ratios in our projections.

Thus to calculate the number of college-educated people in the population required in year 6, we multiply the number of workers with college education required in year −6 by the population labor force ratio for the college stratum in year 0:

$$32.4 \text{ thousand} \times 1.218 = 39.5 \text{ thousand}$$

In other words, only if Planiland in year 6 possesses 39,500 people with a college education will there be 32,400 people at that level in the labor force. Required values for the other levels and years are shown in Table 8-5.

Table 8-5. *Planiland: Educational Structure of the Population Years 0, 6, 12, 18 Required to Attain the Targets of Economic Development (thousands)*

Educational Level	Years			
	0	6	12	18
Without education	744.7	788.0	819.8	803.8
Elementary	1,654.9	1,984.4	2,368.8	2,768.5
High school	191.9	302.9	479.3	769.5
College	26.8	39.5	60.3	93.2
Total	2,618.3	3,114.8	3,728.2	4,435.0

8-3 Net Output Required from the Educational System to Attain the Targets of the Economic Plan

8-3.1 Method to Be Used

The output of the educational system defined in Eqs. 4-14 and 4-15 includes persons who die shortly after they leave the educational system. When these deaths are subtracted we will speak of "net output." A precise definition is given below.

Formula 6-5 gave the relationship between population outside the educational system with a given level of education and the output of the educational system:

$$Pe^i_{t+6} = (1 - v^{i2}) Pe^i_t + (1 - v^{i2})(g^i_t - n^{i+1}_{t+6})$$
$$+ (1 - v^{i3}) a^i_t + (1 - v^{i4}) b^i_{t+6} \qquad [6\text{-}5]$$

This formula will be used below as the starting point for estimates of the student flows required to attain the targets of the economic plan.

8-3.2   Estimation of the Required Net Output of the Educational System

The first step will be the estimation of

$$Pe^i_{t+6} - (1 - v^{i2})\, Pe^i_t$$

This value will be called "required net output" of the educational system.

The required values of Pe^i_t for years 6, 12 and 18 were presented in the Table 8-5. The values of survival ratios $(1 - v^{i2})$ should be provided by a demographer and are presented in Table 8-6. Figures for the required net output of the educational system in years 6, 12, and 18 are given in Table 8-7 along with the values from which these net output figures were calculated.

Table 8-6.   Planiland: Projected Survival Ratios for Six-Year Periods from Year 0 to Year 18

Period	Ratios
Year 0 to 6	0.936
Year 6 to 12	0.952
Year 12 to 18	0.954

Table 8-7.   Planiland: Estimation of Net Output Required from the Educational System to Attain the Targets of Economic Growth (thousands)

	$t = 0$	$t = 6$	$t = 12$	$t = 18$
From Elementary School				
Number required in year t, Pe^1_t	1,654.9	1,984.4	2,368.8	2,768.5
Survivals from numbers in $t - 6$		1,549.0	1,889.1	2,259.8
Required net output		435.4	479.7	508.7
From High School				
Number required in year t, Pe^2_t	191.9	302.9	479.3	769.5
− Survivals from numbers in $t - 6$		179.6	288.4	457.2
Required net output		123.3	190.9	312.3
From College				
Number required in year t, Pe^3_t	26.8	39.5	60.3	93.2
− Survivals from numbers in $t - 6$		25.1	37.6	57.5
Required net output		14.4	22.7	35.7

8-3.3 Distribution of the Net Output Required Among Net Number of Graduates and Dropouts

From Eq. 6-3 we see that

$$Pe_{t+6}^i - (1 - \nu^{i1})\, Pe_t^i = (1 - \nu^{i2})(g_{t+6}^{i+1}) + (1 - \nu^{i3})\, a_t^i + (1\nu^{i4})\, b_{t+6}^i$$

In Table 8-7 we have the values of the left-hand side of this equation. Now our problem is to distribute the total among the three components appearing on the right-hand side. To do so we will use information on the numbers of dropouts and graduates (net of deaths) in the past educational output. Such information appears in Table 8-8. It was prepared, but not

Table 8-8. Distribution of the Net Output of the Educational System Between Years −6 and 0 (thousands)

Line Nos., Table 6-1		Elementary School	High School	College
5	Graduates from educational structure −6	151.00	20.10	1.80
6	− Graduates entering next level	−87.40	−12.80	0.00
7	− Deaths among graduates after they left school	−1.02	−.20	−.05
8	+ Dropouts from structure −6 during and after pivotal year −6	+157.80	+13.10	+2.50
9	− Deaths among dropouts from structure −6 after they left school	−2.52	−.30	−.07
10	+ Dropouts from structure 0 before pivotal year	+378.30	+23.60	+4.40
11	− Deaths among dropouts from structure 0 after they left school	−3.90	−.40	−.10
	Total output from the educational system	592.26	43.10	8.48

presented, in the course of a study of the output of the educational system as it affected the educational structure of the population between years −6 and 0 (Sec. 6-3). A summary of the information is presented in Table 8-9.

The operations to be carried out at this stage are simple. Let us review the steps involved with reference to required elementary school graduates leaving the system between years 0 and 6. Table 8-7 shows that a net output from elementary school of 435,400 must be added to those with elementary education surviving from year 0 in order to reach the economic targets for year 6. Table 8-9 reveals that between years −6 and 0 from an output of 592,260 only 62,580 are graduates, so that the rate of graduates to total net output is

$$\frac{62,580}{592,260} = 0.106$$

Table 8-9. Distribution of the Output Leaving the Educational System from Year −6 to Year 0 and Alive in Year 0 (thousands)

Line Nos., Table 8-8	Components of Total Output	Elementary $i = 1$	High School $i = 2$	College $i = 3$
5, 6, 7	Graduates leaving the system between −6 and 0 alive year 0 = $(1 - \nu^{i2})g^i_{-6} - n^{i+1})$	62.58	7.1	1.75
8, 9	Dropouts between −6 and 0 from structure −6 alive year 0 = $(1 - \nu^{i3})a^i_{-6}$	155.28	12.8	2.43
10, 11	Dropouts between −6 and 0 from structure 0 alive year 0 = $(1 - \nu^{i4})b^i_o$	374.40	23.2	4.3
	Total output	592.26	43.1	8.48

If we assume that this ratio can be used for years 0 to 6, we can say that 0.106 × 435,400 or 46,152 elementary school graduates leaving the system (net of deaths) are required between years 0 and 6. A similar computation with respect to all the other component elements and levels gives the results shown in Table 8-10.

Table 8-10. Distribution of the Net Output Required from the Educational System Among Graduates and Dropouts (thousands)

Structure Year		$(1 - \nu^{i2})$ $(g^i_t - n^{i+1}_t)$	$(1 - \nu^{i3})a^i_t$	$(1 - \nu^{i4})b^i_{t+6}$	Total $Pe^i_{t+6} - (1 - \nu^{i1})Pe^i_t$
			Elementary School $i = 1$		
$t = -6$	(actual)	62.58	155.28	374.40	592.26
$t = 0$	(required)	46.1	114.1	275.2	435.4
$t = 6$	(required)	50.7	125.8	303.2	479.7
$t = 12$	(required)	53.7	133.4	321.6	508.7
			High School $i = 2$		
$t = -6$	(actual)	7.1	12.8	23.2	43.1
$t = 0$	(required)	20.4	36.4	66.5	123.2
$t = 6$	(required)	31.5	56.4	103.0	190.9
$t = 12$	(required)	51.6	92.2	168.5	312.3
			College $i = 3$		
$t = -6$	(actual)	1.75	2.43	4.3	8.48
$t = 0$	(required)	2.96	4.12	7.32	14.4
$t = 6$	(required)	4.67	6.49	11.54	22.7
$t = 12$	(required)	7.35	10.21	18.14	35.7

Estimation of the required total number of graduates and dropouts leaving the school system

We have not yet obtained figures for the total number of graduates and dropouts leaving the school system required by the economic growth targets. Table 8-10 shows only figures on graduates and dropouts surviving to the next pivotal year. Our next step, therefore, is to use the required net output figures to establish required total output figures including subsequent deaths. We know that adding the number of survivors in, for example, year 6 and the number of those who die between years 0 and 6 after leaving school will give us the number of those leaving school between years 0 and 6. We must accordingly begin by estimating the number of deaths occurring before the next pivotal year among students leaving school. For this purpose we make use of the death rates shown in the last column of Table 6-3.

Let us consider an example. In Table 8-10 for high school graduates in structure 0, we see that

$$(1 - v^{22})(g_0^2 - n_6^3) = 20.4$$

Table 6-3 shows us that

$$v^{22} = 0.027$$

As a consequence,

$$(g_0^2 - n_6^3) = \frac{20.4}{(1 - 0.027)} = 20.97$$

The results of similar operations appear in Table 8-11.

Table 8-11. Distribution of the Output Required from the Educational System Among Graduates and Dropouts (thousands)

Year t	$g_t^i - n_{t+6}^{i+1}$	a_t^i	b_{t+6}^i	Total
		Elementary School		
$t = -6$	63.6	157.8	378.3	559.7
$t = 0$	46.8	116.0	278.1	440.0
$t = 6$	51.5	127.8	306.4	485.7
$t = 12$	54.6	135.6	324.9	515.1
		High School		
$t = -6$	7.3	13.1	23.6	44.0
$t = 0$	21.0	37.4	67.7	126.1
$t = 6$	32.4	58.0	104.8	195.2
$t = 12$	53.0	94.8	171.4	319.2
		College		
$t = -6$	1.8	2.5	4.4	8.7
$t = 0$	3.04	4.24	7.46	14.74
$t = 6$	4.80	6.67	11.76	23.23
$t = 12$	7.56	10.50	18.49	36.55

8-4   Student Flows Required to Achieve the Targets of the Economic Plan

8-4.1   Method to Be Used

We know already that the basic instruments for the study of the student flows are Eqs. 4-12 and 4-13.

$$S_t^i = n_t^i + r_t^i - b_t^i - d_t^{1i} \qquad [4\text{-}12]$$

$$S_t^i = g_t^i + a_t^i + r_{t+6}^i + d_t^{2i} \qquad [4\text{-}13]$$

where i = 1 elementary school
$\quad i$ = 2 high school
$\quad i$ = 3 college

As we have already seen, if we can obtain values for four out of five variables in each equation, then we can use the equations themselves to find values for the remaining variable in each equation.

In Table 8-11 the required values of two of these variables a_t^i and b_{t+6}^i are given for each of the three levels of the educational system. Likewise the required values $g_t^i - n_{t+6}^{i+1}$ are given for the three levels. Since the graduates from college do not enter any higher level of education, the values for $g_t^i - n_{t+6}^{i+1}$ given in Table 8-11 for the college level are also the values for g_t^3. Hence, we have the values of three variables for college, namely g_t^3, a_t^3, and b_t^3 (two variables for Eq. 4-13 and one for Eq. 4-12).

The conditions described suggest the following method for estimating the required values of all the variables in Eqs. 4-12 and 4-13 for all three levels. We should begin with the student flows in college where we already have values for three variables.

A method of estimating three variables for Eq. 4-12 and two for Eq. 4-13 is still required. To make such estimates, Eqs. 5-18, 5-20, and 5-21, numbered below 8-1, 8-2, and 8-3 will be used, i.e.,

$$d_t^{13} = \delta^{13} (n_t^3 + r_t^3) \qquad (8\text{-}1)$$

$$r_{t+6} = \rho^3 S_t^3 \qquad (8\text{-}2)$$

$$d_t^{23} = \delta^{23} S_t^3 \qquad (8\text{-}3)$$

where the parameters δ^{13}, δ^{23}, and ρ^3 will have the values observed in the past, presented in Table 5-4.

Equations 4-12, 4-13, 8-1, 8-2, and 8-3, and the values for g_t^3, a_t^3, and b_t^3 in Table 8-11 enable us to obtain the required values for all the variables in Eqs. 4-12 and 4-13 for the college level. Among the values obtained is n_t^3. With this value and that of $g_t^2 - n_{t+6}^2$ in Table 8-11, we can determine the required value of g_t^2. Now we have reached the position with respect to the high school level that we were in with respect to the college level earlier. So, a method similar to the one used above will permit us to evaluate the student flows required for the high school level and will then put us in the position to study the required elementary level flows in the same way.

8-4.2 Required Student Flows at the College Level

Let us consider the problem of determining the required values for the variables in Eq. 4-13 for structure 12.

From Table 8-11 we know that

$$g_{12}^3 = 7.56$$
$$a_{12}^3 = 10.50$$

In addition, with the value of δ^{23} and ρ^3 from Table 5-4, Eqs. 8-2 and 8-3 take the form

$$r_{18}^3 = 0.135 \, S_{12}^3 \qquad\qquad [8\text{-}2]$$

$$d_{12}^{23} = 0.020 \, S_{12}^3 \qquad\qquad [8\text{-}3]$$

Equation 4-13 can now be written in the following form for college level structure 12:

$$S_{12}^3 = 7.56 + 10.50 + 0.135 \, S_{12}^3 + 0.020 \, S_{12}^3$$

giving

$$(1 - 0.135 - 0.020) \, S_{12}^3 = 7.56 = 10.50$$
$$0.845 \, S_{12}^3 = 18.06$$
$$S_{12}^3 = \frac{18.06}{0.845}$$
$$= 21.37$$

With the value of S_{12}^3 and Eqs. 8-2 and 8-3, we can obtain the estimated "required" values for repeaters and deaths:

$$r_{18}^3 = 0.135 \times 21.37 = 2.88$$
$$d_{12}^{23} = 0.020 \times 21.37 = 21.37 = 0.43$$

Similar methods can be applied to Eq. 4-13 for years 0 and 6. This must be done before estimating the values of the variables in Eq. 4-12. The required values in equation 4-13 in structures 0 and 6 appear in Table 8-12. Since in Table 8-11 the required values of g_t^3 and a_t^3 are not presented for years beyond year 12, it is not possible to solve by this method Eq. 4-13 for structures beyond structure 12.

Let us now examine the problem of estimating the required values of variables for relationship 4-12, considering again the case of structure 12.

Table 8-12. *Planiland: Student Flows in the College Level Required to Meet the Needs of Qualified Personnel for the Plan of Economic Growth (thousands)*

Year	Before Pivotal Year				Enrollment, Pivotal Year	After Pivotal Year			
	New Entrants	Repeaters	Dropouts	Deaths		Dropouts	Repeaters	Graduates	Deaths
0	20.19	1.16	7.46	0.32	8.61	4.24	1.16	3.04	0.17
6	31.80	1.83	11.76	0.50	13.57	6.67	1.83	4.80	0.27
12	53.84	2.88	18.49	0.85	21.37	10.50	2.88	7.56	0.43
18					37.38				

From the left-hand side of Table 8-12, we know that

$$b_{12}^3 = 11.76$$
$$S_{12}^3 = 21.37$$
$$r_{12}^3 = 1.83$$

In addition, Eq. 8-1 above can be expressed as

$$d_{12}^{13} = 0.015\,(n_{12}^3 + r_{12}^3)$$

The values and equations given above permit us to state equation 4-12 as

$$21.37 = n_{12}^3 + 1.83 - 11.76 - 0.015\,(n_{12}^3 + 1.83)$$

from which

$$21.37 = (1 - 0.015)\,n_{12}^3 + (1 - 0.015)\,1.83 - 11.76$$
$$= 0.985\,n_{12}^3 + 1.80 - 11.76$$
$$n_{12}^3 = \frac{31.33}{0.985}$$
$$= 31.81$$

This value for n_{12}^3 enables us to establish the value for the number of deaths, as follows

$$d_{12}^{13} = 0.015\,(31.81 + 1.83) = 0.50$$

These results and those obtained in a similar way for structure 6, are shown in Table 8-12. Lack of information about S_t^3 for $t = 18, 24, \ldots$ prevents evaluation of Eq. 4-12 for structures after 12.

It will be seen later that the value of n_t^3 in Eq. 4-12 for structure 18 is required for high school level estimates. For this reason, a method of estimating the required values of the variables in Eq. 4-12, valid only for structure 18 will be presented below. In this case the following equations will be used:

$$b_{18}^3 = \rho^3\,(n_{18}^3 + r_{18}^3)$$
$$d_{18}^{13} \doteq \delta^{13}\,(n_{18}^3 + r_{18}^3)$$
$$S_{18}^3 = n_{18}^3 + r_{18}^3 - b_{18}^3 - d_{18}^{13}$$

We have the following values resulting from previous calculations:

$$b_{18}^3 = 18.43 \quad \text{(from Table 8-11)}$$
$$r_{18}^3 = 2.88 \quad \text{(from Table 8-12)}$$
$$\rho^3 = 0.326 \quad \text{(from Table 5-4)}$$
$$\delta^{13} = 0.015 \quad \text{(from Table 5-4)}$$

With this information the values in Table 8-12 for structure 18 were obtained.

Another method of obtaining values for the variables in Eq. 4-12 for structure 18 may also be noted although it will not be applied here. It involves using rates of growth to project values for g_t^3 and a_t^3 from structure 12 to structure 18. With these values for structure 18, it becomes possible to estimate the values of the other variables in relationship 4-13 for structure 18. Then the variables in relationship 4-12 for structure 18 can be estimated by the method used for structures 6 and 12. The sole reasons for not using this alternative solution here is that it yields a lower value for n_{18}^3 than the method used above. To avoid any possibility of setting our education targets too low, it would seem better to use the higher estimate.

8-4.3   Required Student Flows at High School Level

The first step in the estimation of the required student flows in high school is the following. With the data in Table 8-11 for required values for $g_t^2 - n_{t+6}^3$ and the data in Table 8-12 on the required values of n_t^3, the required values of g_t^2 can be obtained. These values are given in Table 8-13.

With the information on required numbers of high school graduates set out in Table 8-13 and that on dropouts given in Table 8-11, we are in the same position with respect to the high school level as we were before with respect to the college level. We may now use the procedure we used for the college level to estimate required values for all the variables in relations 4-12 and 4-13 in structures 0, 6, and 12 at the high school level.

Table 8-13.   *Planiland: Number of High School Graduates Required for Economic Development (thousands)*

Year	Required Outside the System, Year t $g_t^2 - n_{t+6}^3$ (Table 8-11)	Required as New Entrants in College, Year $t + 6$ n_{t+6}^3 (Table 8-12)	Total g_t^2
$t = 0$	21.0	20.19	41.19
$t = 6$	32.4	31.80	64.20
$t = 12$	53.0	53.84	106.84

For instance, to evaluate the variables in 4-13 for year 12, we have the following system of equations:

$$g_{12}^2 = 106.84 \quad \text{(Table 8-13)}$$
$$a_{12}^2 = 94.8 \quad \text{(Table 8-11)}$$
$$r_{18}^2 = 0.160 S_{12}^2 \text{ with } \rho = 0.160 \quad \text{(Table 5-4)}$$

$$d_{12}^{22} = 0.020 S_{12}^{2} \text{ with } \delta^{22} = 0.020 \qquad (\text{Table 5-4})$$
$$S_{12}^{2} = g_{12}^{2} + a_{12}^{2} + r_{18}^{2} + d_{12}^{22}$$

This system can be solved with exactly the same steps used for the college level. The results for years 12, 6, and 0 appear in Table 8-14.

The next step is to estimate required values of the variables in relationship 4-12 for structures 6 and 12. The following values and equations are needed to estimate the required values of the variables in relation 4-12 for structure 12.

$$b_{12}^{2} = 104.8 \qquad (\text{Table 8-11})$$
$$S_{12}^{2} = 245.90 \qquad (\text{Table 8-14})$$
$$r_{12}^{2} = 23.80 \qquad (\text{Table 8-14})$$
$$d_{12}^{12} = 0.014(n_{12}^{2} + r_{12}^{2}) \text{ with } \delta^{12} = 0.014 \qquad (\text{Table 5-4})$$
$$S_{12}^{2} = n_{12}^{2} + r_{12}^{2} - b_{12}^{2} = d_{12}^{2}$$

Solving this system of equations, and a similar one for year 6, we obtain the results presented in Table 8-14.

The final step consists of estimating the required values for the variables in relationship 4-12 for structure 18. In this case the equations needed are

$$b_{18}^{2} = 0.251(n_{18}^{2} + r_{18}^{2})$$
$$d_{18}^{12} = 0.014(n_{18}^{2} + r_{18}^{2})$$
$$S_{18}^{2} = n_{18}^{2} + r_{18}^{2} - b_{18}^{2} - d_{18}^{12}$$

The values obtained with these equations for the variables in relationship 4-12 for structure 18 are shown in Table 8-14.

As in the case of relationship 4-12 for structure 18 at college level, there is an alternative method of estimation, identical to that outlined at the end of Sec. 8-4.3 for the college level. Since this alternative method again gives lower values for the variables, we do not use the results given by this method.

8-4.4 Required Student Flows in Elementary School

There is no need to repeat here the details of the method used. The results are set out in Table 8-15.

For estimating the required values for the variables in relation 4-12 for structure 18, we again have a choice between two methods, the same as the two described in regard to college flows. This time, however, the second method yields the higher values for the variables; hence the values obtained by this method are given in Table 8-15. Such values for structure 18 are calculated in the following way: Rates of growth are used to estimate $g_{18}^{2} - n_{24}^{2}$, n_{24}^{2}, and a_{18}^{1}.

Table 8-14. Planiland: Student Flows at the High School Level Required to Meet the Needs for Qualified Personnel for the Plan of Economic Growth (thousands)

Year	Before Pivotal Year				Enrollment, Pivotal Year	After Pivotal Year			
	New Entrants	Repeaters	Dropouts	Deaths		Dropouts	Repeaters	Graduates	Deaths
0									
6	202.46	15.33	67.7	3.07	95.84	37.4	15.33	41.19	1.92
12	331.80	23.8	104.8	4.90	149.02	58.0	23.84	64.20	2.98
18	643.53	39.34	171.4	9.56	245.90	94.8	39.34	106.84	4.92

Table 8-15. Planiland: Student Flows at Elementary School Level Required to Meet the Needs for Qualified Personnel for the Plan of Economic Growth (thousands)

Year	Before Pivotal Year				Enrollment, Pivotal Year	After Pivotal Year			
	New Entrants	Repeaters	Dropouts	Deaths		Dropouts	Repeaters	Graduates	Deaths
0					496.28	116.0	125.56	249.26	5.46
6	853.83	125.56	278.1	6.86	694.43	127.8	175.69	383.30	7.64
12	1,273.63	175.69	306.4	10.14	1,132.78	135.6	286.59	698.13	12.46
18	1,897.19	286.59	324.9	15.28	1,843.50	146.58	466.40	1,210.25	20.27

Once the required number of graduates and dropouts is estimated using rates of growth, it becomes possible to estimate the values of all the other variables in relationship 4-13 for structure 18. (The values are shown in Table 8-15.)

After the values of relationship 4-13 for structure 18 are known, we can proceed to estimate the required values for relationship 4-12 for the same structure, using the method used for structures 6 and 12. Results are shown in Table 8-15.

Reference

Correa, H., "Flows of Students and Manpower Planning," *Comparative Education Review*, Vol. 13, No. 2, June 1969.

chapter **9**

The First Stage in Target Setting

9-1 Content of This Chapter

Thus far, two different forecasts of the flows of students have been prepared. In the first, the influences on the flows of students of population and income growth were considered (Chapter 5). The second reflects the needs for qualified labor in economic development (Chapter 6).

In the first stage of target setting the educational planners, using the forecasts as guides, must determine the flows of students that they wish to attain in the future. This target for the flows of students does not need to be equal to either of the forecasts which are to be used as terms of reference. However, this target will probably use elements from both of the forecasts.

For Planiland a reasonable target seems to be the flows of students required for economic growth. However, in determining the flows of students required for economic growth, no attention was paid to the characteristics of the population. It might be that to achieve the required flows of students a school-age population larger than that forecasted (Chapter 2) would be necessary. If this is the case, the required flows of students should be modified before the provisional target of the educational plan is set. The proportion of dropouts and repeaters might also need modification. Once these modifications are completed, the first stage in target setting has been completed.

The targets obtained in this way are only provisional. The planners do not know yet whether it is possible to attain them. That is, it must still be determined if the teachers, buildings, facilities, and financial resources will be available by appropriate time. The provisional targets set in this chapter will permit us to study the availability of the means to reach them.

9-2 Goals and Targets

It is doubtful whether any two planners would agree on precise definitions of the terms "goal" and "target." In order to avoid any confusion, let us begin by setting out the meanings which are attached to these terms in this context.

The world "goal" is used to denote the broad aspirations of countries or their governments. Universal elementary education, for example, represents an educational goal as does improvement in college education. Every country has thousands of such goals for all aspects of society.

Such goals are important in planning, but they are usually too general for use in the actual preparation of plans. The first step in preparing a plan, therefore, is to move from general goals to more precise and concrete targets. While goals are imprecise and usually qualitative, targets are specific and usually quantitative.

In the case of Planiland, the government is committed to socio-economic development. Its economic targets have been expressed in a definite and quantitative form and desired future per capita income and employment levels have been established (Chapter 3).

Our initial task in the course of the preparation of the plan is to help Planiland's government attach a precise meaning to its educational goals. This task was carried out in Chapter 5 with our study of automatic growth of the student flows and in Chapter 8 with our examination of the characteristics which such flows must possess if the educational system is to produce the qualified personnel needed for economic growth. Now a problem appears. We must choose between these two alternatives. Should the country endeavor to create the educational facilities needed to meet the automatic growth of the student flows or should it try to create the means to produce the qualified labor force required for economic growth? In order to answer this question, we must take a closer look at the results of our calculations in Chapters 5 and 8; this is done later in the present chapter. When this analysis is completed, it becomes possible to establish provisional target figures for future student flows at all levels.

Selection of provisional targets for the student flows is only the first step in target-setting. The next step is evaluation of the factors involved in attaining the provisional targets and a determination as to whether or not the provisional targets are feasible. For instance, estimates of the number of teachers required to attain the provisional targets necessarily imply needs for teacher training. If it seems impossible to train enough teachers, then the provisional targets must be adjusted accordingly. This also holds true with regard to constructing classrooms and laboratories, training administrators, and related work.

Estimates of the number of teachers, schools, books, administrators, and so on needed to attain the provisional targets also make it possible to establish the financial costs of reaching the provisional targets. Such an estimate of total costs must be compared with sources of funds—for example, the national income or the government budget. If the costs cannot be met, the targets must be adjusted.

Once it is established that financial costs are in line with governmental financial resources and that the necessary human and economic resources can be made available, the provisional targets become definitive. In the description above, it should be clear that the passage from goals to definite targets is a process of successive approximations. In this process, goal-defining policy-makers and target-setting planners should work closely.

After the impracticable or inconsistent alternatives have been discarded, the remainder of the plan represents what is possible, and all the aspects are equally important. However, in implementing a plan, a sequence of actions must be carried out, some immediately, others a month later, and so on. In other words, in the implementation of a plan not only the importance of a project which must be taken into account, but also the chronological position of that project in the total sequence. This time ordering of the projects attaches a different priority to each of them.

9-3   Determination of the Provisional Targets of Planiland's Educational Plan

The estimates of student flows in Chapter 5 give a concrete quantitative expression to the educational aspirations of Planiland's people and government; those in Chapter 8 show the characteristics of the educational system required if economic growth targets are to be attained. These two elements must now be compared in order to establish the provisional targets of the educational plan.

Two estimates of future student flows at elementary, high school, and college levels are set out in Tables 9-1, 9-2, and 9-3. The upper part of each table gives estimates of future student flows based on the influence of population and per capita income growth (Chapter 5); the lower part gives estimates of student flows required by the economic development plan (Chapter 8). The two estimates set out in each of these three tables will be referred to hereafter as the *automatic growth* of the educational system and the *required growth* of the eductional system respectively.

Let us consider the case of new entrants in the two estimates of student flows for each level.

As regards elementary school, their number is lower in the automatic than in the required projection for structures 12 and 18. The automatic projection for structure 12, for instance, gives a figure of 1,010,700 as

Table 9-1. Planiland: Comparison of the Estimates of Automatic and Required Student Flows for Elementary Education (thousands)

Year	Before Pivotal Year				Enrollment, Pivotal Year	After Pivotal Year			
	New Entrants	Repeaters	Dropouts	Deaths		Dropouts	Repeaters	Graduates	Deaths
Projections of Automatic Growth of the Student Flows (Table 5-25)									
0	875.2	106.2	378.3	7.3	595.8	202.0	129.3	258.0	6.5
6	895.7	129.3	391.5	7.2	626.3	189.8	115.2	314.4	6.9
12	1,010.7	113.2	426.7	7.9	691.3	186.9	107.8	389.0	7.6
18	1,077.9	107.8	445.8	8.3	731.6				
Student Flows Required for Economic Development (Table 8-15)									
0	1,853.83	125.56	278.1	6.86	496.28	116.06	125.56	249.26	5.46
6	1,273.63	175.69	306.4	10.14	694.43	127.89	175.69	383.30	7.64
12	1,897.19	286.59	324.9	15.28	1,132.78	135.69	286.59	698.13	12.46
18					1,843.50	146.58	466.40	1,210.25	20.27

Table 9-2. Planiland: Comparison of the Estimates of Automatic and Required Student Flows for High School Education (thousands)

Year	Before Pivotal Year				Enrollment, Pivotal Year	After Pivotal Year			
	New Entrants	Repeaters	Dropouts	Deaths		Dropouts	Repeaters	Graduates	Deaths
Projections of Automatic Growth of the Student Flows (Table 5-28)									
0	87.4	6.5	23.6	1.3	69.0	22.6	8.6	36.4	1.4
6	165.6	8.6	35.7	2.4	136.1	45.3	12.8	75.3	2.7
12	201.8	12.8	35.8	3.0	175.8	59.4	12.5	100.4	3.5
18	249.7	12.5	35.7	3.7	222.8				
Student Flows Required for Economic Development (Table 8-14)									
0	202.46	15.33	67.7	3.07	95.84	37.4	15.33	41.19	1.92
6	331.80	23.80	104.8	4.90	149.02	58.0	23.87	64.19	2.98
12	643.53	39.34	171.4	9.56	245.90	94.8	39.34	106.84	4.92
18					501.91				

Table 9-3.   Planiland: Comparison of the Estimates of Automatic and Required Student Flows for College Education (thousands)

Year	Before Pivotal Year				Enrollment, Pivotal Year	After Pivotal Year			
	New Entrants	Repeaters	Dropouts	Deaths		Dropouts	Repeaters	Graduates	Deaths
Projections of the Automatic Growth of Student Flows (Table 5-28)									
0	12.8	0.7	4.4	0.2	8.9	5.6	1.2	1.9	0.2
6	25.3	1.2	7.6	0.4	18.5	15.5	2.6	0.0	0.4
12	52.3	2.6	13.9	0.8	40.2	33.7	5.7	0.0	0.8
18	69.7	5.7	16.9	1.1	57.4				
Student Flows Required for Economic Development (Table 8-12)									
0	20.19				8.61				
6	31.80	1.16	7.46	0.32	13.57	4.24	1.16	3.04	0.17
12	53.84	1.83	11.76	0.50	21.37	6.67	1.83	4.80	0.27
18		2.88	18.49	0.85	27.38	10.50	2.88	7.56	0.43

against 1,273,630 in the required projection. Additionally, there is a rapid rise in the relative difference between the two projections. For structure 12, the required number of new entrants is only 1,273.63/1,010.70 = 1.260; that is, 26 percent higher than the automatic number. In the case of structure 18, the required number is 76 percent higher than the automatic. The relative difference between the automatic and required number of new entrants is even greater in the case of high school: for structure 18, the required figure is more than twice the automatic figure. We find exactly the reverse situation at the college level, where the required number of new entrants is lower than the automatic.

The total automatic and required outputs from the various levels of the educational system computed from data in Tables 9-1 to 9-3 are shown in Table 9-4. Again the required output is in most cases higher than the automatic output for the elementary school and high school levels, while the reverse is true for the college level.

Table 9-4.   *Planiland: Comparison of the Output of the Educational System Obtained with the Automatic and the Required Growths of the Student Flows* $O^i_{t+6} = g^i_t + a^i_t + b^i_{t+6}$ (thousands)

Pivoted Year Between	Elementary School $i = 1$		High School $i = 2$		College $i = 3$	
t	Automatic	Required	Automatic	Required	Automatic	Required
6	851.5	643.36	94.7	146.29	15.1	14.74
12	930.9	817.5	156.4	227.00	29.4	23.23
18	1,021.7	1,158.63	195.5	373.04	50.6	36.55

Since the differences between some of the values of variables in the two types of student flows are extensive, adequate attention must be paid to them. However, where differences are small, they may be ignored since the differences fall within the margins of error of our various estimates. For example, whereas we can ignore the small difference between automatic and required outputs for college level structure 6, we must consider the very large differences between automatic and required outputs for high school level structures 12 and 18. Where the two types of estimates differ markedly, a choice must be made between them.

In making this selection, we must remember that the required growth of the student flows will provide the qualified labor force needed for economic growth. We must also remember that, in the automatic growth estimates, factors such as the size of the school-age population are considered. Finally, at this stage, there is no need to consider in detail teachers, buildings, or various costs, but, keeping in mind such factors, we might do well to adopt minimum provisional targets.

Let us see now how the provisional targets for Planiland's educational plan were fixed with the factors mentioned above taken into consideration.

First, in the case of the college level, Table 9-3 shows that the required student flows are lower than the automatic ones. Taking into consideration that it is advisable to save resources wherever possible for use in other levels, the policy-makers adopt the estimates of required flows as provisional targets. They are presented in Table 9-5.

In the case of the high school level, the situation is reversed; that is, the required flows are higher than the automatic ones. Since the government of Planiland is committed to economic growth, the required flows are adopted as provisional targets (Table 9-5).

At the elementary school level, a situation similar to the one at the high school level appears. However, the decision must take into consideration the limit imposed on elementary school enrollment by the number of children of school age in the population.

The number of new elementary school entrants in the required projections is greater than the number of those who could enter the educational system; hence, these required projections cannot be accepted as provisional targets without modifications.

In modifying the required estimates, we must note first that the automatic estimates of numbers of new entrants in elementary school are the maximum possible or very close to it. Therefore they must be accepted in the provisional targets of the plan.

We next observe that the number of graduates (g_{18}^1) required for structure 18 of elementary school (1,210.25 thousand) is greater than the new number of new entrants (n_{18}^1) that could enter structure 18 (1,077.9 thousand). In order to come as close as possible to the number of graduates required, we would need the following situation:

b_{18}^1 = dropouts from structure 18 before pivotal year = 0

a_{18}^1 = dropouts from structure 18 during and after pivotal year = 0

and r_{24}^1 = repeaters from structure 18 proceeding to the next structure = 0

It would not seem possible to attain such values except through a step-by-step reduction in the numbers of dropouts and repeaters. Several trajectories would lead to such a situation for structure 18; the one used here is presented in Table 9-6 and is explained below. We take as our starting point the values

$$b_0^1 = 378.3 \quad \text{(from Table 5-3)}$$

$$a_{-6}^1 = 157.8 \quad \text{(from Table 5-3)}$$

$$r_0^1 = 106.20 \quad \text{(from Table 5-3)}$$

that is, the last observed values for each of the variables in question. All these values must be zero in structure 18. To achieve this result it is assumed that a^1 and r^1 will be reduced by one-fourth passing from one structure to the next, while b^1 will be reduced by one-third from one structure to the next. With this assumption, the results in Table 9-6 were

Table 9-5. Planiland: Provisional Targets for the Students Flows (thousands)

Year	Before Pivotal Year				Enrollment, Pivotal Year	After Pivotal Year			
	New Entrants	Repeaters	Dropouts	Deaths		Dropouts	Repeaters	Graduates	Deaths
Elementary									
0	895.7	79.65	252.2	6.83	452.23	118.35	79.65	249.26	4.97
6	1,010.7	53.10	126.1	7.45	716.32	78.9	53.10	576.44	7.88
12	1,077.9	26.55	0.0	7.73	930.25	39.45	26.55	854.02	10.23
18					1,096.72	0.0	0.0	1,084.66	12.06
High School									
0	202.46	15.33	67.6	3.07	95.84	37.4	15.33	41.19	1.92
6	331.80	23.80	104.8	4.90	149.02	58.0	23.84	64.20	2.98
12	643.53	39.34	171.4	9.56	245.90	94.8	39.34	106.84	4.92
18					501.91				
College									
0	20.19	1.16	7.46	0.32	8.61	4.24	1.16	3.04	0.17
6	31.80	1.93	11.76	0.50	13.57	6.67	1.83	4.80	0.27
12	53.84	2.88	18.49	0.85	21.37	10.50	2.88	7.56	0.43
18					37.38				

Table 9-6. Planiland: Provisional Targets for Repeaters and Dropouts for the Elementary School Level (thousands)

Year t	Dropouts Before Pivotal Year b_t^1	Dropouts During and After Pivotal Year a_t^1	Repeaters r_{t+6}^1
-6		157.8	106.20
0	378.3	118.35	79.65
6	252.2	78.9	53.10
12	126.1	39.45	26.55
18	0	0	0

obtained. Now in addition to n_t^1, we have values of three additional variables in Eqs. 4-12 and 4-13 for elementary level structures.

Our problem now is to use the values of n_t^1, a_t^1, b_t^1 and r_t^1 to obtain the values of the other variables in Eqs. 4-12 and 4-13. In this case, in addition to Eqs. 4-12 and 4-13, the following two equations will be used again:

$$d_t^{11} = 0.007 (n_t^1 + r_t^1) \qquad \text{(from Table 5-4)} \qquad (9\text{-}1)$$

$$d_t^{21} = 0.011 \, S_t^1 \quad \text{(from Table 5-4)} \qquad (9\text{-}2)$$

As an example let us consider the case of structure 6. We have

$$n_6^1 = 895.7 \qquad \text{(from Table 9-1)}$$
$$a_6^1 = 78.9 \qquad \text{(from Table 9-6)}$$
$$b_6^1 = 252.2 \qquad \text{(from Table 9-6)}$$
$$r_0^1 = 79.65 \qquad \text{(from Table 9-6)}$$
$$r_{12}^1 = 53.10 \qquad \text{(from Table 9-6)}$$

$$S_6^1 = n_6^1 + r_6^1 - b_6^1 - d_6^{11} \qquad [4\text{-}12]$$
$$S_6^1 = g_6^1 + a_6^1 + r_{12}^1 + d_{12}^{21} \qquad [4\text{-}13]$$
$$d_6^{11} = 0.007 (n_t^1 + r_t^1)$$
$$d_6^{21} = 0.011 \, S_6^1$$

Hence

$$S_6^1 = 895.7 + 79.65 - 252.2 - 0.007 (895.70 + 79.65)$$
$$= 716.32$$

Then

$$d_6^{21} = 0.011 \times 716.32$$
$$= 7.88$$

and

$$g_6^1 = 716.32 - 53.10 - 78.9 - 7.88$$
$$= 576.44$$

These results and the results of similar calculations for structures 12 and 18 appear in Table 9-5.

Once the provisional targets for an educational plan have been set, preparation of the plan involves evaluating the effort required to achieve these targets. Here, the data in Table 9-5 are of limited use and a better idea of effort required can be obtained by using the indices described in Table 4-9. The provisional target values for all the indices for structures 0, 6, 12, and 18 are given in Tables 9-7, 9-8, and 9-9, computed from Table 9-5.

9-4   Guidelines for Reaching the Provisional Targets

Tables 9-7, 9-8, and 9-9 indicate the characteristics which the educational system must possess if the provisional targets are to be reached.

Table 9-7.   Planiland: Indices of the Provisional Target Student Flows at the Elementary School Level

Definition	Structure 0	Structure 6	Structure 12	Structure 18
$\dfrac{\text{Repeaters}}{\text{Total inputs}}$		0.08166	0.04991	0.02404
$\dfrac{\text{Dropouts before pivotal year}}{\text{Total inputs}}$		0.25857	0.11854	0.000
$\dfrac{\text{Deaths before pivotal year}}{\text{Total inputs}}$		0.007	0.007	0.007
$\dfrac{\text{Dropouts during and after pivotal year}}{\text{Enrollment pivotal year}}$	0.2617	0.11015	0.04241	0.000
$\dfrac{\text{Repeaters passing to next structure}}{\text{Enrollment pivotal year}}$	0.17613	0.07413	0.02854	0.000
$\dfrac{\text{Deaths after pivotal year}}{\text{Enrollment pivotal year}}$	0.01093	0.011	0.011	0.011
$\dfrac{\text{Graduates}}{\text{Enrollment pivotal year}}$	0.55118	0.80472	0.91805	0.98900

Our problem is to determine what must be done in order to create such a system; in other words, we must discover what changes are needed in the present system in order to reach the provisional targets.

The only viable method of analysis is to find an existing educational system with indices similar to those implied by the provisional targets. Then data on teachers, buildings, and overhead in this existing system with the desired index values can be used to estimate the number and type of teachers, buildings, and overhead needed to attain the provisional targets for Planiland. For these purposes, the qualitative subdivisions of the Planiland educational system described in Table 5-6 can be used as existing systems with varying index values.

Table 9-8.   Planiland: Indices of the Provisional Target Student Flows at the High School Level

Definition	Structure 0	Structure 6	Structure 12	Structure 18
$\dfrac{\text{New entrants}}{\text{Graduates elementary school}}$		0.81224	0.57560	0.75353
$\dfrac{\text{Repeaters}}{\text{Total inputs}}$		0.07039	0.06693	0.05761
$\dfrac{\text{Dropouts before pivotal year}}{\text{Total inputs}}$		0.31085	0.29471	0.25100
$\dfrac{\text{Deaths before pivotal year}}{\text{Total inputs}}$		0.014	0.014	0.014
$\dfrac{\text{Dropouts during and after pivotal year}}{\text{Enrollment pivotal year}}$	0.39023	0.38921	0.38552	
$\dfrac{\text{Repeaters passing next structure}}{\text{Enrollment pivotal year}}$	0.15995	0.15995	0.15995	
$\dfrac{\text{Deaths after pivotal year}}{\text{Enrollment pivotal year}}$	0.020	0.020	0.020	
$\dfrac{\text{Graduates}}{\text{Enrollment pivotal year}}$	0.42978	0.43081	0.43448	

Comparison of the indices in Tables 9-7 and 5-6 shows that the ratios for the *provisional elementary level targets are similar to those of stratum A*, while comparison of Tables 9-8 and 5-6 indicates that at the *high school level the target indices are similar to those for stratum B*. This information will be used later when the teachers, buildings, and overhead required to attain the provisional targets of the educational plan are estimated.

9-5   Some Implications of Provisional Targets for Educational Content and Methods

Although the present work does not include any analysis of educational content and methods, some observations on the subject may be usefully made here, first, to reemphasize the close relationship between the quantitative and qualitative aspects of educational planning and, second, to indicate certain direct consequences of the provisional quantitative targets chosen.

One of the main quantitative results of the analysis is that elementary school should cease to be a terminal school and should become instead mainly a preparatory stage for high school. On the other hand, the high

Table 9-9.   Planiland: Indices of the Provisional Target Student Flows at the College Level

Definition	Structure 0	Structure 6	Structure 12	Structure 18
New entrants / Graduates high school		0.490	0.495	0.504
Repeaters / Total inputs		0.054	0.054	0.054
Dropouts before pivotal year / Total inputs		0.35	0.35	0.35
Deaths before pivotal year / Total inputs		0.015	0.015	0.015
Dropouts during and after pivotal year / Enrollment pivotal year	0.49	0.49	0.49	0.49
Repeaters passing next structure / Enrollment pivotal year	0.13	0.13	0.13	0.13
Deaths after pivotal year / Enrollment pivotal year	0.020	0.020	0.020	0.020
Graduates / Enrollment pivotal year	0.35	0.35	0.35	0.35

school level is to be significantly expanded and should become mainly terminal rather than a preparatory stage leading to college.

As a result of these changes the content of elementary and high school education must be changed. Hitherto, vocational and technical skills have been taught in elementary school; henceforth, elementary teaching should be designed to prepare students to proceed to high school. Further, while most high school instruction has been college preparatory, it must now train most high school students in vocational and technical skills.

The problem with respect to the college level is of a different kind. The demand for college education will tend to exceed the levels fixed in the targets as may be observed in the past trends and the projected growth of numbers of high school graduates. Such college level expansion should, however, be limited as far as possible which can be achieved by stiffening entrance requirements.

References

The problem of goals and targets with reference to economic planning is studied in

Tinbergen, J., *Economic Policy: Principles and Design*.   Amsterdam: North Holland Publishing Co., 1956.

The adaptation of the content of education to the needs of social economic development is considered in

Anderson, C. A., "The Adaptation of Education to a Mobile Society," *The Journal of Human Resources*, Vol. 2, No. 2, Spring 1967.

Husén, T., and U. Dahllöf, "An Empirical Approach to the Problem of Curriculum Content," *International Review of Education*, Vol. 11 (1965).

Ministerio de Educación Publica, *Plan Ecuatoriano de Educación*, Quito, 1964.

chapter 10

Demand and Supply
of Teachers

10-1   Content of This Chapter

The first step in assuring the feasibility of the provisional targets set in Chapter 9 is to determine whether there will be enough teachers. This problem can be divided into the following parts:

The first part is to forecast the flows of students being educated as teachers, the output of this education and the current supply of teachers. The methodology for this forecast is quite similar to that employed to forecast the total flows of students, the total output of the educational system and the educational structure of the population.

The second part of the problem is the determination of the number and qualifications of the teachers needed to achieve the targets of the plan and of the supply of teachers from which the required teacher-force will emerge. All the persons with teacher education whether actually teaching or not are included in the current supply of teachers. The methodology used here is similar to that employed in Chapter 7 to estimate the manpower needs and the educational structure of the population from which the required labor force will emerge.

Finally, the forecasted supply of teachers is compared with the required supply. This comparison permits us to determine whether or not there will be available the number of teachers required to achieve the provisional targets of the educational plan.

From the observations above, it follows that the methodology used to prepare an educational plan integrated with an economic plan is conceptually similar to the methodology used to deal with the supply and demand of teachers. There are only differences of magnitude.

Actually, this chapter could be considered an exercise in the application of methods and techniques presented in Chapters 4 to 9.

10-2   Student Flows in Teacher Education

10-2.1   Past Flows of Students in Teacher Training

Two levels of teacher training exist in Planiland: high school and college. Our task is to analyze the flow of students at each level.

The instruments used in analyzing past student flows were described in Chapter 4. The method set out in that chapter is summarized in the basic relationships 4-12 and 4-13. With respect to teacher training in years −12, −6, and 0, the values of the elements in these relationships appear in Table 10-1.

These values provide the bases for computing the indices among the variables shown in Tables 10-2 and 10-3. These indices enable us to detect changes in the characteristics of teacher education and are also useful in preparing projections. Additionally, comparisons between these ratios and those relating to general education at high school and college levels (Tables 5-5 and 5-6) can furnish valuable information.

To complete the analysis of the student flows in teacher education, additional information is required with respect to new entrants. In the case of general education, we began with new entrants in the elementary school level and allowed for the future growth of the population. In the case of the high school and college levels, we used the relationships between new entrants at the higher level and graduates at the lower level in the previous structure.

New entrants to high school level teacher education are graduates of elementary schools. The relationships observed between numbers of new entrants in high school level teacher training and numbers of elementary school graduates in past structures are shown in Table 10-4.

On the other hand, new entrants for college-level teacher training can be either graduates of high school level teacher training institutions or other high school graduates. Data for structures −12, −6, and 0 on these two sources of new entrants in college level teacher training institutions are shown in Table 10-5. These data call for some explanation. The total number of graduates from the high school level is 11,100 for structure −12 and 20,100 for structure −6 (see Table 5-3). These total figures are not shown in Table 10-5; instead, high school level graduates are divided into those coming from ordinary high schools and those coming from teacher training institutions. Likewise, in the table, new entrants to college level teacher training institutions are divided into two groups: those with a general high school education and those from teacher training high schools. Once we know the source and the meaning of the data in Table 10-5, computation of the ratios of new entrants to graduates presents no problem.

Table 10-1.   Planiland: Past Student Flows in Teacher Education Relationships 4-12 and 4-13

Pivotal Year	New Enrollment	Repeaters	Dropouts	Deaths	Total Enrollment, Pivotal Year	Dropouts	Repeaters	Graduates	Deaths
High School Education for Teachers									
-12	8,534	1,024	1,539	124	4,921	925	1,024	2,874	98
- 6	15,473	1,263	2,634	134	7,895	1,084	1,263	5,387	158
0					13,868				
College Education for Teachers									
-12	630	41	164	8	270	92	41	131	6
- 6	1,351	76	358	17	499	95	76	318	10
0					1,052				

Table 10-2. Planiland: Indices for the Students Flows in High-School Level Teacher Education

	Definition	Structure -12	Structure -6	Structure 0
(1)	New enrollment / Graduates from elementary school		$\dfrac{8,534}{84,400} = 0.101$	$\dfrac{15,473}{151,000} = 0.102$
(2)	Repeaters / Total inputs*		$\dfrac{1,024}{8,534 + 1,024} = 0.107$	$\dfrac{1,263}{15,473 + 1,263} = 0.075$
(3)	Dropouts before pivotal year / Total inputs*		$\dfrac{1,539}{8,534 + 1,024} = 0.161$	$\dfrac{2,634}{15,473 + 1,263} = 0.157$
(4)	Deaths before pivotal year / Total inputs*		$\dfrac{124}{8,534 + 1,024} = 0.013$	$\dfrac{234}{15,473 + 1,263} = 0.014$
(5)	Dropouts during and after pivotal year / Enrollment pivotal year	$\dfrac{925}{4,921} = 0.188$	$\dfrac{1,087}{7,895} = 0.138$	
(6)	Repeaters passing to next structure / Enrollment pivotal year	$\dfrac{1,024}{4,921} = 0.208$	$\dfrac{1,263}{7,895} = 0.160$	
(7)	Deaths during and after pivotal year / Enrollment pivotal year	$\dfrac{98}{4,921} = 0.020$	$\dfrac{5,158}{7,895} = 0.020$	
(8)	Graduates / Enrollment pivotal year	$\dfrac{2,874}{4,921} = 0.584$	$\dfrac{5,387}{7,895} = 0.682$	

*Total inputs = new enrollment plus repeaters coming from previous structure.

Table 10-3. Planiland: Indices for the Students Flows in College Education for Teachers

	Definition	Structure −12	Structure −6	Structure 0
(1)	New enrollment / Graduates from high school teacher training		$\dfrac{350}{2,784} = 0.122$	$\dfrac{851}{5,387} = 0.158$
(2)	New enrollment / Graduates from high school general studies		$\dfrac{280}{8,226} = 0.034$	$\dfrac{500}{14,713} = 0.034$
(3)	Repeaters / Total inputs		$\dfrac{41}{630+41} = 0.061$	$\dfrac{76}{1,351+76} = 0.053$
(4)	Dropouts before pivotal year / Total inputs		$\dfrac{164}{630+41} = 0.244$	$\dfrac{358}{1,351+76} = 0.251$
(5)	Deaths before pivotal year / Total inputs		$\dfrac{8}{630+41} = 0.012$	$\dfrac{17}{1,351+76} = 0.012$
(6)	Dropouts during and after pivotal year / Enrollment pivotal year	$\dfrac{92}{270} = 0.341$	$\dfrac{95}{499} = 0.190$	
(7)	Repeaters passing to next structure / Enrollment to pivotal year	$\dfrac{41}{270} = 0.152$	$\dfrac{76}{499} = 0.152$	
(8)	Deaths during and after pivotal year / Enrollment pivotal year	$\dfrac{6}{270} = 0.022$	$\dfrac{10}{499} = 0.020$	
(9)	Graduates / Enrollment pivotal year	$\dfrac{131}{270} = 0.485$	$\dfrac{318}{499} = 0.637$	

Table 10-4.   Planiland: Past Relationship Between Elementary School Graduates and New Entrants in High School Education for Teachers

Year t	Elementary School Graduates from Structure t (Table 5-3)	New Entrants in Structure $t + 6$ (Table 10-1)	$\dfrac{\text{New Entrants}}{\text{Graduates}}$
-12	84,400	8,534	0.101
-6	151,000	15,473	0.102

10-2.2   Projection of Flows of Students in Teacher Training

Such projections call for the same procedures as those used in project-ing the flow of students in general education. Two methods were outlined in Chapter 5, the first allowing for the influence of population growth only and the second taking into account income growth as well as popula-tion growth. Although no use is made here of the former method, it is probable that both methods would have to be employed in preparing an actual plan.   The application of the first method to flows in teacher education is straightforward and will not be explained in detail here.

Nonetheless, a problem remains: Which projections of elementary school and high school graduates should be used in estimating new en-trants for high school and college level teacher training, the required or the automatic values given in Chapter 9? Since we assume, for the time being, that the provisional targets set in Chapter 9 will be attained, we will use Chapter 9's provisional target values for numbers of elementary school and high school graduates.   These target values together with a projection for new entrants in high school education for teachers is given in Table 10-6.   The projections of student flows in college education for teachers are given in Table 10-7.

10-3   Supply of Teachers

As explained in Chapter 6, data on the output of the educational system can be used to determine the growth of a known initial educational structure of the population, i.e., of a known initial supply of qualified persons.

Similar data and methods can be used to study the development of the supply of teachers. Table 10-8 indicates how we estimate the increase of graduates from high school level teacher training schools between year -12 and years -6 and 0, the data for year -12 being derived from a census or sample survey.   This method is identical to that employed in Chapter 6. Using this method, we can obtain the results set out in Table 10-9 where a further distinction between graduates and dropouts is drawn.

Table 10-5. *Planiland: Past Relationship Between Numbers of High School Graduates and Numbers of New Entrants in College Level Education for Teachers*

Year t	General Education			Teacher Training High School Graduates Structure t	Teachers Education	
	General High School Graduates Structure t (Table 5-3)	New Entrants in Structure $t + 6$ (Table 10-1)	$\dfrac{\text{New Entrants}}{\text{Graduates}}$		New Entrants in Structure $t + 6$ (Table 10-1)	$\dfrac{\text{New Entrants}}{\text{Graduates}}$
-12	8,226	280	0.034	2,784	350	0.122
-6	14,713	500	0.034	5,387	851	0.158

Table 10-6. Planiland: Projection of Student Flows in High School Education for Teachers

Year t	Elementary School Graduates Structure t (Table 9-5) a	New Entrants (Table 10-4) $\dfrac{\text{New Entrants}}{\text{Graduates}}$ b	New Entrants Structure $t+6$ $a \times b$
0	249.26	0.102	25.42
6	576.44	0.102	58.80
12	854.02	0.102	87.11

Pivotal Year	New Entrants	Before Pivotal Year			Total Enrollment, Pivotal Year	After Pivotal Year			
		Repeaters	Dropouts	Deaths		Dropouts	Repeaters	Graduates	Deaths
0	25.4	2.2	4.3	0.4	13.9	1.9	2.2	9.5	0.3
6	58.8	3.7	9.8	0.9	22.9	3.2	3.7	15.5	0.5
12	87.1	8.3	15.0	1.3	51.8	7.1	8.3	35.4	1.0
18					79.1	10.9	12.7	53.9	1.6

Table 10-7.　Planiland: Projection of Student Flows in College Education for Teachers

Year t	General Education			Teacher Training High School Graduates Structure t (Table 10-3)	Teacher Education		
	General High School Graduates* Structure t	New Entrants Graduates (Table 10-5)	New Entrants Structure t + 6		New Entrants Graduates (Table 10-6)	New Entrants Structure t + 6	Total
	a	b	c = a × b	d	e	f = d × e	c + f
0	31.7	0.034	1.08	9.5	0.158	1.50	2.58
6	48.7	0.034	1.65	15.5	0.158	2.45	4.10
12	71.4	0.034	2.43	35.4	0.158	5.59	8.02

Pivotal Year	Before Pivotal Year, Relationship 4-12				Total Enrollment, Pivotal Year	After Pivotal Year, Relationship 4-13			
	New Entrants	Repeaters	Dropouts	Deaths		Dropouts	Repeaters	Graduates	Deaths
0					1,052	200	160	671	21
6	2,600	160	673	33	2,059	390	312	1,311	41
12	4,100	312	1,077	53	3,282	624	499	2,093	66
18	8,000	499	2,079	102	6,323	1,201	961	4,035	126

*Value in Table 9-5 minus corresponding value in Table 10-6.

*Table 10-8.   Planiland: Changes in the Supply of Graduates from High School
Level Teacher Training Institutions from Year −12 to Year 0*

	Years		
	−12	−6	0
Graduates with high school level teachers' education year *t*	3,199	5,427	9,477
Survivors in year *t* + 6	2,971	5,063	
Graduates from high school teachers' education structure *t* (Table 10-1)	+2,874	+5,387	
Graduates entering college structure *t* + 6 (Table 10-5)	−350	−851	
Deaths among graduates after they have left school	−68	−122	
Graduates with high school teachers' education year *t* + 6	5,427	9,477	

*Table 10-9.   Planiland: Actual and Projected Supplies of Persons with Teachers'
Education at Different Dates*

Qualifications of Teachers by Amount of Education	Years					
	−12	−6	0	6	12	18
College graduates	106	225	519	1,138	2,357	4,283
College dropouts	342	569	974	1,766	3,117	5,616
High school graduates	3,199	5,427	9,477	16,654	28,553	56,244
High school dropouts	3,572	5,730	8,993	14,493	26,544	46,977

10-4   Number and Qualifications of Teachers Required to Achieve the Targets of the Educational Plan

10-4.1   Basic Instrument for the Analysis of the Demand for Teachers

The basic instrument for the analysis of the demand for teachers is Eq. 4-7:

$$s_h = \frac{h_s \times S}{h_c \times T} \qquad [4\text{-}7]$$

where s_h = average number of students taking each period (weighted student-teacher ratio)
h_s = average number of periods per week per student
h_c = average number of periods taught by each teacher per week
S = number of students
T = number of teachers

10-4.2   Past Experience with Regard to the Demand for Teachers

In Table 5-5 the student flows at elementary and high school levels for structure −6 were divided into four qualitative strata.   In Table 10-10

Table 10-10.   Planiland: Elements in Equation 4-7, Year −6

Index	Elementary School Strata					High School Strata					College
	Total	A	B	C	D	Total	A	B	C	D	Total
Number of teachers, T	9,620	1,924	2,515	2,079	3,102	3,117	143	556	1,989	429	583
Periods per teacher, h_c	28	28	28	28	28	8.60	25.25	15.11	6.72	3.36	5.17
Number of students, S (thousands)	419.6	42.0	105.0	105.0	167.6	40.5	3.95	11.81	22.13	2.61	5.1
Period per student, h_s	28	28	28	28	28	32	32	32	32	32	11.18
Weighted student-teacher ratio	43.61	21.83	41.74	50.50	54.03	48.33	35	45	53	58	18.95

the different elements of formula 4-7 are presented for each of these strata as well as for each of the three levels as a whole. Comparisons of figures in the two tables indicate that the weighted student-teacher ratio has a very definite influence on the quality of education.

The differences among the strata at the elementary and high school levels cannot be attributed, however, solely to the differences in weighted student-teacher ratios. There are many other influential factors, the most important of which is doubtless the qualifications of the teachers.

Table 10-11 shows the qualifications of teachers in Planiland's educational system and shows that qualifications differ considerably even within the same level: for instance, high school teachers include both holders of college degrees and high school dropouts. In Table 10-12, the teachers in the qualitative strata in Table 5-5 are classified according to qualifications.

10-4.3 Teachers Needed to Achieve the Provisional Targets of the Educational Plan

Elementary school total number of teachers required

To find out the total number of teachers needed in years 6, 12, and 18 we have the following data:

(a) Total number of students S_t^1 in year 0 (Table 5-3) and target figures for years 6, 12, and 18 (Table 9-5).

(b) Number of periods per student per week (h_s) and number of periods per teacher per week (h_c). According to past experience (Table 10-10), h_s and h_c will each equal 28 for years 6, 12, and 18.

(c) Actual value of s_h, the weighted student-teacher ratio, in year 0 (41.15) and target value for year 18, i.e., the value for stratum A in year -6. The reason for this is that in order to come as close as possible to meeting requirements for elementary school graduates, planners must bring the entire elementary level of the educational system up to the standards of stratum A.

Once we have actual and target values of s_h for years 0 and 18, we can use a rate of growth to interpolate the values of s_h for years 6 and 12. The results appear in column 4 of Table 10-13. With the necessary target values for four variables (S_t^1, h_s, h_c, and s_h) in Eq. 4-7, we can compute the number of teachers required.

With respect to year 6, for example, we have

$$T = \frac{h_s \times S}{h_c \times s_h} = \frac{28 \times 716,320}{28 \times 33.30} = 21,511$$

This result, together with those for years 12 and 18 appear in Table 10-13.

Table 10-11. Planiland: Teachers in the Different Levels of Education Classified by Types and Number of Periods They Teach

Number	Qualifications	Year −12		Year −6		Year 0	
		Number T	Hours per Week h_c	Number T	Hours per Week h_c	Number T	Hours per Week h_c
	Elementary School						
(1)	Graduates high school teachers' education	1,641	28	2,982	28	5,356	28
(2)	Graduates high school general education	984	28	1,732	28	2,895	28
(3)	Dropouts high school teachers' education	1,642	28	2,694	28	4,343	28
(4)	Dropouts high school general education	1,181	28	1,251	28	1,303	28
(5)	Graduates elementary school	656	28	673	28	434	28
(6)	Dropouts elementary school	459	28	288	28	145	28
	Total	6,563		9,620		14,476	
	High School						
(7)	Graduates college teachers' education	77	17.78	171	17.78	386	17.78
(8)	Graduates college general education	194	17.56	405	17.56	883	17.56
(9)	Dropouts college teachers' education	209	9.63	355	9.63	663	9.63
(10)	Dropouts college general education	139	6.45	237	6.45	442	6.45
(11)	Graduates high school teachers' education	716	6.69	1,013	6.69	1,656	6.69
(12)	Graduates high school general education	251	6.66	468	6.66	828	6.66
(13)	Dropouts high school teachers' education	251	4.09	343	4.09	497	4.09
(14)	Dropouts high school general education	97	3.36	125	3.36	166	3.36
	Total	1,934		3,117		5,521	
	College						
(15)	Graduates college teachers' education	9	6.0	12	6.0	32	6.0
(16)	Graduates college general education	252	5.0	431	5.0	854	5.0
(17)	Dropouts college teacher education	24	4.21	32	4.21	21	4.21
(18)	Dropouts college general education	75	6.45	93	6.45	139	6.45
(19)	Graduates high school teachers' education	11	3.26	14	3.26	21	3.26
	Total	371		582		1,067	

Table 10-12. *Planiland: Number of Teachers in the Qualitative Strata of Elementary and High School Levels Year –6*

Line Nos.. Table 10-11	Qualifications	Total Number of Teachers	Number of Teachers in Strata			
			A	B	C	D
	Elementary Level					
(1)	Graduates high school teachers' education	2,982	1,491	1,491	—	—
(2)	Graduates high school general education	1,732	433	693	520	86
(3)	Dropouts high school teachers' education	2,694	—	269	1,078	1,397
(4)	Dropouts high school general education	1,251	—	62	313	826
(5)	Graduates elementary school general education	673	—	—	168	505
(6)	Dropouts elementary school general education	288	—	—	—	288
	Total	9,620	1,924	2,515	2,079	3,102
	High School Level					
(7)	Graduates college teachers' education	171	45	126	—	—
(8)	Graduates college general education	405	98	307	—	—
(9)	Dropouts college teachers' education	355	—	123	232	—
(10)	Dropouts college general education	237	—	—	218	19
(11)	Graduates high school teachers' education	1,013	—	—	1,004	9
(12)	Graduates high school general education	468	—	—	460	8
(13)	Dropouts high school teachers' education	343	—	—	75	268
(14)	Dropouts high school general education	125	—	—	—	125
	Total	3,117	143	556	1,989	429

Table 10-13.   Planiland: Estimation of the Number of Teachers Required to Attain the Provisional Targets for Elementary Education

Year	Number of Students in Targets Tables 5-3 and 9-5	Number of Periods per Student Stratum *A*	Number of Periods per Teacher Stratum *A*	Weighted Student-Teacher Ratio	Number of Teachers
0	595,800	28	28	41.15	14,476
6	716,320	28	28	33.30	21,511
12	930,250	28	28	26.96	34,505
18	1,096,720	28	28	21.83	50,239

Teacher qualifications

Once we have the total number of teachers required, we can proceed to determine the qualifications they should have. The breakdown of teachers by qualification is known for year 0. We know also that the conditions in stratum *A* of elementary school in year −6 (Table 10-12) must be extended to the entire educational system by year 18. This means that in year 18 the proportion of elementary school teachers with degrees of high school teachers' education was to be the one observed in stratum *A* in year −6. The same is true for the proportion of teachers with degrees from general high school. In Table 10-12 we see that the first proportion must be

$$\frac{1,491}{1,924} = 0.7749$$

and the second must be

$$\frac{433}{1,924} = 0.2251$$

This means that the number of teachers with degrees from high school level teacher-training institutions for year 18 must be

$$0.7749 \times 50,239 = 38,930$$

Elementary school teachers with degrees from high school general education in year 18 must number

$$0.2251 \times 50,239 = 11,309$$

These results appear in Table 10-14.

Next comes the problem of determining the required qualifications of the teachers in years 6 and 12. For this, we notice in Table 10-14 that in year 18 groups 3 to 6 are no longer present. This elimination of less qualified teachers should be gradual.

Table 10-14. Planiland: Number and Qualifications of the Teachers Required to Attain the Provisional Targets for Elementary Education

Line Nos., Table 10-11	Levels of Qualification	Years			
		0	6	12	18
(1)	Graduates from high school teachers' education	5,356	11,266	21,051	38,930
(2)	Graduates from high school general education	2,895	6,093	11,377	11,309
(3)	Dropouts from high school teachers' education	4,343	2,897	1,449	0
(4)	Dropouts from high school general education	1,303	869	435	0
(5)	Graduates from elementary school general education	434	289	144	0
(6)	Dropouts from elementary school general education	145	97	49	0
	Total	14,476	21,511	34,505	50,239

In Table 10-14 it is assumed that one-third of the teachers in groups 3 to 6 leave the educational system between year 0 and year 6, another third between years 6 and 12 and the remainder between years 12 and 18.

Finally, we must estimate the number of teachers required in categories 1 and 2 for years 6 to 12. The method used is as follows: There should be in year 6 a total of 21,511 teachers, 4,152 in categories 3 to 6, and the remaining 17,359 in categories 1 and 2. In order to estimate the number in each of the latter two categories, conditions in year 0 are observed (see Table 10-11). The proportion of teachers in category 1 as compared to those in categories 1 and 2 is

$$\frac{5,356}{5,356 + 2,895} = \frac{5,356}{8,251} = 0.649$$

Thus the required number in category 1 in year 6 is estimated to be

$$0.649 \times 17,359 = 11,266$$

The same method was used to obtain the values for categories 1 and 2 teacher requirements for year 12.

Periods per teacher per week for different types of teachers

In Table 10-13 the estimated average number of periods per teacher per week for years 0, 6, 12, and 18 is presented. Since teachers of all the types teach the same number of periods per week at the elementary school level, there is no problem of differences in periods per week among teachers with different qualifications.

High school total number of teachers required

   In the estimation of the total number of teachers required at the high school level, there is a problem that did not appear in the case of the teachers for the elementary school level. For this reason the process of estimating teacher requirements at this level will be explained in detail.

   The data available are:

(a) Estimated total number of students (S_t^2) for years 0, 6, 12, and 18 (Tables 5-3 and 9-5). These values are reproduced in Table 10-15.

(b) Number of periods per student per week (h_s) for years 0, 6, 12, and 18. The value according to Table 10-10 is

$$h_s = 32$$

(c) Number of periods per teacher per week h_c. For this variable, estimation is not as simple as in the case of the elementary school level. First, we use as target values those for qualitative stratum B in year -6 and these values are different from the values for the level as a whole in year 0. Besides, the number of periods per week for teacher in stratum A is higher than in stratum B; that is, with the period load in stratum A, a smaller number of teachers would be required to provide a given quantity of education. For this reason it is worthwhile to consider two alternatives for the number of periods per week per teacher h_c, the number for stratum A as well as that for stratum B. It should be noted that conditions in stratum C should not be considered in any circumstances since high school education must be at least of stratum B quality in year 18 to assure attainment of output targets for the high school level.

(d) The actual or target values of s_h, the weighted student-teacher ratio for years 0 and 18.

   Again the method of computation of T is based on Eq. 4-7. The values of two variables $(S_t^2$ and $h_s)$ in this equation are known for years 0, 6, 12, and 18, and the required value of two others $(h_c$ and $s_h)$ can be estimated for years 6 and 12 by interpolation using a rate of growth and values for years 0 and 18. With the values of the four variables for years 0, 6, 12, and 18, Eq. 4-7 will yield the number of teachers required in each of these years. For instance, with the first alternative value of h_c, we obtain the following value for T for year 18:

$$T = \frac{h_s \times S}{h_c \times s_h} = \frac{32 \times 501{,}910}{25.25 \times 45} = 14{,}135$$

   The other target values for T and the figures on which they are based are shown in Table 10-15.

Table 10-15   Planiland: Estimation of the Number of Teachers Required to Attain the Provisional Targets for High School Education

Year	Target Number of Students (Tables 5-3 and 9-5)	Number of Periods per Student Stratum B (Table 10-10)	Weighted Student-Teacher Ratio	First Alternative		Second Alternative	
				Number of Periods per Teacher Stratum A (Table 10-10)	Number of Teachers	Number of Periods per Teacher Stratum B (Table 10-10)	Number of Teachers
0	69,000	32	46.5	8.60	5,521	8.60	5,521
6	149,020	32	46.0	12.31	8,421	10.37	9,997
12	245,900	32	45.5	17.63	9,809	12.51	13,824
18	501,910	32	45.0	25.25	14,135	15.11	23,621

Teacher qualifications

Having calculated the total number of teachers required, we can continue a breakdown of teacher requirements by level of qualification, using the same method as in the case of the elementary level (see Table 10-16).

Table 10-16.   Planiland: Number and Qualifications of the Teachers Required to Attain the Provisional Targets for High School Education

Line Nos., Table 10-11	Qualifications	Year			
		0	6	12	18
	First Alternative				
(7)	Graduates college teachers' education	386	1,204	1,721	3,203
(8)	Graduates college general education	883	2,755	3,936	7,805
(9)	Dropouts college teachers' education	663	2,069	2,955	3,127
(10)	Dropouts college general education	442	295	148	0
(11)	Graduates high school teachers education	1,656	1,104	552	0
(12)	Graduates high school general education	828	552	276	0
(13)	Dropouts high school teachers' education	497	331	165	0
(14)	Dropouts high school general education	166	111	56	0
	Total	5,521	8,421	9,809	14,135
	Second Alternative				
(7)	Graduates college teachers' education	386	1,519	2,523	5,353
(8)	Graduates college general education	883	3,475	5,771	13,043
(9)	Dropouts college teachers' education	663	2,610	4,333	5,225
(10)	Dropouts college general education	442	295	148	0
(11)	Graduates high school teachers' education	1,656	1,104	552	0
(12)	Graduates high school general education	828	552	276	0
(13)	Dropouts high school teachers' education	497	331	165	0
(14)	Dropouts high school general education	166	111	56	0
	Total	5,521	9,997	13,824	23,621

Periods per teacher per week for different types of teachers

The estimation of periods per teacher per week is more complex at the high school level than elementary school level. The method to be used for this purpose will be described below with reference to year 6.

We have three sets of data:

(a) H, the total number of periods per week that will be offered by the teachers available in year 6. This can be calculated with the formula

$$H = h_c \times T \qquad [4\text{-}6]$$

For year 6 we have

$$103,662.51 = 12.31 \times 8,421$$

(b) The numbers of teachers of each type required in year 6. These requirements are presented in Table 10-16.

(c) The number of periods that the teachers of each type taught in the *previous* pivotal year; i.e., pivotal year 0 for year 6. These figures appear in Table 10-11.

With the data in (b) and (c), it is possible to calculate the total number of periods per week that would be taught in year 6 if the teachers of each type were to teach the same number of periods per week as each type taught in year 0, i.e., 104,400.97 periods. This total will differ from the total in (a). The factor of change from year 0 to year 6 for the number of periods per week is then obtained by dividing the total in (a) by the total just calculated from (b) and (c). In the case of high school teachers for year 6 this factor of change is

$$\frac{103,662.51}{104,400.97} = 0.992$$

To obtain the number of periods that the teachers of each type must teach in year 6 the factor above should be multiplied by the average number of periods per week taught in pivotal year 0. For instance, the average teacher of type 7 will teach in year 6:

$$17.78 \times .992 = 17.64 \text{ periods per week}$$

The final results of similar calculations for all types of teachers for years 6, 12, and 18 appear in Table 10-17.

Table 10-17. Planiland: Number of Periods Taught per Week Required to Attain the Targets of the Educational Plan

Line Nos., Table 10-11	High School	Year		
		6	12	18
(7)	Graduates college teachers' education	17.64	22.72	25.25
(8)	Graduates college general education	17.42	22.44	25.25
(9)	Dropouts college teachers' education	9.55	12.30	25.25
(10)	Dropouts college general education	6.40	8.24	0
(11)	Graduates high school teachers' education	6.64	8.55	0
(12)	Graduates high school general education	6.61	8.51	0
(13)	Dropouts high school teachers' education	4.06	5.23	0
(14)	Dropouts high school general education	3.33	4.29	0

College total number of teachers required

The method used to estimate the number of teachers required at this level is identical to that outlined for the elementary and high school levels. The results for the college level are set out in Tables 10-18, 10-19, and 10-20.

*Table 10-18.   Planiland: Estimation of the Number of Teachers Required
to Attain the Provisional Targets for College Education*

Year	Target Number of Students (Tables 5-3 and 9-5)	Number of Periods per Student Average (Table 10-10)	Number of Periods per Teacher Average (Table 10-10)	Weighted Student-Teacher Ratio	Number of Teachers
0	8,900	11.18	5.17	18.03	1,067
6	13,570	11.18	5.17	18.95	1,549
12	21,370	11.18	5.17	18.95	2,439
18	37,380	11.18	5.17	18.95	4,266

*Table 10-19.   Planiland: Number and Qualifications of the Teachers Required
to Attain the Provisional Targets for College Education*

Line Nos., Table 10-11	Qualifications	Year			
		0	6	12	18
(15)	Graduates college teachers' education	32	46	73	128
(16)	Graduates college general education	854	1,241	1,952	3,414
(17)	Dropouts college teachers' education	21	30	48	84
(18)	Dropouts college general education	139	202	318	556
(19)	Graduates high school teachers' education	21	30	48	84
	Total	1,067	1,549	2,439	4,266

*Table 10-20.   Planiland: Number of Periods Taught per Week Required to
Attain the Target of the Educational Plan for the College Level*

Line Nos., Table 10-11	Qualifications	Year		
		6	12	18
(15)	Graduates college teachers' education	6.0	6.0	6.0
(16)	Graduates college general education	5.0	5.0	5.0
(17)	Dropouts college teachers' education	4.21	4.21	4.21
(18)	Dropouts college general education	6.45	6.45	6.45
(19)	Graduates high school teachers' education	3.26	3.26	3.26

10-5   Required Supply of People with Teachers' Education

As shown in Sec. 8-2, figures for the required educational structure
of the labor force are not sufficient to enable us to define the necessary
characteristics of the educational system since the system produces educated nonworkers as well as educated members of the labor force.   The
immediate problem, therefore, was to establish the educational structure
of the population as a whole required in order to produce a labor force
with the necessary educational structure.

The same problem arises with respect to people who have attended
teacher training institutions.   Not all those who have been trained as

Table 10-21. Planiland: Relationships Between Persons with Teachers' Education in Teaching Positions and Total Number of Persons with Teachers' Education

Quali-fication Number (Table 10-11)	Qualifications from Teacher Training Institutions	Year − 12			Year − 6			Year 0		
		Total Number (Table 10-9) a	Teaching b	Ratio $\frac{a}{b}$	Total Number (Table 10-9) a	Teaching b	Ratio $\frac{a}{b}$	Total Number (Table 10-9) a	Teaching b	Ratio $\frac{a}{b}$
7, 15	College graduates	106	86	1.233	225	183	1.230	519	418	1.242
9, 17	College dropouts	342	223	1.537	569	387	1.470	974	684	1.424
1, 11, 19	High school graduates	3,199	2,368	1.351	5,427	4,009	1.354	9,477	7,033	1.348
3, 13	High school dropouts	3,572	1,893	1.887	5,730	3,037	1.887	8,993	4,840	1.858

Table 10-22. Planiland: Total Numbers of Persons with Teachers' Education Required to Attain the Provisional Targets of the Educational Plan

Quali-fication Number (Table 10-11)	Qualifications from Teacher Training Institutions	Ratio Table 12–21 a	Year 0		Year 6		Year 12		Year 18	
			Teaching Tables 12–14, 12–16, 12–19 b	Total Number $a \times b$	Teaching Tables 12–14, 12–16, 12–19 c	Total Number $a \times c$	Teaching Tables 12–14, 12–16, 12–19 d	Total Number $a \times d$	Teaching Tables 12–14, 12–16, 12–19 e	Total Number $a \times e$
7, 15	College graduates	1.242	418	519	1,250	1,553	1,794	2,228	3,331	4,137
9, 17	College dropouts	1.424	684	974	2,099	2,989	3,003	4,276	3,211	4,572
1, 11, 19	High school graduates	1.348	7,033	9,480	12,403	16,719	27,051	36,465	38,768	52,259
3, 13	High school dropouts	1.858	4,840	8,993	3,228	5,998	1,614	2,999	0	0

teachers actually teach; the educational system must therefore produce more people qualified to teach than are actually needed in the schools. The value of this required total output of qualified teachers will be estimated below.

The method of estimation is similar to that employed in Sec. 8-2. To begin with, we must determine the past relationships between the total number of those with different types of teacher training and those of each type actually teaching. These relationships are shown in Table 10-21 for each of the four types of qualified teachers with which we are concerned. The table indicates that in year 0 there were 519 graduates from teacher training colleges of whom 418 were teaching. This means that there must be

$$\frac{519}{418} = 1.242$$

people with this level and type of training for each person of this level and type of training actually engaged in teaching.

Assuming that the ratios for year 0 in Table 10-21 will remain constant in the future, we can estimate the total number of people with various types of teacher training required in the future. This involves using not only the ratios in Table 10-21 but also the required numbers of teachers estimated in Sec. 10-4 and shown in Tables 10-14, 10-16, and 10-19. These numbers appear in Table 10-22 along with the required total numbers of those qualified to teach. By way of example, let us consider the number of graduates from teacher-training colleges required in year 18, a figure which is calculated as

$$1.242 \times 3{,}331 = 4{,}137$$

10-6 Comparison Between Forecasted and Required Supplies of Teachers

The comparison between forecasted (Table 10-9) and required (Table 10-22) supplies of teachers will permit us to find out whether or not there will be enough teachers to achieve the provisional targets of the educational plan. From this comparison, it can be seen that there is not a marked difference between the required numbers of those with teachers education and the numbers that will be available as a result of the projections in Table 10-6 and 10-7 of the growth of student flows in teacher training institutions. Hence the projected growth of the student flows in teacher training satisfies the requirements of the educational plan. Were this not so, it would be necessary to set targets for the growth of the student flows in teacher training by means of the methods employed in Chapter 9.

References

Some limitations of the unweighted teacher-student ratios are studied in
Hansen, W. L., "Educational Plans and Teacher Supply," *Comparative Education
Review*, Vol. 6, No. 2 (October 1962).
——, "Human Capital Requirements for Educational Expansion: Teacher
Shortages and Teacher Supply." Paper presented at the Conference on
Education and Economic Development, Comparative Education Center,
University of Chicago, April 1963.

A general analysis of demand and supply of teachers in developed countries
appears in
Caplow, T., and R. McGee, *The Academic Marketplace*. New York: Basic Books,
1958.
Vaizey, J., *The Control of Education*. Part IV. London: Faber and Faber, 1963.

The approach used to adapt the method presented in this chapter to a
computer program appears in
Correa, H., and E. Reimer, *A Simulation Model for Educational Planning in
Puerto Rico*. San Juan: Department of Public Instruction (Mimeographed),
1969.

chapter 11

Buildings and
Other Facilities

11-1   Content of This Chapter

The purpose of this chapter is to determine the physical facilities required to reach the provisional targets of the educational plan. The first step is to study past experience with regards to buildings and other facilities. This analysis gives information about the facilities available and the relationships between the characteristics of the facilities and the flows of students and the output of the educational system. These relationships permit us to determine the characteristics that the school facilities should have in the future if the provisional targets for the flows of students are to be obtained.

11-2   Method

In the determination of the physical facilities required to reach the provisional targets of the educational plan, we will take into account the number of students seeking education, the number of periods per week during which schoolrooms are used, the number of periods during which they could be used and the qualitative characteristics of these rooms. For this we use Eq. 4-9:

$$s_h = \frac{h_s \times S}{h_r \times R} \qquad [4\text{-}9]$$

where s_h = average number of students taking each period; i.e., weighted student-room ratio

h_s = average number of periods per week per student

h_r = average number of periods that each room is used per week

S = number of students

R = number of classrooms and laboratories

It is useful to remember that s_h, h_s, and S in formula 4-7 are the same variables as s_h, h_s, and S in formula 4-9. Hence, some of the results obtained in Chapter 10 can be used here.

In Chapter 4 the following equations were also introduced

$$H = h_c T \qquad\qquad [4\text{-}6]$$

$$H = h_r R \qquad\qquad [4\text{-}8]$$

where H = number of periods of education offered
  h_c = average number of periods taught by each teacher per week
  T = number of teachers
  h_r = average number of periods that each room is used per week
  R = number of classrooms and laboratories

In Chapter 10 we have already determined target values for each level for the number of periods per teacher per week h_c and number of teachers T for years 6, 12, and 18. Equation 4-6 allows us to calculate from these figures target values for H for each level for years 6, 12, and 18.

In order to estimate the number and characteristics of classrooms and laboratories required to attain the targets of the educational plan, we can use Eq. 4-9 or Eqs. 4-6 and 4-8. In both cases the results already obtained in Chapter 10 must be taken into consideration. Due to their simplicity, we will use mainly Eqs. 4-6 and 4-8.

11-3 Past Experience with Regard to Buildings and Other Facilities

In Table 11-1, the year -6 values of different variables in formulas 4-8 and 4-9 for the three levels of education and their qualitative subdivision are presented.

The Table 11-2 gives more detailed data on types of classrooms in use in years -12, -6, and 0 and Table 11-3 gives data on types of classrooms used in the various qualitative strata at the elementary and high school levels in year -6. In these tables, classrooms are classified according to number of square meters of classroom space available per pupil in an average-sized class.

It will be observed that, at elementary and high school levels, the space available ranges from 0.8 to 3.8 square meters per student while, at college level, it varies from 2.3 to 4.3 square meters per student. The space available per student is estimated by dividing the area of each room by the average number of students taught in that room in each period.

It will be noted also that in Table 11-2 classrooms have been classified as "owned" and "not owned," an important distinction inasmuch as the financing required for owned buildings is quite different from that required for rented buildings.

Table 11-1. Planiland: Values of the Variables Appearing in Eqs. 4-8 and 4-9

Index	Elementary School					High School					College
	Total	A	B	C	D	Total	A	B	C	D	Total
Number of rooms, R	8,339	2,020	2,466	1,669	2,184	914	158	293	418	45	184
Periods per room, h_r	32.31	26.27	28.58	34.88	39.77	29.34	22.85	28.67	32.00	32.00	16.35
Number of periods of education offered, H	269,410	53,872	70,470	58,212	86,856	26,819	3,611	8,401	13,366	1,441	3,009
Number of students, S (thousands)	419.6	42.0	105.0	105.0	167.6	40.5	3.95	11.81	22.13	2.61	5.1
Periods per student, h_s	28	28	28	28	28	32	32	32	32	32	11.18
Weighted student-room ratio, s_h	43.61	21.83	41.74	50.50	54.03	48.33	35	45	53	58	18.95

Table 11-2. Planiland: Inventory of School Facilities, Size and Ownership of Rooms for Classes and Laboratories

Square Meters per Student	Year 0			Year –6			Year –12		
	Owned	Not Owned	Total	Owned	Not Owned	Total	Owned	Not Owned	Total
Elementary School									
0.8–1.3	1,446	215	1,661	1,981	299	2,280	1,435	315	1,750
1.3–1.8		350	350		338	338		240	240
1.8–2.3	1,191	580	1,771	1,515	185	1,700	1,244	104	1,348
2.3–2.8	2,340	390	2,730	477	260	737	387	116	503
2.8–3.3	2,980		2,980	1,360		1,360	674		674
3.3–3.8	3,520		3,520	1,294		1,924	1,020		1,020
Total	11,477	1,535	13,012	7,257	1,082	8,339	4,760	775	5,535
High School									
0.8–1.3	110	15	125	110	27	137	80	21	101
1.3–1.8	40	83	123	45	45	90	34	26	60
1.8–2.3	231	128	359	243	81	324	164	52	216
2.3–2.8	570		570	95		95	41		41
2.8–3.3	265		265	125		125	48		48
3.3–3.8	208		208	143		143	53		53
Total	1,424	226	1,650	761	153	914	420	99	519
College									
2.3–2.8	9		9	9		9	11		11
2.8–3.3	32		32	22		22	19		19
3.3–3.8	199		199	110		110	73		73
3.8–4.3	97		97	43		43	75		75
Total	337		337	184		184	178		178

Table 11-3.   Planiland: Number of Classrooms and Laboratories by Size of Classroom and Qualitative Strata Year −6

Square Meters per Student	Total Number of Rooms	No. of Rooms in Schools of Strata			
		A	B	C	D
Elementary School					
0.8–1.3	2,280	96			2,184
1.3–1.8	338			338	
1.8–2.3	1,700		369	1,331	
2.3–2.8	737		737		
2.8–3.3	1,360		1,360		
3.3–3.8	1,924	1,924			
Total	8,339	2,020	2,466	1,669	2,184
High School					
0.8–1.3	137	15	52	70	
1.3–1.8	90			45	45
1.8–2.3	324		21	303	
2.3–2.8	95		95		
2.8–3.3	125		125		
3.3–3.8	143	143			
Total	914	158	293	418	45

In the case of classrooms and laboratories (as in the case of teachers), it is not enough to know the various types of existing facilities. In the preparation of a plan, information must also be available concerning the influence which the different physical facilities have on the quality of education. This is particularly true of the elementary and high school levels where qualitative changes must be introduced.

Information on the relationship between physical facilities and educational quality can be obtained only by analyzing actual experience within a country. Data for the qualitative strata at the elementary and high school levels in Planiland in year −6 are set out in Table 11-3.

11-4   Classrooms and Laboratories Needed to Achieve the Provisional Targets of the Educational Plan

11-4.1   Elementary School Total Number of Rooms Needed

In Table 11-4 the target numbers of periods of education to be offered (in elementary education) in years 0, 6, 12, and 18 are presented. These values are calculated from the data in Table 10-13 by means of formula 4-6, i.e.,

$$H = h_c T \qquad [4\text{-}6]$$

Table 11-4.   Planiland: Number of Classrooms and Laboratories Required to Attain the Provisional Targets for Elementary Education

Year	Number of Periods of Education Offered H	First Alternative		Second Alternative		Third Alternative	
		Periods per Room h_r	Number of Rooms R	Periods per Room h_r	Number of Rooms R	Periods per Room h_r	Number of Rooms R
0	405,328	31.15	13,012	31.15	13,012	31.15	13,012
6	602,308	29.57	20,369	33.11	18,191	35.14	17,140
12	966,140	28.08	34,407	35.20	27,447	39.70	24,336
18	1,406,692	26.67	52,744	37.33	37,680	44.80	31,400

The target values of H in Table 11-4 and the formula 4-8 ($H = h_rR$) will be used below to determine the total number of rooms (R) required.

Three different alternatives will be considered. For the first alternative, the number of periods per week per room h_r in stratum A in year -6 (i.e., $h_r = 26.67$) is used as a target value for year 18. Since the values of h_r for years 0 and 18 are now known, target values for years 6 and 12 can be estimated by interpolation. The results appear in Table 11-4.

Once the target values of H and h_r are obtained, target values of R can be obtained by using formula 4-8; for instance, for year 6 we have

$$R = \frac{H}{h_r} = \frac{602,308}{29.57} = 20,369$$

The second and third alternatives require some preliminary comments. They are based on the notion that the physical facilities used in education may be used more frequently without any loss in educational quality.

Planiland elementary schools in year 0 for instance are in use 28.78 hours per week or 5.76 hours per day in a five-day week. They could, however, be used during at least 10 or 12 hours per day without loss of educational efficiency. On the other hand, not all schools can be put to more intensive use since there may not be enough students to justify it. This applies, for example, to schools in lightly populated rural areas. Thus maximum possible utilization of classrooms and laboratories is directly related to the location of the schools. In fact, the two problems should be tackled together. Unfortunately, however, this would be complicated from a mathematical point of view.

In the case of the second alternative, it is assumed that half of the 1,406,692 periods in year 18 will be provided in rooms used during 28 periods per week and the remainder in rooms used during 56 hours per week. Hence, the number of rooms to be used during 28 hours per week in year 18 is

$$\frac{703,346}{28} = 25,120$$

while those to be used during 56 hours per week amount to

$$\frac{703,346}{56} = 12,560$$

The total number of rooms,

$$25,120 + 12,560 = 37,680$$

is shown in the "second alternative" column for year 18, Table 11-4.

Assuming that 1,406,692 periods are offered in 37,680 rooms, the average number of periods per room is

$$\frac{1,406,692}{37,680} = 37.33$$

This figure also appears in Table 11-4.

Knowing the average number of periods per room h, in years 0 and 18, we can now use the rate of growth between these two years to estimate h, for years 6 and 12. With these values and those of H, the target values of R for the second alternative are calculated (Table 11-4).

The third alternative is obtained by assuming that one-third of the periods H in year 18 will be offered in rooms used for 28 periods per week and two-thirds will be offered in rooms used for 56 hours per week. The results of this assumption are also given in Table 11-4. Again interpolation is used to estimate h, for years 6 and 12, and formula 4-8 is used to estimate R for these years.

There are two possibilities open to us in connection with these three alternatives: either to proceed with the analysis of all three or to select one from among them. Since at this stage we have no criteria for selecting among the three alternatives, we should proceed with the analysis of all three; but, although this would be essential in practice, it will suffice here to complete our analysis using the third alternative only.

Our problem, now, is to determine the sizes of classrooms and laboratories required to meet the provisional targets of the plan. This step is similar to that taken in analyzing the types of teachers required in the various qualitative strata. The method used below follows the lines of the method applied in Chapter 10 to teacher qualifications.

We must begin with the required distribution of the total number of rooms for year 18 among the different classroom size classifications. We use here the fact that in year 18 all rooms must have the characteristics of stratum A rooms in year −6. These characteristics are shown in Table 11-3 and indicate that in stratum A the proportion of rooms with between

3.3 and 3.8 square meters per pupil is

$$\frac{1,924}{2,020} = .952$$

If this proportion is to apply to the total number of elementary school rooms in year 18, the number of rooms with 3.3 to 3.8 square meters per pupil will have to be

$$0.952 \times 31,400 = 29,893$$

Since in year -6 the rooms in stratum A schools were in either the 0.8 to 1.3 square-meter classification or the 3.3 to 3.8 square meter classification and since the same conditions are to hold for the entire elementary school level in year 18, the number of rooms in the 0.8 to 1.3 square-meter interval can be established by a simple subtraction:

$$31,400 - 29,893 = 1,507$$

There are to be no rooms in any of the other intervals. These results are set out in Table 11-5.

Table 11-5. Planiland: Number and Sizes of Classrooms and Laboratories Required to Attain the Provisional Targets for Elementary Education (third alternative)

Meters per Student	Year			
	0	6	12	18
0.8–1.3 in A	96	294	573	1,507
0.8–1.3	1,565	1,044	522	0
1.3–1.8	350	233	116	0
1.8–2.3	1,771	1,182	592	0
2.3–2.8	2,730	1,820	910	0
2.8–3.3	2,980	1,987	994	0
3.3–3.8	3,520	10,580	20,629	29,893
Total	13,012	17,140	24,336	31,400

The next problem is to determine how the number of rooms in the four intervals between 1.3 and 3.3 square meters will decline between year 0 and year 18. The simplest approach is to assume that in each six-year period one-third of the rooms will cease to be used. With regard to the 2,730 rooms in the 2.3 to 2.8 square-meter interval, for instance,

$$\frac{1}{3} \times 2,730 = 910$$

rooms will go out of service between year 0 and year 6. Thus there will be

$$2,730 - 910 = 1,820$$

rooms in use in year 6, then 910 in year 12, and 0 in year 18.

The same method is applied to the other intervals between 1.3 and 3.3 square meters. For the 0.8 to 1.3 square-meter interval, the problem is more complicated. In year −6, there was a total of 2,280 rooms in that interval; but we cannot conclude that no rooms of this size need to be constructed between years 0 and 18. A glance at Table 11-3 indicates that 2,184 of these rooms were in stratum D schools; it is improbable that stratum D buildings can be used in year 18 since they will be too old and the rooms in the 0.8 to 1.3 square-meter interval must be in the same buildings as rooms in the 3.3 to 3.8 square-meter interval.

To sum up: the 1,565 rooms in the 0.8 to 1.3 square-meter interval in stratum D schools will be gradually abandoned between year 0 and year 18; while, on the other hand, the 96 stratum A rooms of this size must be increased to 1,507. We interpolate values for the number of 0.8 to 1.3 square-meter rooms in stratum D schools in years 6 and 12.

The foregoing observations indicate the danger involved in studying room requirements separately from school requirements. This methodological division simplifies the mathematical operations but we do not know the magnitude of the error thereby introduced.

Our last problem consists of determining the number of rooms required in the stratum A 0.8 to 1.3 and 3.3 to 3.8 intervals in years 6 and 12. In year 6, for example, a total of 17,140 rooms are needed. In the other room size intervals for year 6 (including stratum D 0.8 to 1.3 square-meter rooms) the number of rooms used will be

$$1,044 + 233 + 1,182 + 1,820 + 1,987 = 6,266$$

Thus for the two intervals with which we are concerned, the number of rooms needed in year 6 is

$$17,140 - 6,266 = 10,874$$

The division of the total figure of 10,874 between the two room sizes is made by maintaining the same proportional division as in year 0 when, out of a total of 3,616 rooms of the stratum A 0.8 to 1.3 and 3.3 to 3.8 square-meter intervals, there were 3,520 in the 3.3 to 3.8 square-meter interval, i.e., a proportion of

$$\frac{3,520}{3,616} = 0.973$$

By preserving the same proportion in year 6, we obtain the following for the number of 3.3 to 3.8 square-meter rooms:

$$0.973 \times 10,874 = 10,580$$

The number of rooms in the 0.8 to 1.3 interval may then be established through a simple subtraction:

$$10,874 - 10,580 = 294$$

A similar method is used for year 12; the results are given in Table 11-5.

11-4.2   High School Total Number of Rooms Needed

The method used to estimate the number and sizes of rooms required to meet provisional targets at high school level is similar to the method employed with respect to the elementary school level: the first step is to estimate the total number of rooms required and the second is to determine the sizes required.

Once again, three alternatives are considered in estimating the total number of rooms needed. In the first case, rooms in year 18 are assumed to be in use for the same number of periods as stratum **B** rooms in year −6; in the second case, half of the periods are assumed to be offered in rooms used for 32 hours per week and the other half in rooms used 64 hours per week; in the third case, one-third of the periods are assumed to be provided in rooms used for 32 hours per week and two-thirds in rooms used for 64 hours per week. Target values for these three alternatives are shown in Table 11-6.

Table 11-6.   Planiland: Number of Classrooms and Laboratories Required to Attain the Provisional Targets for High School Education

Year	Number of Periods of Education Offered H	First Alternative		Second Alternative		Third Alternative	
		Periods per Room h_r	Number of Rooms R	Periods per Room h_r	Number of Rooms R	Periods per Room h_r	Number of Rooms R
0	47,480.60	28.78	1,650	28.78	1,650	28.78	1,650
6	103,662.51	28.75	3,606	32.84	3,157	34.85	2,975
12	172,932.67	28.71	6,024	37.47	4,615	42.20	4,098
18	356,908.75	28.67	12,449	42.67	8,365	51.20	6,971

Required sizes of the rooms are set out in Table 11-7, with the calculations made for the third alternative only. In constructing this table, allowance was made for the fact that, in order to reach the educational output targets, all schools in year 18 must have at least the same facilities as stratum **B** schools had in year −6. It is also assumed that all strata A and B rooms in year 0 can be retained up to year 18 whereas this does not hold for strata C and D rooms, even if some of them may have characteristics in common with strata A and B rooms needed. For example, there are rooms providing between 0.8 and 1.3 square meters per student in strata A, B, and C; those in strata A and B can be retained but those in stratum C must be abandoned since the buildings themselves must be abandoned. The same applies to the rooms in intervals 1.3 to 1.8, 1.8 to 2.3 and 2.3 to 2.8.

Stratum A rooms are better than those required to meet the provisional targets and therefore will be not only retained but even increased in number although financial considerations may subsequently make it necessary to limit such increases.

Table 11-7.   Planiland: Number and Sizes of the Classrooms and Laboratories Required to Attain the Provisional Targets for High School Education (third alternative)

Square Meters per Student	Year			
	0	6	12	18
0.8–1.3 in A–B	61	151	229	411
0.8–1.3 in C	64	42	21	0
1.3–1.8 in C–D	123	82	41	0
1.8–2.3 in B	19	47	71	125
1.8–2.3 in C	340	226	113	0
2.3–2.8 in C	85	56	28	0
2.3–2.8 in A–B	485	1,200	1,820	3,258
2.8–3.3 in B	265	656	994	1,781
3.3–3.8 in A	208	515	781	1,396
Total	1,650	2,975	4,098	6,971

The procedure used in estimating the figures in Table 11-7 is identical to that employed above with respect to elementary schools.

11-4.3   College Total Number of Rooms Needed

Estimates of the number of rooms required to reach the provisional targets for the college level are presented in Table 11-8. Three alternatives are again considered.

Table 11-8.   Planiland: Number of Classrooms and Laboratories Required to Achieve the Provisional Targets for the College Level

Year	Number of Periods of Education Offered H	First Alternative		Second Alternative		Third Alternative	
		Periods per Room h_r	Number of Rooms R	Periods per Room h_r	Number of Rooms R	Periods per Room h_r	Number of Rooms R
0	5,516.39	16.35	337	16.35	337	16.35	337
6	8,008.33	16.35	482	20.45	385	22.00	358
12	12,609.63	16.35	759	25.59	485	29.62	419
18	22,055.22	16.35	1,327	32.00	678	40.00	542

The number of periods per week during which a room may be used at college level does not depend on the concentration of the population, in contrast to the case of the elementary and high school levels where some schools are in rural or semirural districts with enough students to justify no more than one shift.

All colleges are situated in cities but a limitation on hours of classroom utilization might nonetheless be imposed very often by the fact that large numbers of college students have jobs and find it difficult to attend classes during working hours.   Planners must therefore evaluate the possibility of inducing a change in this situation before determining the number of periods per week during which rooms may be used.

The operations used to obtain the values in Table 11-8 are identical with those used to calculate the value in Tables 11-4 and 11-6 for the elementary and high school levels.

It is easier in the case of the college level than in the case of elementary and high school levels to establish the sizes of rooms required because the conditions prevailing in year 0 must prevail in year 18. Thus, all that is necessary is to preserve the year 0 proportions in years 6, 12, and 18. Required numbers of different-sized classrooms are shown for the third alternative in Table 11-9.

Table 11-9. Planiland: Numbers and Sizes of the Classrooms and Laboratories Required to Attain the Provisional Targets for the College Level (third alternative)

Square Meters per Student	Year			
	0	6	12	18
2.3–2.8	9	10	11	14
2.8–3.3	32	34	40	51
3.3–3.8	199	211	247	320
3.8–4.3	97	103	121	157
Total	337	358	419	542

11-5   Some Additional Problems

Besides determining the numbers and sizes of the school rooms needed to achieve the provisional targets of the educational plan, the planner must solve other problems related to buildings and facilities.

One problem concerns the concentration of rooms for classes and laboratories. The choice is between small schools with a few single-section grades and large schools in which each grade is divided into several sections. The solution of this problem is closely related to the problem of the location of schools since, clearly, large schools are needed wherever there is a heavy concentration of the population.

There is then a second problem: the materials used in building schools and the frequency with which schools must be replaced. Brief comments will be made below with respect to these two problems.

11-5.1   Optimum Size and Location of a School

In determining the sizes of classes and the characteristics of classrooms and laboratories required to attain educational planning targets we have so far used the *quality* of education as our basic criterion.

However, if we shift our attention from classrooms to schools, the problem is rather different. It seems reasonable to assume that by itself the size of schools probably has little influence on educational quality or, at any rate, much less influence than the characteristics of teachers and rooms. Let us consider two schools, one with three times as many students as the other but both with teachers and rooms of similar characteristics and with the same number of students attending each period. The larger school has three first grades, three second grades and so on; the other has one of each. It would seem a justifiable conclusion that the quality of education in both schools is the same. Qualitative criteria therefore cannot be used to determine the appropriate size of schools. Any decision as to the size of schools is dependent on the decision as to the number of schools; and both decisions are closely related to the problem of location.

Since there is no qualitative criterion with which to determine size of schools, it may be asked why they should not be reduced to a minimum dimension—that is, one-grade schools or, conversely, enlarged to the maximum extent, one high school for the whole country. The reason for rejecting these extremes is obvious. When a school is unduly small, certain facilities such as laboratories and libraries are only partially utilized so that, for a given quality of education, excessively small schools are also excessively costly. On the other hand, if schools are unduly large, some students must travel long distances to school and there is thus a corresponding rise in transportation costs.

The problem confronting us is to find a way of minimizing the total costs involved in building and operating a school. What must be borne in mind is that it is worthwhile to enlarge a school to the point at which additional savings effected through a more rational use of equipment become less than the additional cost of transporting students from farther away.

In these calculations we must also consider the further complicating facts that transport costs are paid each day throughout the entire life of school buildings and that it is sometimes possible to provide substitutes for transport, such as student dormitories.

It is clear then that large schools are suitable for densely populated areas and small schools are suitable for areas with a sparse population. The question of the appropriate size for a school cannot, therefore, be decided unless something is known of the population in the area where it is to be located. Similarly, with respect to the ideal location of a school of a given size, a basic consideration is to reduce transport costs to a minimum.

It should be noted in this context that the cost of transporting students accounts for the vertical integration of schools; i.e., the fact that schools usually are composed of several grades rather than several sections of one grade. Within an area of reasonable size, it is easier to find enough students for several grades than for several sections of one grade.

Hence transportation costs will be lower in the case of vertically integrated schools. The need for such integration may be regarded merely as a particular form of the problem of optimum school size.

11-5.2 Determination of the Number and Location of Schools

The educational planner is familiar with the characteristics of the rooms that must be constructed, the relation between laboratory periods and class periods required to provide education of a certain quality, and the geographical distribution of the population. His problem now is to decide how to combine laboratories and classrooms to form school buildings so that the cost of constructing schools and transporting students is held to a minimum. His final solution should include the number of schools required, the facilities which each must possess; the number of students to be taught in each school and the geographic location of the schools.

Since we are concerned here with overall educational planning, we shall not pursue further such questions which are primarily of interest to those preparing detailed educational plans.

11-5.3 Determination of Materials to be Used in Constructing Schools

Specific details obviously cannot be given in this regard. Often the central planning authority should make the decision on type of construction, since materials suitable for one type of school in one area may not be suitable for other types of schools in other areas.

Nonetheless, all buildings have one characteristic in common: they must be maintained. Maintenance costs vary with the age of buildings and the materials used in their construction. As a general rule, the older the building and the lower the quality of the building materials, the higher the maintenance costs. Thus if construction costs are increased there is likely to be a long-run reduction in maintenance costs.

The planner, therefore, is confronted with the problem of balancing increased construction costs against reduced maintenance costs in order to find the type of construction which minimizes total costs in the long run.

References

Correa, H., "Optima for Size and Number of Schools," *Scientia Paedagogica Experimentalis*, Vol. 3, No. 1 (1966).

The approach described in this chapter is also used in
Correa, H., and E. Reimer, A Simulation Model for Education Planning in Puerto Rico. San Juan: Department of Public Instruction (Mimeographed), 1969.

Costing and Financing the Educational Plan

12-1 Content of This Chapter

In a study of the costs and financial aspects of an educational plan two basic elements must be considered: (a) the sources of the funds and (b) the uses of the funds. The method of analysis of these two aspects is similar to that of previous chapters. With respect to the sources of funds, we will study their characteristics in the past and the factors determining the funds available to education. Next, the relationship between the sources of the funds and the factors determining them must be established. With this information and that of the development of the determining factors, it is possible to project the funds that will be available to education. A similar analysis should be made with respect to the use of the funds.

An additional step is required in the study of sources and use of educational funds. The past relationships between sources and use must be analyzed.

With the studies described above, we will be able to estimate the cost of meeting the educational targets; then we will be in a position to determine if these costs can be met out of funds likely to be available to education.

If estimated values for funds needed and funds available are in harmony or if the difference between them is not too large, it is likely that it will be possible to finance the educational plan as it is. If this is not the case, it will be necessary to study the possibility of reducing the expenditures on education while still attaining the provisional targets. If this were not possible, the targets themselves might need to be revised.

Unfortunately, the revision process would not stop there. If the educational targets could not be attained, there might be bottlenecks of qualified manpower preventing the full implementation of the economic plan. Thus it might be necessary to revise the economic plan also. If the economic plan had to be revised, the initial estimate of resources available for education might also have to be altered. With this, we would be right back to the place where we started, and the process of successive approximations would have to be continued.

12-2   Past and Present Costs of Education

12-2.1   Cost Categories

Educational expenditures will be discussed below under three main headings: teachers, buildings, and equipment and other costs.

12-2.2   Past and Present Expenditures on Teachers

Figures on the number and qualifications of teachers and the number of hours that they teach in each of the levels of the educational system in Planiland were presented in Table 10-11. The data on salary per period for the teachers with different qualifications appear in Table 12-1. The

Table 12-1.   Planiland: Teachers' Salaries per Period
(thousands of year 0 dollars)

Line Nos., Table 10-11	Qualifications	Year		
		−12	−6	0
	Elementary School			
(1)	Graduates high school teachers' education	12.09	14.75	17.80
(2)	Graduates high school general education	9.25	11.25	13.75
(3)	Dropouts high school teachers' education	6.14	7.50	9.05
(4)	Dropouts high school general education	3.51	4.25	5.10
(5)	Graduates elementary school	3.05	3.75	4.25
(6)	Dropouts elementary school	2.99	3.50	4.00
	High School			
(7)	Graduates college teachers' education	20.30	25.00	30.25
(8)	Graduates college general education	20.42	25.00	30.25
(9)	Dropouts college teachers' education	16.35	20.00	25.00
(10)	Dropouts college general education	16.52	20.00	25.00
(11)	Graduates high school teachers' education	12.39	15.00	18.00
(12)	Graduates high school general education	9.95	12.00	14.25
(13)	Dropouts high school teachers' education	6.70	8.00	9.50
(14)	Dropouts high school general education	4.20	5.00	5.75
	College			
(15)	Graduates college teachers' education	40.00	50.00	60.50
(16)	Graduates college general education	40.00	50.00	60.50
(17)	Dropouts college teachers' education	25.00	30.00	36.00
(18)	Dropouts college general education	25.00	30.00	36.00
(19)	Graduates high school teachers' education	17.50	20.00	23.00

data in these two tables permit us to calculate the total amount paid to teachers in years − 12, − 6, and 0. The operations used for this calculation are so simple that they are not described. The results appear in Table 12-2.

Table 12-2.   *Planiland: Total Expenditures on Teachers' Salaries (thousands of year 0 dollars)*

Level	Year		
	− 12	− 6	0
Elementary school	67,765	134,713	267,201
High school	11,899	26,163	62,819
College	3,526	6,984	15,963

The study of past experience with regard to the expenditures on teachers' salaries does not end with the results presented in Table 12-2. Actually, the main objective of this analysis has not yet been attained since we have not discussed past relationships between expenditures on teachers' salaries and the main factors determining the level of these expenditures.

In the computation of the total expenditures for teachers' salaries, the main determinants of these expenditures were considered: i.e., number of teachers, number of periods that each teacher teaches and salary per period. In Chapter 10, remarks were made about the factors determining the demand for teachers, so attention will be paid here only to the question of salaries per period.

Economists in general and labor economists in particular have studied a great many factors determining the changes of salaries. When, in the preparation of an educational plan, the time comes to study teachers' salaries, it is advisable to consult the economists. However, if the planner cannot, for any reason, benefit from such expert advice, he himself can use the economists' most elementary technique: comparison of the rate of growth of teachers' salaries with the rate of growth of per capita income.

Table 12-3.   *Comparison of Growth Rates of Salaries of Type 1 Teachers with Growth Rates of Per Capita Income*

Year	Annual Salaries, Type 1 Teachers		Per Capita Income (Table 3-6)	
	Salaries	Rate of Growth	Income	Rate of Growth
− 12	17,306		2,299	
		0.241		0.210
− 6	21,476		2,783	
		0.207		0.203
0	25,917		3,349	

Such a comparison for salaries of teachers with qualification level 1 is presented in Table 12-3. We see that salaries for this type of teacher and per capita income have grown at almost the same rate. The same result can be obtained with regard to all other types of teachers. This information will be used in the estimation of the future growth of teachers' salaries per period.

12-2.3   Past and Present Expenditures for Buildings and Equipment Including Construction and Equipment

The numbers of classrooms and laboratories of different dimensions owned by the educational system was shown in Table 11-2. These figures permit us to estimate the number of rooms constructed and equipped in the periods between years −12 and −6 and between years −6 and 0. For this, we use two steps which will be explained with reference to the period between years −12 and −6. First, from the number of rooms in year −12, the number still in use in year −6 must be determined. Second, the number of rooms constructed can be found by subtracting from the number available in year −6 those surviving from year −12.

The first step is always more or less arbitrary. In some cases it is omitted, based on the assumption that a building well maintained will last forever. In any case, there is no scientific rule to determine the proportion of the buildings that will cease to be usable in any period. Here we have assumed that each building lasts 75 years and that over each six-year period 8 percent of the buildings cease to be useable. In Table 12-4, the number of surviving rooms and the number constructed in two periods between years −12 and 0 are presented.

In the same table the dollar costs of constructing and equipping classrooms and laboratories of different sizes are presented. It might seem surprising that the same prices are valid for construction in both the time periods considered. We should remark that we are dealing with "constant prices"; that is, the actual prices are deflated by means of a price index. Even in this case, it is likely that some changes in the prices will occur, but as a first approximation, if no other information is available, the prices of year 0 are taken as valid for years −6 and −12.

Another point that deserves comment is that the salaries of teachers measured in constant dollars change, while the costs of constructing buildings do not change. This might seem a contradiction, but actually it is the essence of welfare growth as measured in terms of per capita income in constant dollars. Real salaries increase because the productivity of labor increases; consequently the "constant dollar" prices of goods remain more or less unchanged.

Multiplying cost per room by the number of rooms constructed and equipped, we calculate total expenditure on construction and equipment in six years. A rough estimate of expenditure in one year is obtained by

Table 12-4.   Planiland: Classrooms and Laboratories
Constructed and Equipped

Size, Square Meters per Student	Construction Cost per Unit (year 0 dollars)	Between −12 and −6		Between −6 and 0	
		Surviving from −12 in −6	Constructed in Period	Surviving from −6 in 0	Constructed in Period
Elementary School					
0.8–1.3	10,822	1,320	661	1,822	
1.3–1.8	17,927	—	—	—	
1.8–2.3	25,032	1,144	371	1,394	
2.3–2.8	31,138	356	121	439	1,901
2.8–3.3	38,243	620	740	1,251	1,729
3.3–3.8	45,349	938	986	1,770	1,750
Total			2,879		5,380
High School					
0.8–1.3	13,385	74	36	101	9
1.3–1.8	21,513	31	14	41	—
1.8–2.3	30,027	151	92	223	8
2.3–2.8	27,363	38	57	87	483
2.8–3.3	45,689	44	81	115	150
3.3–3.8	54,015	49	94	132	76
Total			374		726
College					
2.3–2.8	39,800	10	—	8	1
2.8–3.3	49,791	17	5	20	12
3.3–3.8	57,954	67	43	101	98
3.8–4.3	68,116	14	29	40	57
Total			77		168

dividing the six-year totals by six. Estimates of yearly construction expenditures for years −6 and 0 may be made in this way.

This method cannot be used to make estimates for year −12. Data for this year must be obtained from other sources. Yearly construction figures for all three years are in Table 12-5.

Table 12-5.   Planiland: Estimated Annual Expenditure for
Construction (thousands of year 0 dollars)

Level	Year		
	−12	−6	0
Elementary school	8,324	15,537	34,106
High school	976	2,409	4,894
College	311	786	1,700

Expenditures for renting classrooms and other equipment

In Table 11-2 we see that some of the facilities used by the educational system are rented. Figures on the rents paid are presented in Table 12-6; the total amounts of rental payments are given in Table 12-7. The rents per room in years -12, -6, and 0 are constant as were the construction costs, and for a similar reason.

Table 12-6. Planiland: Yearly Rent per Room for Years
-12, -6, and 0 (thousands of year 0 dollars)

Size, Square Meters per Student	Rents
Elementary School	
0.8–1.3	541
1.3–1.8	896
1.8–2.3	1,252
2.3–2.8	1,557
High School	
0.8–1.3	669
1.3–1.8	1,075
1.8–2.3	1,502

Table 12-7. Planiland: Annual Expenditures on Rent
(thousands of year 0 dollars)

Level	Year		
	-12	-6	0
Elementary school	696	1,101	1,763
High school	120	188	291
College	—	—	—

Maintenance expenditures

The information available on maintenance expenditures in Planiland is presented in Table 12-8.

Table 12-8. Planiland: Maintenance Expenditures
(thousands of year 0 dollars)

Level	Year		
	-12	-6	0
Elementary school	3,923	6,404	11,758
High school	399	711	1,617
College	322	323	601

12-2.4   Other Expenditures

In Table 12-9 figures on all the categories of expenditures not previously considered are presented. No special analysis of the information
in this table is required.

Table 12-9.   Other Current Expenditures
(thousands of year 0 dollars)

Type of Expenditure	Year		
	−12	−6	0
Elementary School			
Supervision	4,973	6,585	7,913
Administration	13,937	20,666	27,816
School materials	8,297	10,984	13,200
Libraries	7,543	9,985	12,000
Restaurants for students	15,765	17,450	25,080
Board for students	—	—	—
Scholarships	—	—	—
Total	50,525	65,670	86,009
High School			
Supervision	2,234	3,814	5,242
Administration	7,299	13,424	21,504
School materials	1,397	2,294	3,281
Libraries	984	1,616	2,312
Restaurants for students	—	—	—
Board for students	1,995	3,405	4,680
Scholarships	2,236	3,668	5,248
Total	16,145	28,221	42,267
College			
Supervision	420	706	1,176
Administration	1,824	3,285	6,233
School materials	181	291	493
Libraries	80	130	220
Restaurants	—	—	—
Board for students	375	630	1,050
Scholarships	363	583	985
Total	3,243	5,625	10,157

12-2.5   Summary

A summary of the results presented in Tables 12-2, 12-5, 12-7, and
12-9 appears in Table 12-10. In this table, the total expenditures by level
of education and the total expenditures on education in Planiland are
presented.

Table 12-10.   *Planiland: Total Educational Expenditure*
(thousands of year 0 dollars)

Type of Expenditure	Year		
	−12	−6	0
Elementary School			
Teachers	67,765	134,713	267,201
Other current	50,525	65,670	86,009
Rents	696	1,101	1,763
Maintenance	3,923	6,404	11,758
Construction	8,324	15,537	34,106
Total	131,233	223,425	400,837
High School			
Teachers	11,899	26,163	62,819
Other current	16,165	28,221	42,267
Rents	120	188	291
Maintenance	399	711	1,617
Construction	976	2,409	4,894
Total	29,559	57,692	111,888
College			
Teachers	3,526	6,984	15,963
Other current	3,243	5,625	10,157
Rents	—	—	—
Maintenance	322	323	601
Construction	311	786	1,700
Total	168,194	294,835	541,146

12-3   Past and Present Sources of the Funds Used in Education

The contributions from different sources to past educational expenditure appear in Table 12-11. A main subdivision is that between national and foreign sources. The funds from national sources can come from

Table 12-11.   *Planiland: Sources of the Funds Used in Education*
(thousands of year 0 dollars)

Sources	Year		
	−12	−6	0
Total National	143,301	237,342	412,894
Government	133,413	206,250	330,728
Private·	9,888	31,092	82,166
Total Foreign Aid	24,894	57,493	128,252
Bilateral	15,011	34,151	78,490
Multilateral	9,883	23,342	49,762
Total	168,194	294,835	541,146

Table 12-12.   Planiland: Sources and Uses of Educational Funds (thousands of year 0 dollars)

Sources	Elementary School			High School			College			Total
	Current	Capital	Total	Current	Capital	Total	Current	Capital	Total	
Government sector	301,899	13,504	315,403	10,298	1,514	11,812	3,513	—	3,513	330,728
Private sector	64,832	3,773	68,605	13,210	351	13,561	—	—	—	82,166
National total	366,731	17,277	384,008	23,508	1,865	25,373	3,513	—	3,513	412,894
Bilateral foreign aid	—	13,830	13,830	47,152	1,199	48,351	14,809	1,700	16,309	78,490
Multilateral foreign aid	—	2,999	2,999	36,324	1,830	38,164	8,599	—	8,599	49,762
Foreign aid total	—	16,829	16,829	83,486	3,029	86,515	23,208	1,700	24,908	128,252
Grand total	366,731	34,106	400,837	106,994	4,894	111,888	26,721	1,700	28,421	541,146

either the government or private citizens and organizations. In some cases, it may be useful to subdivide further government funds into those from the national government and those from provincial and local governments. However, this additional subdivision does not appear in Table 12-11.

Foreign assistance for education may come from either bilateral or multilateral aid-giving agencies. Bilateral foreign aid is that given by one country to another; multilateral aid is that given by an international organization such as UNESCO, ILO, or the World Bank (IBRD). A more detailed analysis of the data in Table 12-11 for year 0 is presented in Table 12-12.

The main reason for the study of the sources of funds used in education is to analyze the factors influencing the amount of money available for education.

One of the main determinants of the expenditure on education from national sources is the total amount of national output, i.e., GDP. A comparison of national expenditure on education and GDP appears in Table 12-13. In the same table, the expenditures from the public and pri-

Table 12-13. Planiland: Comparison of National Resources Available and Expenditures on Education (millions of year 0 dollars)

Year	Total Economy			Public Sector			Private Sector		
	GDP a	Education b	$\frac{b}{a} \times 100$	Total c	Education d	$\frac{d}{c} \times 100$	Total e	Education f	$\frac{f}{e} \times 100$
−12	6,805	143	2.10	1,194	133	11.13	5,611	10	0.18
−6	9,782	237	2.42	1,762	206	11.69	8,020	31	0.39
0	13,932	413	2.96	2,492	331	13.28	11,440	82	0.72

vate sectors (elaborated from Tables 3-2 and 3-3) are compared with the total resources available to each sector. In some cases it is useful to divide even further the items in Table 12-13; for example, all items in the table could be subdivided into investment, on the one hand, and consumption and current expenditure, on the other.

The results in Table 12-13 will be used for estimating the future automatic development of the resources available for education.

12-4   Educational Expenditures Required to Attain the Targets of the Educational Plan

12-4.1   Expenditures for Teachers

To estimate the expenditures on teachers required to attain the targets of the educational plan, we must have three sets of information:
(a) Number and qualifications of teachers required in years 0, 6, 12, and

18. This information, obtained in Sec. 10-4.3, appears in Tables 10-14, 10-16, and 10-19.
(b) Future development of the number of periods taught by teachers of the different types. This information is presented in Tables 10-17 and 10-20.
(c) Future development of the salaries per period for the teachers of the different types. This information is obtained below.

Future development of teachers' salaries

For an estimate of the required expenditures on teachers, a projection of the future development of teachers' salaries is needed. In Sec. 12-2.2 we noted that the person best qualified to prepare such a projection is a labor economist. Here, only the most elementary method used by labor economists will be employed.

In Table 12-3 the rate of growth of the salaries of teachers of type 1 was compared with the rate of growth of per capita income. Commenting

Table 12-14.   Planiland: Future Development of Salaries Per Period (year 0 dollars)

Line Nos., Table 10-11	Qualifications	Year		
		6	12	18
	Elementary School			
(1)	Graduates high school teachers' education	21.64	26.36	32.10
(2)	Graduates high school general education	16.72	20.36	24.80
(3)	Dropouts high school teachers' education	11.00	13.40	16.32
(4)	Dropouts high school general education	6.20	7.55	9.20
(5)	Graduates elementary school	5.17	6.30	7.67
(6)	Dropouts elementary school	4.86	5.92	7.21
	High School			
(7)	Graduates college teachers' education	36.78	44.80	54.56
(8)	Graduates college general education	36.78	44.80	54.56
(9)	Dropouts college teachers' education	30.40	37.03	45.10
(10)	Dropouts college general education	30.40	37.03	45.10
(11)	Graduates high school teachers' education	21.89	26.66	32.47
(12)	Graduates high school general education	17.33	21.11	25.71
(13)	Dropouts high school teachers' education	11.55	14.07	17.13
(14)	Dropouts high school general education	6.99	8.51	10.37
	College			
(15)	Graduates college teachers' education	73.57	89.61	109.14
(16)	Graduates college general education	73.57	89.61	109.14
(17)	Dropouts college teachers' education	43.78	53.32	64.95
(18)	Dropouts college general education	43.78	53.32	64.95
(19)	Graduates high school teachers' education	27.97	34.07	41.49

on this comparison, we observed that the salaries of all types of teachers in Planiland grew in the past at a rate similar to the growth rate of per capita income. For this reason, the estimates of the future development of teachers' salaries are made on the assumption that teachers' salaries will grow in the future at the same rate as per capita income. These projections of teachers' future salaries appear in Table 12-14.

It is probable that in some countries the rates of growth of the salaries of teachers is different from the rate of growth of per capita income. In this case, it is advisable to use the elasticities of the teachers salaries with respect to per capita income. These elasticities are

$$\frac{\text{Rate of growth of teachers salaries}}{\text{Rate of growth of per capita income}}$$

Since the use of elasticities to estimate the future values of a variable has been explained several times, no further elaboration of this procedure is presented here.

Estimation of future expenditures on teachers

There is no need to explain the operations used to estimate the required expenditures for teachers. The projections appear in Table 12-15.

Table 12-15. Planiland: Expenditures on Teachers' Salaries Required to Attain the Targets of the Educational Plan (thousands of year 0 dollars)

Level	Year		
	6	12	18
Elementary school	560,386	1,179,987	2,227,813
High school	179,200	379,045	973,753
College	28,190	54,043	115,134

12-4.2   Expenditures for Buildings and Other Equipment

In Sec. 11-3 the number of rooms required to attain the targets of the educational plan was estimated; such estimates may be found in Tables 11-5, 11-7, and 11-9. Using these figures, we must estimate construction and equipment costs, expenditures in rents and maintenance costs over future years.

Expenditures on construction, equipment, and rents

To pass from the data concerning the number of rooms and laboratories needed to an estimate of construction and equipment costs, two sets of estimates are necessary: the number of rooms that must be constructed in future years and the future construction and equipment costs per room. With these, we may proceed to the determination of the total expenditures for construction and equipment necessary to attain the targets of the educational plan.

Number of rooms that must be constructed

In order to estimate the number of rooms that must be constructed, we need to know the proportion of new rooms that will be rented rather than owned. We assume here that, as a matter of policy, all the new rooms required for the educational system will be owned. The rooms rented in previous years can be maintained if required; but, if a new room of a specified type is required, it must be constructed. With this assumption it is possible for us to determine the number of rooms that will have to be constructed as well as the number of rooms that will have to be rented. The steps required are explained with respect to the rooms to be constructed for elementary school between years 0 and 6.

The first step for this estimation is to determine the number of rooms existing in year 0 which will still be usable in year 6. The methods used for this estimation and their limitations are discussed in Sec. 12-2.3.

Next, comparing the number of year 0 rooms being used in year 6 to the number required in year 6 (see Tables 11-5, 11-7, and 11-9), we can determine the number of rooms that have to be constructed, rented and abandoned between years 0 and 6. These figures are all found in Table 12-16.

Future development of construction and equipment costs and of rents

As mentioned in Sec. 12-2.3, the use of year 0 dollar prices of goods and services in cost calculations allows us to suppose that the construction and equipment costs and rents in future years will remain at about the same level as in year 0. Hence, the values in Table 12-4 for construction and equipment costs and in Table 12-6 for rents will be assumed to be the values prevailing up to year 18.

It should be observed that the construction and equipment costs given in Table 12-4 include the cost of the land on which buildings are built. However, some of the new buildings to be constructed to achieve the targets of the educational plan might be constructed on land already owned by the educational system. But, in this case other special types of expenditure are likely to be required. Since the computations in this book are intended to give an approximate picture, no modifications are introduced to handle such complications.

The data introduced above permit us to estimate construction and equipment costs for six-year periods. As before, a rough estimation of yearly costs is obtained by dividing the six-year values by six. Estimated yearly cost figures appear in Table 12-17.

Table 12-16. Planiland: Number of Classrooms and Laboratories That Must be Constructed to Attain the Targets of the Educational Plan

Square Meters per Student	Between 0 and 6				Between 6 and 12				Between 12 and 18			
	Surviving Year 6 from Year 0	Required	New to be Constructed	Rented	Surviving Year 12 from Year 6	Required	New to be Constructed	Rented	Surviving Year 18 to Year 12	Required	New to be Constructed	Rented
Elementary School												
0.8–1.3 in A	88	294	206	—	270	573	303	—	527	1,507	980	—
0.8–1.3 not in A	1,242	1,044	—	—	960	552	—	—	480	—	—	—
1.3–1.8	—	233	—	233	—	116	—	116	—	—	—	—
1.8–2.3	1,096	1,182	—	86	1,008	592	—	—	545	—	—	—
2.3–2.8	2,153	1,820	—	—	1,674	910	—	—	837	—	—	—
2.8–3.3	2,742	1,987	—	—	1,800	994	—	—	914	—	—	—
3.3–3.8	3,238	10,580	7,342	—	9,734	20,629	10,859	—	18,979	29,893	10,914	—
High School												
0.8–1.3 in A–B	56	151	95	—	139	229	90	—	211	411	200	—
0.8–1.3 in C	45	42	—	—	39	21	—	—	19	—	—	—
1.3–1.8 in C–D	37	82	—	45	34	41	—	7	31	125	60	—
1.8–2.3 in B	17	47	30	—	43	71	28	—	65	—	—	—
1.8–2.3 in C	195	226	—	31	179	113	—	—	104	—	—	—
2.3–2.8 in C	446	1,200	754	—	1,104	1,820	716	—	1,674	3,258	1,584	—
2.3–2.8 in A–B	78	56	—	—	52	28	—	—	26	—	—	—
2.8–3.3 in B	244	656	412	—	604	994	390	—	914	1,781	867	—
3.3–3.8 in A	191	515	324	—	474	781	307	—	719	1,396	677	—
College												
2.3–2.8	8	10	2	—	9	11	2	—	10	14	4	—
2.8–3.3	29	34	5	—	31	40	9	—	37	51	14	—
3.3–3.8	183	211	28	—	194	247	53	—	227	320	93	—
3.8–4.3	89	103	14	—	95	121	26	—	111	157	46	—

*Table 12-17.   Planiland: Construction and Equipment Expenditure and
Rental Payments Required to Attain the Targets of the Educational Plan
(thousands of year 0 dollars)*

Level	Year					
	6		12		18	
	Construc-tion	Rent	Construc-tion	Rent	Construc-tion	Rent
Elementary school	55,640	316	82,283	104	83,920	—
High school	11,067	95	10,491	7	23,214	—
College	482	—	891	—	1,557	—

Maintenance costs

The data in Table 12-8 permit us to evaluate maintenance costs per classroom in years −12, −6, and 0. Figures for these costs appear in Table 12-18.

*Table 12-18.   Planiland: Maintenance Costs per Room
(thousands of year 0 dollars)*

Year	Elementary School			High School			College		
	Total	Number of Rooms, Table 11-3	Dollars per Room	Total	Number of Rooms, Table 11-3	Dollars per Room	Total	Number of Rooms, Table 11-3	Dollars per Room
−12	3,923	4,760	824	399	420	950	322	178	1,809
−6	6,404	7,757	882	711	761	934	323	184	1,755
0	11,758	11,477	1,024	1,617	1,424	1,135	601	337	1,783

For the estimation of future maintenance costs it is assumed that the level of costs prevailing in year 0 will hold for future years. Table 12-18 shows that per room maintenance costs in constant dollars generally rose over past years; but with a higher proportion of new buildings after year 0, average maintenance costs should not continue to rise. Hence, year 0 cost levels can be used in rough estimates of future maintenance costs.

*Table 12-19.   Planiland: Maintenance Expenditure Required to
Attain the Targets of the Educational Plan
(thousands of year 0 dollars)*

Level	Year		
	6	12	18
Elementary school	17,551	24,920	32,154
High school	3,377	4,651	7,912
College	638	747	966

With figures for maintenance costs per room and the number of rooms needed to attain the provisional targets of the educational plan, it is possible to estimate the total maintenance costs in future years. Such estimates appear in Table 12-19.

12-4.3   Other Expenditures

Finally, we have to estimate the amount of "other expenditures" required to attain the targets of the educational plan. To do so, the most appropriate method would be to study the factors determining these expenditures, the relationship between these factors and the expenditures, and the future changes in the determining factors. That is, to estimate the future changes of the other expenditures we should apply the method that we used for estimating the cost of teachers and buildings.

However, in this book we will obtain a first rough approximation on the assumption that the "other expenditures" maintain a constant relationship to total expenditure on teachers and buildings.

The relationships holding in past years are shown in the left half of Table 12-20. Assuming that the proportion observed in year 0 will be maintained in the future, it is possible to estimate "other expenditures" in years 6, 12, and 18. These estimates are presented in the right half of Table 12-20.

12-4.4   Summary of the Previous Estimates of Expenditures Required to Attain the Targets of the Educational Plan

A summary of the results presented in previous tables appears in Table 12-21.

12-5   Sources of the Funds Required to Attain the Targets of the Educational Plan

12-5.1   Introduction

A very important step in the preparation of an educational plan is the study of the possibility of obtaining the funds required to attain the targets of the plan. For this, it is necessary to estimate the future changes in the funds available for education, on the assumption that conditions similar to those existing in the past will exist in the future. This kind of estimation is called here "automatic projection."

12-5.2   Automatic Projection of the National Funds Available for Education

In Table 12-13, expenditures on education from total national production, the public sector and the private sector, were compared to GDP,

Table 12-20.   Planiland: "Other Expenditure" Past Experience and Value Required to Attain Targets of the Plan
(thousands of year 0 dollars)

Type of Expenditure	Years					
	-12	-6	0	6	12	18
			Elementary			
(a) Other current	50,525	65,670	86,009	173,053	351,429	639,881
(b) Teachers and buildings	80,708	157,755	314,828	633,893	1,287,285	2,343,887
a/b	0.626	0.416	0.273	0.273	0.273	0.273
			High School			
(a) Other current	16,165	28,221	42,267	117,600	239,276	609,962
(b) Teachers and buildings	13,394	29,471	69,621	193,739	394,194	1,004,879
a/b	1.206	0.957	0.607	0.607	0.607	0.607
			College			
(a) Other current	3,243	5,625	10,157	16,296	30,959	65,417
(b) Teachers and buildings	4,159	8,093	18,264	29,310	55,681	117,657
a/b	0.779	0.695	0.556	0.556	0.556	0.556

Table 12-21.   Planiland: Total Expenditures Required to Attain the Targets of the Educational Plan (thousands of year 0 dollars)

Type of Expenditure	Year		
	6	12	18
Elementary School			
Teachers	560,386	1,179,978	2,227,813
Other current	173,053	351,429	639,881
Rents	316	104	—
Maintenance	17,551	24,920	32,154
Construction	55,640	82,283	83,920
Total	806,946	1,638,714	2,983,768
High School			
Teachers	179,200	379,045	973,753
Other current	117,600	239,276	609,962
Rents	95	7	—
Maintenance	3,377	4,651	7,912
Construction	11,067	10,491	23,214
Total	311,339	633,470	1,614,841
College			
Teachers	28,190	54,043	115,134
Other current	16,296	30,959	65,417
Rents	—	—	—
Maintenance	638	747	966
Construction	482	891	1,557
Total	45,606	86,640	183,074
Grand total	1,163,891	2,358,824	4,781,683

total governmental expenditure and total private expenditure.   Since public and private education expenditures seem to follow two different growth patterns, it is better to make separate projections for public and private expenditures on education.

The division of GDP into public and private sectors is the concern of the economists.   The division of the Planiland GDP was shown in Table 3-9.

Private and public resources likely to be available for education are projected using elasticities.   The details of the method have already been explained and do not need to be repeated here.   The values of the elasticities used are presented in Table 12-22.   The projections of national funds available for education are shown in Table 12-23.

In order to judge the reliability of the results in Table 12-23, it is useful to compare them with data from other countries.   From such comparisons, it can be seen that the proportion of national resources available

Table 12-22

Average Elasticity of Private Funds Available to Education with Respect to Total Private Resources	Average Elasticity of Public Funds Available to Education with Respect to Total Public Resources
4.378	1.308

for education is projected to reach levels higher than proportions found in most of the countries of the world. The reason for this is that the rapid past growth in the private resources for education in Planiland is assumed to continue in the future. It may be decided that a more refined projection of the national resources available to education is required. However, this and other refinements should wait until the complete picture is drawn; at that time, we will have some idea of the financial feasibility or unfeasibility of the plan.

Table 12-23. *Planiland: Projection of National Resources Available for Education (millions of year 0 dollars)*

Year	Total Economy			Public Sector			Private Sector		
	GDP a	Education b	$\frac{b}{a} \times 100$	Total c	Education d	$\frac{d}{c} \times 100$	Total e	Education f	$\frac{f}{e} \times 100$
6	19,782	760	3.84	3,620	530	14.64	16,162	230	1.42
12	28,098	1,480	5.26	5,226	835	15.97	22,872	645	2.82
18	39,885	3,143	7.88	7,658	1,343	17.53	32,227	1,800	5.58

12-5.3 Automatic Projection of Foreign Aid Funds Available for Education

To project the future amounts of foreign aid for education, we need to know the factors determining the amount of foreign aid for education received. Unfortunately no study of these determining factors is available.

The method to be used here can serve for a rough first approximation. We make the assumption that the aid-giving countries try to match the efforts of the aid-receiving country. Thus the growth of foreign aid is related to the increase in the amount of national resources devoted to education. In this case, the elasticity of foreign aid with respect to na-

Table 12-24. Planiland: Automatic Projection of Foreign Aid for Education (millions of year 0 dollars)

Year	Value
6	325
12	889
18	2,704

tional expenditures on education is used; its value is 1.829. Using this elasticity, we obtain the projected values shown in Table 12-24.

12-5.4 Summary

In Table 12-25, the automatic projection of total funds available for education is presented.

Table 12-25. Planiland: Automatic Projection of Funds Available for Education (millions of year 0 dollars)

Year	Total	National	Foreign Aid
6	1,085	760	325
12	2,369	1,480	889
18	5,847	3,143	2,704

12-6 Study of the Financial Feasibility of the Plan

In Table 12-21, the total expenditures necessary to attain the targets of the educational plan were calculated. In Table 12-25, the automatic projection of the resources that can be used in education is presented. A comparison of the two sets of information is made in Table 12-26.

The results shown in this table give reasons for an optimistic attitude toward the problem of the financial feasibility of the educational plan. At least we see that no major revision of the targets is required.

Table 12-26. Planiland: Comparison of the Resources Required to Attain the Targets of the Educational Plan and the Automatic Properties of the Resources Available (millions of year 0 dollars)

Year	Resources Required (Table 12-21)	Resources Available (Table 12-25)
6	1,164	1,085
12	2,359	2,369
18	4,782	5,847

However, we must remember that the automatic projection of resources available for the plan has several serious defects. For this reason, a wise policy is to accept the provisional targets introduced in Chapter 12 while making every possible effort to reduce costs.

References

General studies on costs and educational finance appear in

Benson, C. S., *The Economics of Public Education*. Boston: Houghton Mifflin, 1968.
Vaizey, J., *The Costs of Education*. London: Allen and Unwin, 1958.

On foreign aid:

Cerych, L., *Problems of Aid to Education in Developing Countries.* New York: Praeger, 1965.

An application of the method of analysis presented in this chapter appears in

Poignant, R., and J. Hallak, *Les Aspects Financiers de l'Education en Côte-d'Ivoire.* Paris: UNESCO, 1966.

A computerized version of the model in this chapter appears in

Correa, H., and H. Reimer, *A Simulation Model for Educational Planning in Puerto Rico.* San Juan: Department of Public Instruction (Mineographed), 1969.

chapter 13

Planning When Alternative Ways to Achieve the Targets Are Explicitly Considered

13-1 Approaches to the Technical Preparation of a Plan
Content of This Chapter

In Chapter 1 it was mentioned that two approaches can be used in the technical preparation of a plan. The first one has been presented in the previous chapters where it is assumed that there is only one way to obtain the desired ends. For instance, in the chapter dealing with manpower requirements, no attention is paid to the possibility of substitution between persons with different kinds of qualifications. In the chapter dealing with costs, the possibility of reducing costs using different educational methods is not even raised. Actually, similar examples can be presented with respect to the topic of each one of the chapters of this book.

Another limitation of the previous chapters is that they omit one of the main problems of educational planning and its integration with economic planning; that is, the problem of adaptation to limited human and financial resources. When the targets for the economic plan and those for the educational plan were set, it was observed that these targets were provisional because it was not known if there would be enough human and financial resources to reach them. Step by step we verified that there were such resources. First, we saw that the level of enrollment was high enough to provide the educated personnel required by the economy. Next, the availability of teachers was verified, and, finally, that of financial resources. However, this process of verification was made somewhat outside the main trend of the analysis. In addition, there is no clearly outlined approach when it is found that, for example, the number of professors available will not be enough to attain the targets for enrollment. In the extreme case, it is necessary to revise downward the enrollment targets; but no practical method to do so is presented in the previous pages. The only possibility is a time-consuming trial-and-error approach.

In the second approach to the technical preparation of a plan, the different methods to obtain a desired end and the limitations of resources are explicitly taken into consideration, with the purpose of selecting the best possible method for the objectives in mind. A simple example which shows the characteristics and possibilities of this approach is presented below. Limitations of space do not permit us to go into all the details of this second approach. The interested reader should consult the references at the end of this chapter.

13-2   Quantity Versus Quality in Teachers' Education

In this section one of the mathematical techniques used to study the problem of choice among alternatives is applied to the problem of choice between quantity and quality in teachers' education.

Three main steps must be considered in the statement of the problem. The first is to define with precision the product of education; it should be noted that it is always possible to make a definition useful for practical purposes. The second step is to relate the product of education to the inputs used to obtain it. Finally, the cost of the inputs and the limitations on financial resources are considered.

Below, to simplify the analysis, we assume that it is possible to train two types of teachers. The first are well qualified, the second not so well qualified. The cost of training these two types is not the same; it will be more expensive to train the qualified type than the nonqualified type.

In order to be able to choose between these two types of teacher training, it is necessary to relate them to the product of education. It is assumed that a group of students enrolls and without any dropouts attends school up to a certain level. Once this level is reached, all of the would-be dropouts actually leave school. The reduced group continues in school until graduation. Thus

n_i = number of students who can be enrolled using teachers of type i, part of whom will drop out later, $i = 1, 2$

g_i = number of students who can be graduated with teachers of type i

The distinction between the number of students enrolled up to a certain level and the number of graduates does not characterize with enough precision the product of education. A simple method to quantify the qualitative differences among the different types of graduates and dropouts is to consider the income that they will receive.

In Table 13-1 the income levels of dropouts and graduates from educational types 1 and 2 are presented.

*Table 13-1.   Lifetime Income for Persons
with Different Types of Education
(thousands of dollars)*

Level of Education	Type of Education	
	Type 1	Type 2
Dropouts	180	150
Graduates	250	200

With the income figures in Table 13-1 the total product of education is

$$Z = 180n_1 + 70g_1 + 150n_2 + 50g_2 \qquad (13\text{-}1)$$

In Eq. 13-1 we use 50 and 70 as coefficients of the number of graduates g_1 and g_2 because it is simpler to consider the graduates and the dropouts together forming total enrollment n_i. Thus, to the total income obtained by those enrolled, the additional income of those graduating is added. With this, Z in Eq. 13-1 represents total income to be produced by the educated persons.

Educators will not be happy about using income as a measure of the quality of education, and there is no need to do so. Another simple measurement would be years of study. In this case, if one graduate attends school for six years and one dropout three, one graduate is worth twice as much as one dropout. The meaning of Z, then, in Eq. 13-1 will be the total number of years in school.

If the number of years spent in school are not equivalent, it could be said, for instance, that one year with type 1 teachers is equivalent to 1.5 years with type 2 teachers. Corrections of this sort can be introduced until the person who must make the decision is satisfied. In principle, this is possible as long as criticism of one measure is accompanied by some idea of how it can be improved. In any case, the mathematical method would be the same as that already used; that is, the number of graduates and total enrollment will be multiplied by some weights. Thus Eq. 13-1 is general. The coefficients of n_i and g_i must be known if teacher training is to be evaluated and a choice among the different types of teacher training must be made. Perhaps a useful task would be to find the best possible weights to be used under different circumstances.

Once the function Z is defined, that is, once appropriate weights have been found, the optimum use of the resources available for teacher training can be clearly stated. This optimum use is to maximize Z. There is no question about the usefulness of this procedure if the coefficients have been properly defined.

Another of the differences caused by the different types of teacher training is in the maximum proportion of graduates that can be obtained from a given enrollment. Let us suppose that at most 70 percent of the student teachers of type 1 and 50 percent of the students having teachers with type 2 reach graduation level. These proportions are characteristics of the methods used for training teachers; they are assumed to be known. The fact that they are the maximum proportion of graduates means that

$$g_1 \leq 0.7n_1 \tag{13-2}$$

$$g_2 \leq 0.5n_2 \tag{13-3}$$

The main characteristics of the product of education have been considered. Now it is necessary to relate the desired output to the factor or factors that will be used to produce them. To simplify the problem, here teachers are considered to be the only factor.

To establish the relationship between output and input, the weighted student-teacher ratio will be used. From the weighted student-teacher ratio, it is possible to obtain the coefficient relating the number of teachers to the number of students. The procedure was explained in Chapter 10. Let us suppose that $1/50$ is the coefficient for teachers of type 1 and $1/40$ for teachers of type 2. These values permit us to find that the number of teachers of type 1 required is

$$\frac{n_1}{50}$$

and that of type 2 is

$$\frac{n_2}{40}$$

The third step in our analysis is to relate the required input of teachers to costs and financial limitations. Let us suppose that $250,000 and $200,000 are the costs of teachers of types 1 and 2 respectively. In these costs, the training and salaries are included. For training only the part corresponding to a six-year period is considered since that is the time the student will spend in the school level under consideration.

Hence, the total cost of the teacher will be

$$250,000 \frac{n_1}{50} + 200,000 \frac{n_2}{40}$$

That is,

$$5,000n_1 + 5,000n_2$$

Finally, let us assume that 100 million dollars are available for the level of education under consideration over the six-year period. Hence, the following condition must be satisfied by the costs:

$$5{,}000n_1 + 5{,}000n_2 \leq 100{,}000{,}000$$

That is,

$$5n_1 + 5n_2 \leq 100{,}000 \qquad (13\text{-}4)$$

At this stage, it is useful to summarize the problem; it is to maximize

$$Z = 180n_1 + 70g_1 + 150n_2 + 50g_2 \qquad [13\text{-}1]$$

subject to

$$g_1 \leq 0.7n_1 \qquad [13\text{-}2]$$
$$g_2 \leq 0.5n_2 \qquad [13\text{-}3]$$
$$5n_1 + 5n_2 \leq 100{,}000 \qquad [13\text{-}4]$$
$$n_i \geq 0 \qquad g_i \geq 0. \qquad (13\text{-}5)$$

The mathematical process for solving the model in Eqs. 13-1 to 13-5 will not be presented here. Rather, we shall use an intuitive approach.

Let us first consider conditions 13-2 and 13-3. We can observe that by increasing the number of graduates g_1 and g_2 we increase Z; therefore, it is advisable to do so. The maximum number of graduates that can be produced is

$$g_1 = 0.7n_1 \qquad (13\text{-}6)$$
$$g_2 = 0.5n_2 \qquad (13\text{-}7)$$

Thus, instead of the conditions 13-2 and 13-3, Eqs. 13-6 and 13-7 will be used.

If Eqs. 13-6 and 13-7 are substituted in Eq. 13-1, we obtain

$$Z = 180n_1 + 70 \times 0.7n_1 + 150n_2 + 50 \times 0.5n_2$$

That is,

$$Z = 229.0n_1 + 175.0n_2 \qquad (13\text{-}8)$$

and the problem becomes maximized; Eq. 13-8, subject to conditions 13-4 and 13-5.

Let us consider now condition 13-4. It tells us that we cannot use more than a fixed amount of resources. It seems clear that we can push Z to higher values if all the available resources are used. Thus, condition 13-4 should be transformed to

$$5n_1 + 5n_2 = 100{,}000 \text{ or } n_1 + n_2 = 20{,}000 \qquad (13\text{-}9)$$

Now condition 13-9 points out an essential problem. The only way to increase type 1 students is to trade them for type 2 students, and vice versa. To increase the number of students of any type means a cost in students for the other type of teachers. So to trade teachers is to trade students.

The fact that students of one type of teachers are traded for students of the other type of teachers can be expressed more clearly in the following way:

$$n_1 = 20,000 - n_2 \qquad (13\text{-}10)$$

Now it can be seen that any increment in n_2 has to bring about a reduction in n_1 and vice versa.

The trade of students of one type of teachers for those of the other type of teachers might or might not pay. The payment that we want to receive is in the values of the criterion function Z. Therefore, we have to check the effect on Z of changing the number of students. Putting in Eq. 13-8 the value of n_1 in Eq. 13-10 we have:

$$Z = 229\,(20,000 - n_2) + 175n_2$$
$$Z = 4,580,000 - 229n_2 + 175n_2$$
$$Z = 4,580,000 - 54n_2 \qquad (13\text{-}11)$$

From Eq. 13-11 it is clear that Z will be maximum if $n_2 = 0$. So, from Eq. 13-10, it follows that $n_1 = 20,000$. The solution to our problem is to train teachers of type 1 only, and in this case, income of students will be

$$Z = 4,580,000$$

the number of students enrolled

$$n_1 = 20,000$$

and the number of graduates

$$S_1 = 14,000$$

The simple exercise presented has two advantages: First, it settles the problem of quality versus quantity in teacher training in an operational way. This means that we can actually decide in a concrete situation which is the best option, in agreement with what we want to accomplish. For this, the values assumed to be known in the model must be determined. This is a question of a sample survey or some other type of procedure to collect data.

The other advantage of the method is that it can be generalized to consider more types of teacher training and more products of education; for instance, levels or courses, etc., and finally, more limitations, such as the capacity of the existing institutions for teacher training.

13-3 Concluding Remarks

In this book some basic aspects of educational planning have been presented. However, even after all the steps presented above are completed, there is a long distance to cover before a complete educational plan is obtained. A description of the steps required is presented in Chapter 1 and will not be repeated here.

References

The main applications of decision models to educational planning appear in the following papers:

Adelman, I., "A Linear Programming Model of Educational Planning: A Case Study of Argentina," in I. Adelman, and E. Thorbecke (eds.), *The Theory and Design of Economic Development.* Baltimore, Md.: Johns Hopkins Press, 1966.

Benard, J., "Un modèle d'affectation optimale des ressources entre l'economie et le système e'ducatif," *Metroeconomica,* Vol. 19, No. 1 (January, April 1967).

Bowles, S., "The Efficient Allocation of Resources in Education," *The Quarterly Journal of Economics*, Vol. 81, No. 2 (May 1967).

Correa, H., *The Economics of Human Resources.* Amsterdam: North Holland Publishing Co., 1967.

———, "Quantity vs. Quality in Teacher Education," *Comparative Education Review,* Vol. 8, No. 2 (October 1964).

———, "Optimum Choice Between General and Vocational Education," *Kyklos,* Vol. 18, Fasc. 1 (1965).

———, "Planning the Educational Curriculum," *Kyklos*, Vol. 18, Fasc. 4 (1965).

———, "Optima for Size and Number of Schools," *Scientia Paedagogica Experimentalis,* Vol. 3, No. 1 (1966).

———, "More Schools or Better Schools," *Scientia Paedagogica Experimentalis*, Vol. 3, No. 2 (1966).

———, "A Survey of Mathematical Models in Educational Planning," *Mathematical Models in Educational Planning.* Paris: O.E.C.D., 1967.

———, "An Optimum Enrollment Policy for Developing Countries," in R. H. P. Kraft (ed.), *Education and Economic Growth.* Tallahassee: The Florida State University, 1968.

Correa, H., and E. Reimer, "Planning a Literacy Campaign and Other Educational Programs," *Scientia Paedagogica Experimentalis* (to be published).

Davis, R., *Planning Human Resource Development: Models and Schemata.* Chicago: Rand McNally, 1966.

Tu, P. N. V., "Optimal Educational Investment Program in an Economic Planning Model," *The Canadian Journal of Economics II,* No. 1 (February 1969).

Van Weizsacker, C. C., "Training Policies Under Conditions of Technical Progress: A Theoretical Treatment," *Mathematical Models in Educational Planning.* Paris: O.E.C.D., 1967.

Glossary of Symbols

Symbol	Meaning	Page References
a_t^j	dropouts after pivotal year t, level j	58, 59
α^j	(alpha) dropouts during and after pivotal year/enrollment pivotal year	62, 102
b_t^j	dropouts before pivotal year t, level j	58, 59
β^j	(beta) dropouts before pivotal year/total inputs	62, 102
d_t^{1j}	deaths before pivotal year t, level j	58, 62
d_t^{2j}	deaths after pivotal year t, level j	58, 62
ϵ_i^i	(epsilon) elasticity of educational strata i of the labor force respect to total labor force	123
ϵ_τ	elasticity of the ratio τ (tau) respect to per capita income	96
η^j	(eta) proportion of dropouts from level j before the pivotal year that are considered a part of the output of the previous level	64
g_t^j	graduates, level j	58, 62
γ^j	(gamma) proportion of dropouts from level j during and after the pivotal year that are considered a part of the output of the previous level	64
GDP	Gross Domestic Product	29
H	number of periods of education offered per unit of time	45
h_c	average number of periods taught by each teacher per week	50
h_r	average number of periods each room is used per week	52
h_s	average number of periods of education received by each student	45

Symbol	Meaning	Page References
L_t	total number of persons in the labor force in year t	16
L_t^i	total number of workers with educational level i in year t	16
l_t	inverse productivity of employed worker	121
l_t^i	inverse productivity for workers with educational level i	121
N	number of periods of education received by all the students	45
n_t	number of new entrants	57
n_{hj}^1	new elementary school entrants of age j in year h	85
ν	(nu) mortality rate	84
O_t^i	output of the educational system of persons of level $i = 1, 2, 3$ between pivotal years $t - 6$ and t	64
P_t	total population year t	13
P_{ht}	population in the age interval h in year t	13
Pe_t^i	number of persons other than students with educational level i in year t	110
R	number of classrooms and laboratories	52
r_t	number of repeaters from the previous school period	58
ρ^j	(rho) repeaters passing to next structure/enrollment pivotal year	62, 102
S_t	number of students at time t	57
s_h	average size of a class	45
T	number of teachers	50
τ_{hj}	(tau) proportion of persons of age j in year h becoming new entrants in elementary school	85
Y_t	gross domestic product at constant prices in year t	33
y_t	per capita income in year t	38
Z	objective function	228

Indexes

Author Index

Subject Index